HAWTHORNE

TWENTIETH CENTURY VIEWS

The aim of this series is to present the best in contemporary critical opinion on major authors, providing a twentieth century perspective on their changing status in an era of profound revaluation.

Maynard Mack, *Series Editor*
Yale University

HAWTHORNE

A COLLECTION OF CRITICAL ESSAYS

Edited by
A. N. Kaul

Prentice-Hall, Inc. A SPECTRUM BOOK *Englewood Cliffs, N. J.*

Contents

HAWTHORNE

Introduction

by A. N. Kaul

I

In a lifetime devoted almost entirely to writing, Hawthorne produced comparatively little: four novels, three collections of tales and sketches, a juvenile romance, some unfinished fragments, and a quantity of miscellaneous, occasional, or simply pot-boiling prose. Yet quantitative standards, almost always irrelevant, seem particularly so when applied to Hawthorne. Not only do the major novels and tales stand in significant relation to one another—itself an achievement of genius—but most of them individually, as the discussions included in this volume demonstrate, are successes of a high imaginative order. Even the failures can be seen as those of a great writer, particularly when one considers that he wrote without the usual assurances of a live literary tradition in the immediate background. In the true pioneer or renaissance spirit, within a relatively small body of work, Hawthorne experimented extensively with literary forms and techniques, trying out or discovering for himself, as Q. D. Leavis points out, a wide variety of possible modes ranging from the whimsical, the legendary, and the allegorical to the panoramic, the pictorial, and the dramatic. Through this process (quite unlike Cooper, who was content to entrust his radical intuitions to the first available literary vehicle) Hawthorne fought his way to the creation of an authentic American literature, discovering many areas where the logic of his individual imagination, the resources of past literature, and the vital rhythms of a new culture could meet in a creative interplay. In the course of two centuries, American life had acquired a visible shape of its own, but Hawthorne, more than any other writer, apprehended what, in Hopkins' term, one might call the "inscape" of that life, and thus grappled with its history by starting the finer argument of its literary history.

A deeply "American" writer, Hawthorne is also a peculiarly "modern" writer. It is true that often he deliberately, even perversely, shrouds his narratives in a sort of nameless, dateless archaism, and delights too in calling up figures that seem to belong anywhere but in the real world. Occasionally, as in "The Custom House" sketch at the beginning of *The*

Scarlet Letter, he was himself perplexed by this seeming perversity. And yet this archaism appears to have been a necessary condition for the richest engagement of his imagination, and also, paradoxically, for his deepest intuitions of the modern spirit. His true interests and concerns, far from being antiquarian, anticipate the spiritual problems and discoveries of modern life as well as of modern literature. Even his notorious "Gothicism" is essentially a device for creating in the background a medieval ethos against which the realities of the post-renaissance or modern world can make their effective point. To it one may apply Henry James's comment on the "almost exclusively *imported* character of the sense of sin in Hawthorne's mind," namely, that "it seems to exist there merely for an artistic or literary purpose."

The sense of sin itself is another thing again. Unlike "Gothic" mystery, it is undoubtedly central to Hawthorne's world, although not in the way supposed by a persistent line of his critics who have tended to regard him as a sort of Calvinistic Dante. Hawthorne is not a Dante, if only because his are not the orthodox or traditional categories of sin; those who think otherwise simply confuse him with some of his characters. There is almost always in Hawthorne a radical difference between the sin that is actually committed and the sin that the characters *believe* they have committed. Hawthorne's irony, in fact, often turns precisely on this incongruity between the realities of living and the orthodoxies of belief. To take the most obvious example, it is Arthur Dimmesdale and not his creator for whom the "sin" of adultery is the chief issue of *The Scarlet Letter.* And yet, if the ironic distance between the author and his character points to the meaning of the novel, it does not explain the novel's dramatic power, which arises rather from a complementary attribute of the historical imagination: its ability to enter into the inner life of the character, to view the world through his eyes, to represent his "sin" in his own terms, dramatically—not as the dubious mechanism it might be to a later or a more disengaged observer but as the potent force it actually was in shaping Dimmesdale's life.

Because Hawthorne was much given to evasions, mystifications, and prevarications of various sorts, because he repeatedly confuses the issues by shying away from them, because he often talks of his fiction in terms of misty legends and faded blooms, because, in short, he seems frequently to disclaim his own vital interests, we must take care not to lose from sight those aspects of his work that are most essential to his vision and of most immediate relevance to modern life and literature. He was preeminently a "psychological" novelist—"burrowing, to his utmost ability, into the depths of our common nature, for the purposes of psychological romance," as he puts it himself in the preface to *The Snow Image*—long before the psychological novel is officially supposed to have been born. He was deeply preoccupied with the modern themes of alienation, isolation, and guilt consciousness—and with modern spiritual problems generally. In his half-cautious, half-daring way he sensed the relation between sex and socio-political ideology, and, as Irving Howe has shown (*Politics and the Novel,* 1957), attempted the theme of politics itself in *The Blithedale Romance*—a novel charged with potentially explosive energy, although it evades the central question of ideology by approaching it from the phenomenal extremities of corrupted fanaticism on the one side and utopian idealism on the other. A highly conscious artist himself, he explored in a remarkable group of tales dealing with artists (chiefly in "The Artist of the Beautiful," discussed here by Fogle), that conflict between the aesthetic impulse and the predominant drives of a utilitarian culture which has since come to be exploited and deplored by nearly every American who can write. This conflict was very much his own, and he dramatized it by refusing, against all expectations, to enter a recognized profession. In an effort to apprehend and adequately reflect the new complexity of man's life, he molded the venerable—in his case directly inherited—allegorical method into the modern technique of symbolism. Moreover, he introduced into the art of prose narrative a severe, if not always sustained, sense of structure as well as the rigorous economies and concentrations of effect upon which the novel prides itself today but which, before his time, were mostly confined to the arts of drama and poetry.

For all these reasons we need not be surprised that twentieth century criticism has accorded Hawthorne considerable attention. What may surprise us more is the fact that so few creative writers have turned to him apart from his own countrymen—or, if others have in fact turned to him, that they have left so few reports of their discoveries. Aside from Trollope's "The Genius of Nathaniel Hawthorne" (*North American Review,* September 1879) and a few casual, mostly deprecatory remarks by André Gide and François Mauriac, the record contains, among non-American contributions, only the essays of D. H. Lawrence on *The Scarlet Letter* and *The Blithedale Romance,* surely the least rewarding of all the pieces in Lawrence's otherwise revelatory and influential *Studies in Classic American Literature* (1923). Lawrence's special insight in this volume, so far as Hawthorne criticism is concerned, lies in his insistence on the American novelist's "duplicity"—the crucial discrepancy between the logic of rhetoric and the logic of imagination in his work. But this insight, derived from Lawrence's over-all view of classic American writing, is neither developed nor even fully articulated in the two essays specially devoted to Hawthorne. It is expressed, in fact, most effectively in the introductory chapter of the volume, "The Spirit of Place":

And you can please yourself, when you read *The Scarlet Letter,* whether you accept what that sugary, blue-eyed little darling of a Hawthorne has to say for himself, false as all darlings are, or whether you read the impeccable truth of his art speech. . . .

The artist usually sets out—or used to—to point a moral and adorn a tale. The tale, however, points the other way, as a rule. Two blankly opposing morals, the artist's and the tale's. Never trust the artist. Trust the tale.

In America, on the other hand, Hawthorne's contemporaries and immediate successors were not slow to recognize his achievement. To name only major novelists, Melville wrote an eloquent tribute in *The Literary World* in 1850 (August 17 and 24), and Henry James published his *Hawthorne* in the same year as Trollope's essay. The discovery of Hawthorne was for both men a lesson in self-discovery, although James did not exploit the lesson fully until much later in his career. At the time of writing his Hawthorne study James was aligning himself with that school of European realists whose method, as he himself noted, differed so radically from Hawthorne's. But because this sense of detachment operated in James's fine critical mind together with his deeper and more pervasive sympathy, he could write what remains, in spite of its many limitations and its leisurely format, one of the best studies of the novelist that we have. Its sanity of perspective stands as a corrective to certain excesses of today's Hawthorne criticism, and its insights have been further elaborated to great advantage by later critics. James not only knew how to ask the right questions but often had the right answers. Discussing Hawthorne's fictional technique, for example, he puts his finger on the recurrent problem of allegory, draws attention to Hawthorne's symbolism (though with the minor caveat that occasionally it is overdone—as it certainly is), and concludes with a searching comment on the essentially poetic nature of Hawthorne's method: "Hawthorne is perpetually looking for images which shall place themselves in picturesque correspondence with the spiritual facts with which he is concerned, and of course the search is of the very essence of poetry." Simultaneously, recognizing the deep psychological and historical aspects of Hawthorne's theme, James saw that, Hawthorne's method being what it is, "the historic consciousness" must operate in him without "the apparatus of an historian."

James's tone in the essay, half-tender, half-condescending, as if he were speaking of a beloved but somewhat crotchety forbear, is taken over intact in T. S. Eliot's "The Hawthorne Aspect" (*The Little Review,* August 1918). Here Eliot studies the James-Hawthorne relationship, and finds the older novelist's achievement superior in only one respect: "In one thing alone Hawthorne is more solid than James: he had a very acute historical sense. . . . Both men had that sense of the past which is peculiarly American, but in Hawthorne this sense exercised itself in a grip on the past itself; in James it is a sense of the sense." The same attitude, respectful but in the end patronizing, marks most other early twentieth century estimates of Hawthorne's work, including that of the usually shrewd W. C. Brownell (*American Prose Masters,* 1909). Since, as James had noted, Hawthorne lacked the realism with which the novel was coming to be increasingly identified, his fiction seemed in these years hardly more than an interesting curiosity. Nor did the concern of critics with "social relevance" during the twenties and early thirties help matters. In the critical context of the time, only *The House of the Seven Gables* was thought to deserve mature scrutiny, for it was the only work that answered at least partially to the current idea of what a novel should be. Eliot's discussion focuses on it, so far as it focuses on any single work, and even Matthiessen's criticism continues to give it pride of place. No critic could, of course, quite ignore *The Scarlet Letter*, but whatever joy was taken in it was implacably haunted by the guilty ghost of allegory. As for the other two novels and the great tales, their critical recovery is an event of very recent date. In a way it was mainly the relationship with James that won Hawthorne such serious attention as he received for several decades.

This is not to suggest that he ever suffered the obscurity that overtook his friend and fellow novelist, Herman Melville. On the contrary, in Hawthorne's case a reputation of sorts was noisily kept up by ceremonial applause during the years following his death. Between 1864 and 1900, he rapidly assumed the status of a Venerable Presence in the American schoolroom and before the American public. Longfellow read obituary verses at his grave, Holmes composed memorial verses, E. C. Stedman gave a public ode at Harvard. These, together with a score of estimates in prose, either celebrated his wizardry or attempted to pluck out the secret of his elusive personality. But whether he was viewed as Matthew Maule or Ariel, Romantic concern with his personal genius effectively prevented critical contact with his works. The tale was ignored in favor of the artist.

It is only recently that Hawthorne's literary art, together with that of some of the other older American writers, has come fully into its own. Indeed, during the last three decades his achievement as an artist has found so many stout champions that inevitably some of them have proved "gray champions," standing up for him so somberly as to make heavy weather of even the lightest and brightest things in him. All the same, the landmarks of a sharper understanding are plainly visible. Newton Arvin's critical biography (1929) and Randall Stewart's edition of the *American Notebooks* three years later (with Stewart's introductory discussion of recurrent themes in Hawthorne) were perhaps the first signs. A good deal, though by no means all, of what followed is represented in this anthology. Hawthorne as allegorist, as poet, as symbolist, as aspiring creator of tragedy, as culture critic and evaluator of democratic possibilities, as subtle narrative artist and native mythographer, as dramatizer of the artist's situation in society—these are the major themes explored by the essayists in this volume. Collectively they demonstrate the capacity of his best work to sustain and reward rigorous scrutiny from several distinct perspectives, literary as well as ideological. His seemingly fragile imagination seizes upon crucial issues and then responds to them with satisfying complexity.

II

If we should ask at this point, what are the overarching continuities in Hawthorne's work, the unities of interest that run through the various experimentations and make even the most tentative effort reflect upon the most assured success, we should not be able to answer, I suspect, without pointing to those two aspects of his nature which constituted for James and Eliot the chief distinction of his imagination: a passionate interest in "the deeper psychology" and an equally passionate "historic consciousness." Our knowledge of each of these aspects has since been extended—in the former case most recently and provocatively by Frederick C. Crews in the Freudian interpretation of "Roger Malvin's Burial" included here. But so far critics do not seem to have recognized that the two interests are seldom disjunct for Hawthorne. His theme, if for the moment one stays close to the Jamesian terms, is something like historical psychology or deeper historicity. As he puts it in "The Custom House," the artist's task of "dressing up of the tale" is primarily one of "imagining the motives and modes of passion" which, in a particular age, could have the power of influencing people's character and thereby of shaping their destiny. And this is precisely the cast of the forces, indistinguishably both historical and spiritual, that are dramatized in the main story of *The Scarlet Letter*. Consider, for example, the climactic forest scenes and the tragic dream that is born there of escape into the larger world of freedom and happiness. It is a dream that Pearl lives to achieve almost effortlessly, but only because Hawthorne has conceived her more in the spirit of his own times and less in that of the historical period in which the novel is set. The facts of her adult career, which the novelist so carefully intimates in the concluding chapter and which anticipate the fortunes of many a Jamesian heroine, identify her with an even later and more expansive milieu. In the Puritan world of *The Scarlet Letter* she functions as a revealing anachronism. Although born into this society and living under its stern authority, she owes no personal allegiance to its laws, and can therefore with ease repudiate its ban and remain exempt from that deeper conflict which is the chief source of her parents' anguish. For the simple but intensely tragic truth about Hester and Dimmesdale is that they cannot escape their age because spiritually they belong to it. Dimmesdale's commitment to it—"supporting, while it confined him within its iron framework"—is the sole organizing principle of his life and personality. Nor, unlike Hester, has he undergone any "experience calculated to lead him beyond the scope of generally received laws. . . . At the head of the social system, as the clergymen of that day stood, he was only the more trammelled by its regulations, its principles, and even its prejudices." Hester, who inwardly strives beyond the crippling perspectives of the day—recognizing at one particularly rebellious moment that "the whole system of society is to be torn down, and built up anew"—still remains too much its creature to be the prophetess of a new epoch. Dimmesdale's and Hester's struggle is historical, but it is not merely a struggle against the outside world. Their own divided souls are an equally decisive arena for the conflict, and ultimately their defeat comes from themselves. As Hawthorne develops it with deep psychological insight, the interest of the story centers not on the failure of the lovers' dream but on its *unreality,* its unreality to themselves, even at the wildest moment of hope.

Hawthorne is good at showing a character thus poised as it were on the farthest edge of his age, intellectually looking through and past the reigning *zeitgeist,* but being all the while, like the figure in Eliot's Preludes, rooted in the "certain certainties" of his time. Such is the situation of Miles Coverdale as dramatized through his involvement in Blithedale, an experiment of which he says: "But, considered in a profounder relation, it was part of another age, a different state of society, a segment of an existence peculiar in its aims and methods, a leaf of some mysterious volume interpolated into the current history which time was writing off." This controlled interplay between the historical and the anachronistic is what gives Hawthorne's pages their grim complexity; his ironies are generated by a powerful sense of reality clashing with equally powerful personal sympathies. Thus the subject of *The Blithedale Romance* is again not the failure of the idealistic, forward looking experiment, but rather its unreality; and again it is an unreality that stems from history but is experienced by the protagonists themselves in the form of irreducible personal tensions and psychological paralyses. Even in *The House of the Seven Gables,* Clifford's futile impulse to jump headlong into the crowded street, or his and Hepzibah's abortive train ride into the brave new world, trace the curve of a psychological escape that fails. Clifford's attempt is to reach out from an arrested past to the realities of the actual, living, bustling present—a present which is the natural habitat of Holgrave or Phoebe but to which he and Hepzibah belong as little as Hester does to the world of Pearl. These are the scenes that rightly make, and have always made, the profoundest impression on Hawthorne's readers. It is this little drama and not the obvious historicity of the chronicle of the Pyncheon generations that reveals, so far as *The Seven Gables* is concerned, the depth of Hawthorne's imaginative penetration.

What sort of truth, then, do we have here—psychological, social, or historical? In its quality of being inextricably all of these, it exemplifies a special glory available to the art of fiction at its best. It presents man in his time and yet not wholly confined by his time, man living under the real forces of the day but not so crippled by them as to be unable to rise into a world of new values and belief. The truth of such poetry, though not of the same order, is yet more valid than the truth of history. At least no records of actuality have the power to interpret the real world at the level of spiritual movement and immediacy of experience as these "romances" do.

This is not to deny that in many places Hawthorne explores the so-called eternal verities, the permanent afflictions of the unchanging human heart, rather than historically concrete issues such as these. But it is precisely in these generalized moral statements that he sometimes blurs or loses altogether the authenticity of artistic truth, which derives not from abstraction but from intensity of particularization. However, even his allegories—his allegorizing of self and pride, not to mention science and solitude—when taken in their context, acquire some specificity and accumulate to form a circumstantial portrait of historical man. The tendency to universalize by vehement abstraction, observable in much nineteenth century literature, should not deceive us into supposing that the spirit of the morality plays was there reborn. Dickens, too, for example, took Self and Pride for his themes, one in *Martin Chuzzlewit* and the other in *Dombey and Son,* proclaiming their abstract quality in capital letters without losing their existential force.

Martin Chuzzlewit (1844) is especially relevant because a portion of it seems to have been directly echoed a few years later in *The Blithedale Romance.* In Dickens, the theme is characteristically pursued along several lines of action only loosely held together in one plot: the melo-dramatic action centering upon Anthony and Jonas Chuzzlewit; the comic action involving Pecksniff; and the sentimental-romantic story of young Martin. Furthermore, whereas the first action ends in murder and suicide, the second in the exposure of Pecksniff's intransigent hypocrisy, Dickens characteristically assigns the business of articulate discovery to the hero of the sentimental action. And it is in an American colony called Eden, a deadly wilderness of marshes and disease, that young Martin makes his discovery while watching over his faithful retainer, Mark Tapley:

> It was natural for him to reflect—he had months to do it in—upon his own escape, and Mark's extremity. This led him to consider which of them could be the better spared, and why? Then the curtain slowly rose a very little way; and Self, Self, Self, was shown below.
>
> He asked himself, besides, when dreading Mark's decease (as all men do and must, at such a time), whether he had done his duty by him, and had deserved and made a good response to his fidelity and zeal. No. Short as their companionship had been, he felt in many, many instances, that there was blame against himself; and still inquiring why, the curtain slowly rose a little more, and Self, Self, Self, dilated on the scene.
>
> It was long before he fixed the knowledge of himself so firmly in his mind

that he could thoroughly discern the truth; but in the hideous solitude of that most hideous place, with Hope so far removed, Ambition quenched, and Death beside him rattling at the very door, reflection came, as in a plague-beleaguered town; and so he felt and knew the failing of his life, and saw distinctly what an ugly spot it was.

(Ch. XXXIII)

A similar discovery—this time likewise in a colony that was supposed to be the type of second paradise—is made by Zenobia as she turns upon Hollingsworth in *The Blithedale Romance*:

"It is all self!" answered Zenobia, with still intenser bitterness. "Nothing else; nothing but self, self, self! The fiend, I doubt not, has made his choicest mirth of you these seven years past, and especially in the mad summer which we have spent together. I see it now! I am awake, disenchanted, disinthralled! Self, self, self!"

(Ch. XXV)

There are, to be sure, differences of radical importance between Dickens' understanding of this theme and Hawthorne's. In Hawthorne the romantic, comic, and melodramatic elements are all merged in a single action whose main cast is tragic rather than sentimentally hopeful. Moreover, while both novelists are obviously manipulating a system of Christian ethics for their purposes, Hawthorne's image of the fiend enjoying his subversive victory at Blithedale, evokes the interpretative Puritan myth that is peculiarly his. Dickens' concern is more directly socio-economical. Developing the theme of self in various modes, he presents not merely the domestic selfishness of young Martin and the sanctimonious avarice of Pecksniff, but also, more grimly and with the intense melodramatic energy of his art, the commercial ethic that rules and eventually dehumanizes and destroys from within the lives of Anthony and Jonas Chuzzlewit. And yet, in spite of the differences, or even perhaps because of them, the two novels remain mutually illuminating. Dickens' integrating theme—the domination of individuals by impersonal "things" and the consequent breakdown of human values and relationships, and even, incipiently, of human communication and control—is also the underlying theme of Hawthorne in *The Blithedale Romance*.

At bottom, most of Hawthorne's work possesses this quality of historical and critical evaluation. His imagination, though less extensively engaged than that of Dickens, shows a profounder concern with the ultimate nature of the spiritual and material forces that were coming to a head in his day. These forces have since become intensified and the future of what used to be called "humanity" is doubtless more precarious now than even Hawthorne supposed. Yet his problems remain ours, and though contemporary writers have explored these problems perhaps more pungently, one may doubt on rereading Hawthorne that they have yet surpassed his sensitivity and depth.

III

In accounting for the content and arrangement of this collection, the first word must be one of apology. There are a number of studies which I would have liked to, but for obvious reasons of space could not, present here. These are listed in the brief bibliography at the end. The anthology opens with four general essays each discussing the major novels as well as some of the important tales in the light of a distinctive and influential thesis. The tales exclusively form the subject of the next group of three essays. Following this there is a comment on "The Custom House," followed by four separate studies of the individual novels in chronological order. Although, for the reasons noticed earlier, most of the contributions are by Americans, three come from outsiders—one from England, one from Germany, one from India. Possibly they are a token of an increasing interest in Hawthorne beyond the boundaries of the American mind.

Maule's Curse, or Hawthorne and
the Problem of Allegory

by Yvor Winters

"At the moment of execution—with the halter about his neck and
while Colonel Pyncheon sat on horseback, grimly gazing at the scene
—Maule had addressed him from the scaffold, and uttered a
prophecy, of which history as well as fireside tradition, has preserved the very words. 'God,' said the dying man, pointing his finger,
with a ghastly look, at the undismayed countenance of his enemy,
'God will give him blood to drink!' "
—The House of the Seven Gables

Of Hawthorne's three most important long works—*The Scarlet
Letter, The House of the Seven Gables,* and *The Marble Faun*—the first
is pure allegory, and the other two are impure novels, or novels with
unassimilated allegorical elements. The first is faultless, in scheme and in
detail; it is one of the chief masterpieces of English prose. The second
and third are interesting, the third in particular, but both are failures,
and neither would suffice to give the author a very high place in the
history of prose fiction. Hawthorne's sketches and short stories, at best,
are slight performances; either they lack meaning, as in the case of
Mr. Higginbotham's Catastrophe, or they lack reality of embodiment, as
in the case of *The Birthmark,* or, having a measure of both, as does
The Minister's Black Veil, they yet seem incapable of justifying the intensity of the method, their very brevity and attendant simplification,
perhaps, working against them; the best of them, probably, is *Young
Goodman Brown.* In his later romances, *Septimius Felton, Dr. Grim-
shaw's Secret, The Ancestral Footstep,* and *The Dolliver Romance,* and
in much of *The Blithedale Romance* as well, Hawthorne struggles un-
successfully with the problem of allegory, but he is still obsessed with it.

Hawthorne is, then, essentially an allegorist; had he followed the
advice of Poe and other well-wishers, contemporary with himself and

posthumous, and thrown his allegorizing out the window, it is certain that nothing essential to his genius would have remained. He appears to have had none of the personal qualifications of a novelist, for one thing: the sombre youth who lived in solitude and in contemplation in Salem, for a dozen years or more, before succumbing to the charms and propinquity of Miss Sophia Peabody and making the spasmodic and only moderately successful efforts to accustom himself to daylight which were to vex the remainder of his life, was one far more likely to concern himself with the theory of mankind than with the chaos, trivial, brutal, and exhausting, of the actuality. Furthermore, as we shall see more fully, the Puritan view of life was allegorical, and the allegorical vision seems to have been strongly impressed upon the New England literary mind. It is fairly obvious in much of the poetry of Emerson, Emily Dickinson, Bryant, Holmes, and even Very—Whittier, a Quaker and a peasant, alone of the more interesting poets escaping; Melville, relatively an outsider, shows the impact of New England upon his own genius as much through his use of allegory as through his use of New England character; and the only important novelist purely a New Englander, aside from Hawthorne, that is, O. W. Holmes, was primarily concerned with the Puritan tendency to allegory, as its one considerable satirist, yet was himself more or less addicted to it.

These matters are speculative. That New England predisposed Hawthorne to allegory cannot be shown; yet the disposition in both is obvious. And it can easily be shown that New England provided the perfect material for one great allegory, and that, in all likelihood, she was largely to blame for the later failures.

The Puritan theology rested primarily upon the doctrine of predestination and the inefficaciousness of good works; it separated men sharply and certainly into two groups, the saved and the damned, and, technically, at least, was not concerned with any subtler shadings. This in itself represents a long step toward the allegorization of experience, for a very broad abstraction is substituted for the patient study of the minutiae of moral behavior long encouraged by Catholic tradition. Another step was necessary, however, and this step was taken in Massachusetts almost at the beginning of the settlement, and in the expulsion of Anne Hutchinson became the basis of governmental action: whereas the wholly Calvinistic Puritan denied the value of the evidence of character and behavior as signs of salvation, and so precluded the possibility of their becoming allegorical symbols—for the othodox Calvinist, such as Mrs. Hutchinson would appear to have been, trusted to no witness save that of the Inner Light—it became customary in Massachusetts to regard as evidence of salvation the decision of the individual to enter the Church and lead a moral life. "The Puritans," says Parkes, "were plain blunt men with little taste for mysticism and no talent for speculation. A new conception was formulated by English theologians, of whom William Ames was the most influential. The sign of election was not an inner assurance; it was a sober decision to trust in Christ and obey God's law. Those who made this sober decision might feel reasonably confident that they had received God's grace; but the surest proof of it was its fruit in conduct; complete assurance was impossible. It was assumed that all was the work of grace; it was God, without human cooperation, who caused the sober decision to be made. But in actual practice this doctrine had the effect of unduly magnifying man's ability to save himself, as much as Calvin's conception had unduly minimized it; conversion was merely a choice to obey a certain code of rules, and did not imply any emotional change, any love for God, or for holiness, or any genuine religious experience; religion in other words was reduced to mere morality." [1] Objective evidence thus took the place of inner assurance, and the behavior of the individual took on symbolic value. That is, any sin was evidence of damnation; or, in other words, any sin represented all sin. When Hester Prynne committed adultery, she committed an act as purely representative of complete corruption as the act of Faustus in signing a contract with Satan. This view of the matter is certainly not Catholic and is little short of appalling; it derives from the fact, that although, as Parkes states in the passage just quoted, there occurred an exaggeration of the will in the matter of practical existence, this same will was still denied in the matter of doctrine, for according to doctrine that which man willed had been previously willed by God.

The belief that the judgment of a man is predestined by God, and the corollary that the judgment of a good man, since all men are either good or bad, purely and simply, is the judgment of God, may lead in the natural course of events to extraordinary drama; and this the more readily if the actors in the drama are isolated from the rest of the world and believe that the drama in which they take part is of cosmic importance and central in human destiny. Andrews writes: "The belief that God had selected New England as the chosen land was profoundly held by the Puritans who went there. Winthrop himself in 1640 wrote to Lord Saye and Sele of 'this good land which God hath found and given to his people,' adding that 'God had chosen this country to plant his people in.' Cotton in his sermon, *God's Promise to His Plantation* (London, 1634), devotes much space to the same idea—'This place is appointed me of God.' " [2] And Schneider writes on the same subject: "No one can live long in a Holy Commonwealth without becoming sensitive, irritable, losing his sense of values and ultimately his balance. All acts are acts either of God or of the devil; all issues are matters of religious faith; and all conflicts are holy wars. No matter how trivial an opinion

---

[1] H. B. Parkes, "The Puritan Heresy," *The Hound and Horn*, II (Jan.-March 1932), 173-74.

[2] Charles M. Andrews, *The Colonial Period of American History* (Yale University Press, 1934), I, 386, note 2.

might appear from a secular point of view, it became vital when promulgated as a theological dogma; no matter how harmless a fool might be, he was intolerable if he did not fit into the Covenant of Grace; no matter how slight an offense might be, it was a sin against Almighty God and hence infinite. Differences of opinion became differences of faith. Critics became blasphemers, and innovators, heretics." [3] And again: ". . . the mind of the Puritan was singularly unified and his imagination thoroughly moralized. The clergy were, of course, the professional moral scientists, but the laymen were no less dominated by such mental habits. The common man and illiterate shared with the expert this interest in divining God's purposes in the course of events. No event was merely natural; it was an act of God and was hence charged with that 'numinous' quality which gives birth to both prophetic insight and mystic illumination." [4] And again: "Nature was instructive to them only in so far as it suggested the hidden mysterious operations of designing agents. God and devil were both active, scheming, hidden powers, each pursuing his own ends by various ministrations, and natural events were therefore to be understood only in so far as they showed evidence of some divine or diabolical plot." [5]

Now according to the doctrine of predestination, if we interpret it reasonably, Hester merely gave evidence, in committing adultery, that she had always been one of the damned. This point of view, if really understood, could never have led to the chain of events which Hawthorne described in *The Scarlet Letter*; neither could it have led to the events of the actual history of New England. It is at this point that we must consider that fluid element, history, in connection with dogma, for Hester, like the witches who so occupied the Mathers, was treated as if she had wilfully abandoned the ways of God for the ways of Satan. This final illogicality introduces the element of drama into the allegory of *The Scarlet Letter* and into the allegorical morality of the Puritans.

The English Puritans who settled Massachusetts were socially the product of centuries of the type of ethical discipline fostered by the Catholic and Anglo-Catholic Churches. They may have denied the freedom of the will and the efficaciousness of good works by lip, but by habit, and without really grasping the fact, they believed in them and acted upon them. Edwards exhorts sinners to repent while preaching the doctrine of the inability to repent; the Mathers wrestled with demons physically and in broad daylight, and quite obviously felt virtuous for having done so; in fact, to such a pass did Puritanism come, that Melville's Ahab, who wilfully embarks upon the Sea of Unpredictability in order to overtake and slay the Spirit of Evil—an effort in which he is predestined and at the end of which he is predestined to destruction—

[3] H. W. Schneider, *The Puritan Mind* (Henry Holt, 1930), pp. 51-52.
[4] *Ibid.*, p. 48.
[5] *Ibid.*, pp. 42-43.

appears to us merely the heroic projection of a common Puritan type. The Puritan may be said to have conceived the Manicheistic struggle between Absolute Good and Absolute Evil, which he derived through the processes of simplification and misunderstanding which have already been enumerated, as a kind of preordained or mechanical, yet also holy combat, in which his own part was a part at once intense and holy and yet immutably regulated.

There were at least two motives in the new environment which tended to intensify the effect of habit in this connection: one was the inevitable impulse given to the will by the exaltation attendant upon a new religious movement; the other was the impulse given by the supremely difficult physical surroundings in which the new colonies found themselves. Foster writes on these points: "The first Puritans, sure in their own hearts that they were the elect of God, found the doctrine necessary to sustain them in the tremendous struggle through which they passed. . . . Hence the doctrine nerved to greater activity; and it produced a similar effect during the first period of the promulgation of Calvinism, among every nation which accepted the system." [6] The force of the will was strengthened at the beginning, then, at the same time that its existence was denied and that reliance upon its manner of functioning (that is, upon good works) was, from a doctrinal standpoint, regarded as sin. The will, highly stimulated, but no longer studied and guided by the flexible and sensitive ethical scholarship of the Roman tradition, might easily result in dangerous action.

Andrews speaks of this subject as follows: "The dynamic agency . . . the driving force which overrode all opposition, legal and otherwise, was the profound conviction of the Puritan leaders that they were doing the Lord's work. They looked upon themselves as instruments in the divine hand for the carrying out of a great religious mission, the object of which was the rebuilding of God's church in a land—the undefiled land of America—divinely set apart as the scene of a holy experiment that should renovate the church at large, everywhere corrupt and falling into ruins. This new and purified community was to be the home of a saving remnant delivered from the wrath to come and was to serve as an example to the mother church of a regenerated form of faith and worship. It was also to become a proselyting center for the conversion of the heathen and the extension of the true gospel among those who knew it not. In the fulfillment of this mission the Puritans counted obstacles, moral and physical, of no moment. Theirs was a religious duty to frustrate their enemies, to eradicate all inimical opinions, religious and political, and to extend the field of their influence as widely as possible. Once they had determined on their rules of polity and conduct, as laid down in the Bible and interpreted by the clergy, they had

<hr />

[6] Frank Hugh Foster, *A Genetic History of the New England Theology* (University of Chicago Press, 1907), p. 29.

no doubts of the justness and rightness of their course. The means employed might savor of harshness and inequity, but at all costs and under all circumstances, error, sin, and idolatry, in whatever form appearing and as determined by themselves, must be destroyed. In the process, as events were to prove, a great many very human motives played an important part in interpreting the law of God, and personal likes and dislikes, hypocrisy, prejudice, and passion got badly mixed with the higher and more spiritual impulses that were actively at work purging the church of its errors." [7]

Over a long period, however, the doctrine of predestination would naturally lead to religious apathy, for it offered no explicit motive to action; and this is precisely that to which it led, for after the Great Awakening of the middle of the eighteenth century, itself a reaction to previous decay in the Church, the Church lost power rapidly, and by the opening of the nineteenth century was succumbing on every hand to Unitarianism, a mildly moralistic creed, in which the element of supernaturalism was minimized, and which, in turn, yielded rapidly among the relatively intellectual classes to Romantic ethical theory, especially as propounded by the Transcendentalists. "It has never been a good way to induce men to repent," says Foster, "to tell them that they cannot." [8] Or at least the method has never been highly successful except when employed by a rhetorician of the power of Edwards, or by an orator of the effectiveness of Whitefield; and the effect can scarcely be expected long to outlive the immediate presence of the speaker. The Unitarians, in depriving the ethical life of the more impressive aspects of its supernatural sanction, and in offering nothing to take the place of that sanction, all but extinguished intensity of moral conviction, although their own conviction—we may see it portrayed, for example, in *The Europeans,* by Henry James, and exemplified in the lucid and classical prose of W. E. Channing—was a conviction, at least for a period, of the greatest firmness and dignity. Emerson eliminated the need of moral conviction and of moral understanding alike, by promulgating the allied doctrines of equivalence and of inevitable virtue. In an Emersonian universe there is equally no need and no possibility of judgment; it is a universe of amiable but of perfectly unconscious imbeciles; it is likewise a universe in which the art of the fictionist—or for that matter, any other art—can scarcely be expected to flourish. A fictionist who has been in any considerable measure affected by Emersonian or allied concepts, or even who is the product of the historical sequence which gave rise to Emerson, is likely to find himself gravely confused and may even find himself paralyzed; and we have only to read such a document, to cite a single example, as *The New Adam and Eve,* to realize that Haw-

[7] Charles M. Andrews, *op. cit.,* I, 430-31.
[8] Frank Hugh Foster, *op. cit.,* p. 29.

thorne's own moral ideas, in spite of his intense but conflicting moral sentiments, and in spite of his professed dislike for Emerson's philosophy, were much closer to the ideas of Emerson than to those of Edwards.

Now in examining Hawthorne, we are concerned with two historical centers: that of the first generation of Puritans in New England, in which occurs the action of *The Scarlet Letter*; and that of the post-Unitarian and Romantic intellectuals, in which was passed the life of Hawthorne.

Hawthorne, by nature an allegorist, and a man with a strong moral instinct, regardless of the condition of his ideas, found in the early history of his own people and region the perfect material for a master-piece. By selecting sexual sin as the type of all sin, he was true alike to the exigencies of drama and of history. In the setting which he chose, allegory was realism, the idea was life itself; and his prose, always remarkable for its polish and flexibility, and stripped, for once, of all superfluity, was reduced to the living idea, it intensified pure exposition to a quality comparable in its way to that of great poetry.

The compactness and complexity of the allegory will escape all save the most watchful readers. Let us consider the following passage as a representative example. Hester has learned that the magistrates and clergy are considering whether or not she ought to be separated from her child, and she waits upon Governor Bellingham in order to plead with him:

> On the wall hung a row of portraits, representing the forefathers of the Bellingham lineage, some with armor on their breasts, and others with stately ruffs and robes of peace. All were characterized by the sternness and severity which old portraits so invariably put on; as if they were the ghosts, rather than the pictures, of departed worthies, and were gazing with harsh and intolerant criticism at the pursuits and enjoyments of living men.
>
> At about the center of the oaken panels, that lined the hall, was suspended a suit of mail, not, like the pictures, an ancestral relic, but of the most modern date; for it had been manufactured by a skillful armorer in London, the same year in which Governor Bellingham came over to New England. There was a steel head-piece, a cuirass, a gorget, and greaves, with a pair of gauntlets and a sword hanging beneath; all, especially the helmet and breast-plate, so highly burnished as to glow with white radiance, and scatter an illumination everywhere about the floor. This bright panoply was not meant for mere idle show, but had been worn by the Governor on many a solemn muster and training field, and had glittered, moreover, at the head of a regiment in the Pequod war. For, though bred a lawyer, and accustomed to speak of Bacon, Coke, Noye, and Finch as his professional associates, the exigencies of this new country had transformed Governor Bellingham into a soldier as well as a statesman and ruler.
>
> Little Pearl—who was as greatly pleased with the gleaming armor as she

had been with the glittering frontispiece of the house—spent some time looking into the polished mirror of the breast-plate.

"Mother," cried she, "I see you here. Look! Look!"

Hester looked, by way of humoring the child; and she saw that, owing to the peculiar effect of the convex mirror, the scarlet letter was represented in gigantic and exaggerated proportions, so as to be greatly the most prominent feature of her appearance. In truth, she seemed absolutely hidden behind it. Pearl pointed upward, also, at a similar picture in the headpiece; smiling at her mother with the elfish intelligence that was so familiar an expression on her small physiognomy. That look of naughty merriment was likewise reflected in the mirror, with so much breadth and intensity of effect, that it made Hester Prynne feel as if it could not be the image of her own child, but of an imp who was seeking to mold itself into Pearl's shape.

The portraits are obviously intended as an apology for the static portraits in the book, as an illustration of the principle of simplification by distance and by generalization; the new armor, on the other hand, is the new faith which brought the Puritans to New England, and which not only shone with piety—"especially the helmet and breast-plate," the covering of the head and heart—but supported them in their practical struggles with physical adversaries, and which in addition altered their view of the life about them to dogmatic essentials, so that Hester was obliterated behind the fact of her sin, and Pearl transformed in view of her origin. Governor Bellingham, in his combination of legal training with military prowess, is representative of his fellow colonists, who displayed in a remarkable degree a capacity to act with great strength and with absolutely simple directness upon principles so generalized as scarcely to be applicable to any specific moral problem, which mastered moral difficulties not by understanding them, but by crushing them out.

Historically and relatively considered, Richard Bellingham might conceivably have been spared this function in the story, for of his group he was one of the two or three most humane and liberal; but the qualities represented were the qualities of the group of which he was a leader, and were extremely evident in most of the actions of the colony. Perhaps the best—or in another sense, the worst—embodiment of these qualities is to be found in John Endecott, of whom Andrews gives the following characterization:

Endecott had few lovable qualities. He was stern, unyielding, and on some subjects a zealot. Johnson apostrophizes him as "strong, valiant John," whom Christ had called to be his soldier, but the Old Planters, most if not all of whom were Anglicans and demanded service according to the Book of Common Prayer, deemed themselves slaves and took in very bad part his determination to suppress the Church of England in the colony. They preferred Roger Conant, who though a less forcible man was one much easier to get along with. Endecott's later career discloses his attitude toward those who differed with him—the heathen Indian, the Quaker, the prisoner before him for judgment, and the Brownes and other upholders of the Anglican service who were disaffected with the Puritan government. It also shows his dislike of forms and devices that offended him—the Book of Common Prayer, the cross of St. George, and the Maypole. He was hard, intolerant, and at times cruel. Even the Massachusetts government caused him "to be sadly admonished for his offense" in mutilating the flag at Salem in 1635, charging him with "rashness, uncharitableness, indiscretion, and exceeding the limits of his calling"; and again in the same year "committed" him for losing his temper. Endecott once apologized to Winthrop for striking "goodman Dexter," acknowledging that he was rash, but saying that Dexter's conduct "would have provoked a very patient man." The best that can be said of him has been said by Chapple ("The Public Service of John Endecott," Historical Collections, Essex Institute), an essay in the best Palfrey manner. It is odd that Endecott should have chosen for his seal a skull and crossbones.[9]

It is interesting to observe in such a passage, as in many others, that the Puritans cannot be discussed, nor can they discuss each other, without the language employed exceeding the limits proper to predestinarians and invoking the traditional morality of the older churches; yet the attempt to ignore this traditional morality as far as might be, and, in the matter of formal doctrine, to repudiate it, unquestionably had much to do with the formation of such characters as Professor Andrews here describes and as Hawthorne in the last passage quoted from him symbolizes. The imperceptive, unwavering brutality of many of the actions committed in the name of piety in the Massachusetts colonies more than justified the curse and prophecy uttered by Matthew Maule, that God would give these Puritans blood to drink; in the name of God, they had violently cut themselves off from human nature; in the end, that is in Hawthorne's generation and in the generation following, more than one of them drank his own heart's blood, as Hawthorne himself must have done in his ultimate and frustrated solitude, and more than one of them shed it.

It is noteworthy that in this passage from *The Scarlet Letter* Hawthorne turns his instrument of allegory, the gift of the Puritans, against the Puritans themselves, in order to indicate the limits of their intelligence; it is noteworthy also that this act of criticism, though both clear and sound, is negative, that he nowhere except in the very general notion of regeneration through repentance establishes the nature of the intelligence which might exceed the intelligence of the Puritans, but rather hints at the ideal existence of a richer and more detailed under-

---

[9] Charles M. Andrews, *op. cit.,* I, 361, note 3.

standing than the Puritan scheme of life is able to contain. The strength
of *The Scarlet Letter* is in part safeguarded by the refusal to explore this
understanding; the man who was able in the same lifetime to write *The
New Adam and Eve,* to conceive the art-colony described in *The Marble
Faun,* and to be shocked at the nude statues of antiquity, was scarcely
the man to cast a clear and steady light upon the finer details of the soul.

The conception of the book in general is as cleanly allegorical as is
the conception of the passage quoted. Hester represents the repentant
sinner, Dimmesdale the half-repentant sinner, and Chillingworth the
unrepentant sinner. The fact that Chillingworth's sin is the passion for
revenge is significant only to the extent that this is perhaps the one
passion which most completely isolates man from normal human
sympathies and which therefore is most properly used to represent an
unregenerate condition.

The method of allegorization is that of the Puritans themselves; the
substance of the allegory remained in a crude form a part of their
practical Christianity in spite of their Calvinism, just as it remained in
their non-theological linguistic forms, just as we can see it in the language
of the best poems of so purely and mystically Calvinistic a writer as
Jones Very, a living language related to a living experience, but over-
flowing the limits of Calvinistic dogma; Hawthorne's point of view was
naturally more enlightened than that of the Puritans themselves, yet it
was insufficiently so to enable him to recover the traditional Christian
ethics except in the most general terms and by way of historical sympathy, for had a more complete recovery been possible, he would not have
been so narrowly bound to the method of allegory and the frustration of
the later romances would scarcely have been so complete.

Once Hawthorne had reduced the problem of sin to terms as general
as these, and had brought his allegory to perfect literary form, he had,
properly speaking, dealt with sin once and for all; there was nothing further to be said about it. It would not serve to write another allegory with
a new set of characters and a different sin as the motive; for the particular sin is not particular in function, but is merely representative of sin
in general, as the characters, whatever their names and conditions may
be, are merely representative of the major stages of sin—there is no escape from the generality so long as one adheres to the method. There
was nothing further, then, to be done in this direction, save the composition of a few footnotes to the subject in the form of sketches.

The only alternative remaining was to move away from the allegorical
extreme of narrative toward the specific, that is, toward the art of the
novelist. The attempt was made, but fell short of success. In *The House
of the Seven Gables* and in *The Marble Faun* alike the moral understanding of the action—and there is a serious attempt at such understanding, at least in *The Marble Faun*—is corrupted by a provincial senti-
mentalism ethically far inferior to the Manicheism of the Puritans, which

was plain and comprehensive, however brutal. And Hawthorne had small gift for the creation of human beings, a defect allied to his other defects and virtues: even the figures in *The Scarlet Letter* are unsatisfactory if one comes to the book expecting to find a novel, for they draw their life not from specific and familiar human characteristics, as do the figures of Henry James, but from the precision and intensity with which they render their respective ideas; the very development of the story is neither narrative nor dramatic, but expository. When, as in *The Marble Faun* or *The House of the Seven Gables,* there is no idea governing the human figure, or when the idea is an incomplete or unsatisfactory equivalent of the figure, the figure is likely to be a disappointing spectacle, for he is seldom if ever a convincing human being and is likely to verge on the ludicrous. Hawthorne had not the rich and profound awareness of immediacy which might have saved a writer such as Melville in a similar predicament.

His effort to master the novelist's procedure, however, was not sustained, for his heart was not in it. In *The Blithedale Romance,* he began as a novelist, but lost himself toward the close in an unsuccessful effort to achieve allegory; the four unfinished romances represent similar efforts throughout.

His procedure in the last works was startlingly simple; so much so, that no one whom I can recollect has run the risk of defining it.

In *The Scarlet Letter* there occurs a formula which one might name the formula of alternative possibilities. In the ninth chapter, for example, there occurs the following passage:

The people, in the case of which we speak, could justify its prejudice against Roger Chillingworth by no fact or argument worthy of serious refutation. There was an aged handicraftsman, it is true, who had been a citizen of London at the period of Sir Thomas Overbury's murder, now some thirty years agone; he testified to having seen the physician, under some other name, which the narrator of the story had now forgotten, in company with Dr. Forman, the famous old conjuror, who was implicated in the affair of Overbury. Two or three individuals hinted, that the man of skill, during his Indian captivity, had enlarged his medical attainments by joining in the incantations of the savage priests; who were universally acknowledged to be powerful enchanters, often performing seemingly miraculous cures by their skill in the black art. A large number—many of them were persons of such sober sense and practical observation that their opinions would have been valuable in other matters—affirmed that Roger Chillingworth's aspect had undergone a remarkable change while he had dwelt in the town, and especially since his abode with Dimmesdale. At first, his expression had been calm, meditative, scholar-like. Now, there was something ugly and evil in his face, which they had not previously noticed, and which grew still more obvious to sight the oftener they looked upon him. According to the vulgar idea, the fire in his laboratory had been brought from the lower regions, and was fed with infernal fuel; and so, as might be expected, his visage was getting sooty with smoke.

In such a passage as this, the idea conveyed is clear enough, but the embodiment of the idea appears far-fetched, and Hawthorne offers it whimsically and apologetically, professing to let you take it or leave it. Another example occurs in the eighteenth chapter; Dimmesdale and Hester are sitting in the forest, planning the flight which ultimately is never to take place, and Pearl, the symbolic offspring of the untamed elements of human nature, and hence akin to the forest, which, in the Puritan mind, was ruled by Satan in person, plays apart: "A fox, startled from his sleep by her light footstep on the leaves, looked inquisitively at Pearl, as doubting whether it were better to steal off or renew his nap on the same spot. A wolf, it is said—but here the tale has surely lapsed into the improbable—came up and smelt of Pearl's robe, and offered his savage head to be patted by her hand. The truth seems to be, however, that the mother-forest, and these wild things which it nourished, all recognized a kindred wildness in the human child." Similarly, in *The Marble Faun,* one never learns whether Donatello had or had not the pointed ears which serve throughout the book as the physical symbol of his moral nature; the book ends with the question being put to Kenyon, who has had opportunities to observe, and with his refusing to reply.

This device, though it becomes a minor cause of irritation through constant recurrence, is relatively harmless, and at times is even used with good effect. If we reverse the formula, however, so as to make the physical representation perfectly clear but the meaning uncertain, we have a very serious situation; and this is precisely what occurs, in some measure toward the close of *The Blithedale Romance,* and without mitigation throughout the four unfinished romances. We have in the last all of the machinery and all of the mannerisms of the allegorist, but we cannot discover the substance of his communication, nor is he himself aware of it so far as we can judge. We have the symbolic footprint, the symbolic spider, the symbolic elixirs and poisons, but we have not that of which they are symbolic; we have the hushed, the tense and confidential manner, on the part of the narrator, of one who imparts a grave secret, but the words are inaudible. Yet we have not, on the other hand, anything approaching realistic fiction, for the events are improbable or even impossible, and the characters lack all reality. The technique neither of the novelist nor of the allegorist was available to Hawthorne when he approached the conditions of his own experience: he had looked for signals in nature so long and so intently, and his ancestors before him had done so for so many generations, that, like a man hypnotized, or like a man corroded with madness, he saw them; but he no longer had any way of determining their significance, and he had small talent for rendering their physical presence with intensity.

Percy Boynton,[10] in quoting the following passages from *Septimius Felton,* refers to it as a self-portrait:

> As for Septimius, let him alone a moment or two, and then they would see him, with his head bent down, brooding, brooding, his eyes fixed on some chip, some stone, some common plant, any commonest thing, as if it were the clew and index to some mystery; and when, by chance startled out of these meditations, he lifted his eyes, there would be a kind of perplexity, a dissatisfied, foiled look in them, as if of his speculations he found no end.

It is in this generation and the next that we see most clearly and bitterly the realization of Maule's prophecy. These men were cut off from their heritage, from their source of significance, and were abnormally sensitive to the influence of European Romanticism. In Emerson[11] the terms of New England mysticism and of Romantic amoralism were fused and confused so inextricably that we have not yet worked ourselves free of them. In Poe, a man born without a background, New England or any other, Romantic doctrine was introduced directly, in a form free of theological terminology, but in a form none the less which would tend in the long run to support the influence of Emerson. In Melville, the greatest man of his era and of his nation, we find a writer superior at certain points in his career—in books such as *Moby Dick* and *Benito Cereno,* for example—to the confusion and apparently understanding it; at other points—in books like *Mardi* and *Pierre*—succumbing to the confusion; at all points in his career made to suffer for the confusion of contemporary literary taste; and at the end, settling himself in silence, a figure more difficult to face than the later Hawthorne—more difficult, because more conscious, more controlled, and more nearly indifferent.

In Henry Adams we see the curse at work most clearly: intellectual but inconsecutive, unable to justify any principle of action, yet with a character of the highest, a character which demanded not only just action but its justification, he was damned to a kind of restless torment; in which, though an historian of great learning and of high academic distinction, he transformed the Middle Ages by a process of subtle falsification, into a symbol of his own latter-day New England longing; in which, though a stylist of great power and precision, he propounded the aesthetic theory that modern art must be confused to express confusion;[12] in which, though a philosopher of a sort, he created one of the most unphilosophical theories of history imaginable, as a poetic symbol of his own despair.

[10] Percy H. Boynton, *Literature and American Life* (Ginn and Co., 1936), p. 518.

[11] This subject is fully discussed by H. B. Parkes, *The Hound and Horn* IV (July-Sept. 1932), 581-601.

[12] See the last three or four pages of *Mont Saint-Michel and Chartres.*

In the suicide of Henry Adams' wife it is conceivable that we see the logical outcome of his own dilemma, an outcome in his own case prevented by the inheritance of character, which, like the inheritance of confusion, was bequeathed him by early New England.[13]

In *The Scarlet Letter,* then, Hawthorne composed a great allegory; or, if we look first at the allegorical view of life upon which early Puritan society was based, we might almost say that he composed a great historical novel. History, which by placing him in an anti-intellectual age had cut him off from the ideas which might have enabled him to deal with his own period, in part made up for the injustice by facilitating his entrance, for a brief time, into an age more congenial to his nature. Had he possessed the capacity for criticizing and organizing conceptions as well as for dramatizing them, he might have risen superior to his disadvantages, but like many other men of major genius he lacked this capacity. In turning his back upon the excessively simplified conceptions of his Puritan ancestors, he abandoned the only orderly concepts, whatever their limitations, to which he had access, and in his last work he is restless and dissatisfied. The four last romances are unfinished, and in each successive one he sought to incorporate and perfect elements from those preceding; the last, *The Dolliver Romance,* which he had sought to make the best, had he lived, is a mere fragment, but on the face of it is the most preposterous of all. His dilemma, the choice between abstractions inadequate or irrelevant to experience on the one hand, and experience on the other as far as practicable unilluminated by understanding, is tragically characteristic of the history of this country and of its literature; only a few scattered individuals, at the cost of inordinate labor, and often impermanently, have achieved the permeation of human experience by a consistent moral understanding which results in wisdom and in great art. If art is to be measured by the greatness of the difficulties overcome—and the measure is not wholly unreasonable, for there can scarcely be virtue without a comprehension of sin, and the wider and more careful the comprehension the richer the virtue—then these few writers are very great indeed. Hawthorne, when he reversed his formula of alternative possibilities, and sought to grope his way blindly to significance, made the choice of the later Romantics; and his groping was met wherever he moved by the smooth and impassive surface of the intense inane.

[13] This idea is very ably defended by Katherine Simonds, *The New England Quarterly* (December 1936).

Hawthorne as Poet

by Q. D. Leavis

I

For an English person to offer an opinion on Hawthorne, much more an evaluation of his *oeuvre,* must be felt in America to be an impertinence. But the excuse that would justify writing on Hawthorne in an English context—that he is, except as author of one "Puritanical" novel, unread and unrecognized, will, it seems to me, serve here too if somewhat modified. To me, a tremendous admirer of long standing of much of Hawthorne's work, it appears that the essential nature of his achievement has not been isolated and established critically, in spite of the immense amount that has been published on Hawthorne the man, Hawthorne as material for the psychologist, the Hawthorne period and all the rest. I should like to present my own reading of his work, if only to get endorsement from others. In England one can never assume an intelligent knowledge of Hawthorne in the professional world of letters —witness the complacently stupid whole-page article in our august *Times Literary Supplement* two years ago when Mr. Randall Stewart's book came up for review. And in the English academic world Hawthorne's existence as a considerable writer is not even acknowledged. But what is one to conclude when faced with the account of Hawthorne in that admirable American work *The American People* (1949) by Professor H. B. Parkes? Here Hawthorne is characterized as

> a man of low emotional pressure who adopted throughout his life the role of an observer. Remaining always aloof from the world around him, he was able to record what he felt with a remarkable balance and detachment. . . . But since he lacked the compulsive drive of the writer who is himself the victim of conflict and must find a way of salvation, his work lacked force and energy. Carefully and delicately constructed, it was devoid of color and drama and almost passionless. Hawthorne's obsessing personal

"Hawthorne as Poet," by Q. D. Leavis. Part I, *The Sewanee Review,* LIX (Spring 1951), 179-205; Part II, *The Sewanee Review,* LIX (Summer 1951), 426-58. Copyright 1951 by the University of the South. Reprinted by permission of *The Sewanee Review* and Q. D. Leavis.

problem was his sense of isolation. He came to regard isolation as almost the root of all evil, and made it the theme of many of his stories. But Hawthorne's treatment of the subject was always too conscious and deliberate; he expressed it allegorically and not in symbols; and consequently he was unable to say anything about it that enlarges our understanding either of human nature or of the society in which Hawthorne lived.

This is in effect the account of Hawthorne that has always been in currency—stated for instance with more authority and more persuasively by Mr. Yvor Winters in the interesting essay "Maule's Curse, or Hawthorne and the Problem of Allegory," where, though he claims that *The Scarlet Letter* is "faultless, in scheme and detail; it is one of the chief masterpieces of English prose," yet he classifies it as "pure allegory," and dismisses all "Hawthorne's sketches and short stories [as] at best slight performances." Even Henry James, whose monograph on Hawthorne is felt, and was clearly intended, to be the tribute of an artist to the predecessor from whom he inherits, even James demurs at what he calls "allegory, quite one of the lighter exercises of the imagination." But it is clear that James is deploring Hawthorne's merely fanciful pieces; he exempts the works "redolent of a rich imagination." The standard account relegates Hawthorne along with Bunyan to an inferior class of writer who depends for his effects on "allegory," something mechanical and inferior, as Dr. Johnson implied when he wrote "allegory is perhaps one of the most pleasing vehicles of instruction." But when James wrote "Hawthorne is perpetually looking for images which shall place themselves in picturesque correspondence with the spiritual facts with which he is concerned, and of course the search is of the very essence of poetry," he admits, however inadequately, that Hawthorne's intention is a poetic one, nothing less. Similarly, in general acceptance Hawthorne is a "delicate" writer, but when he is praised for his "delicacy" it is intended to stamp his art as something minor. I should prefer to have the purity of his writing noted instead. Nor is the epithet "charming," selected by Henry James, appropriate.

The account, as endorsed by Mr. Parkes, contrives to be unjust to Hawthorne's object and to ignore the very nature of his art. Hawthorne's less interesting work bulks large, no doubt, but it is easily cut free from what is his essential contribution to American literature. The essential Hawthorne—and he seems to me a great genius, the creator of a literary tradition as well as a wonderfully original and accomplished artist—is the author of *Young Goodman Brown, The Maypole of Merry Mount, My Kinsman Major Molineux, The Snow Image, The Blithedale Romance, The Scarlet Letter,* and of a number of sketches and less pregnant stories associated with these works such as *The Gray Champion, Main Street, Old News, Endicott and the Red Cross, The Artist of the Beautiful.* This work is not comparable with the productions of the eighteenth-century "allegorical" essayists nor is it in the manner of Spenser, Milton, or Bunyan—whom of course it can be seen he has not merely studied but assimilated. The first batch of works I specified is essentially dramatic, its use of language is poetic, and it is symbolic, and richly so, as is the dramatic poet's. In fact I should suggest that Hawthorne can have gone to school with no one but Shakespeare for his inspiration and model.[1] Mr. Wilson Knight's approach to Shakespeare's tragedies—each play an expanded metaphor—is a cue for the method of rightly apprehending these works of Hawthorne's, where the "symbol" is the thing itself, with no separable paraphrasable meaning as in an allegory: the language is directly evocative. Rereading this work, one is certainly not conscious of a limited and devitalized talent employing a simple-minded pedestrian technique; one is constantly struck by fresh subtleties of organization, intention, expression and feeling, of original psychological insight and a new minting of terms to convey it, as well as of a predominantly dramatic construction. Yet of the above-mentioned works, apart from *The Scarlet Letter* which has had a good deal of inadequate attention, I can't find any serious *literary* criticism, even in *American Renaissance* where Hawthorne was evidently intended by Professor Matthiessen in some way to be a focus and key-figure. Mr. Quentin Anderson at the end of his article "Henry James and the New Jerusalem" (*Kenyon Review,* Autumn, 1946) offers a metaphysical account of both *The Snow Image* and *Major Molineux*—but these seem to me subjective interpretations (the second misses Hawthorne's meaning entirely) and not literary criticism rooted in the texts. The recent spate of Hawthorne books has not yet reached England but I am told—though I should be glad to hear that I have been told wrongly—that they add nothing.

The aspect of Hawthorne that I want to stress as the important one, decisive for American literature, and to be found most convincingly in the works I specified, is this: that he was the critic and interpreter of American cultural history and thereby the finder and creator of a literary tradition from which sprang Henry James on the one hand and Melville on the other. I find it impossible to follow Mr. Parkes's argument[2] that

> what is lacking in [Hawthorne's] framework of experience is any sense of society as a kind of organic whole to which the individual belongs and in which he has his appointed place. And lacking the notion of social continuity and tradition, [he] lacks also the corresponding metaphysical concep-

---

[1] I find support for this in "Our Old Home," in which Hawthorne wrote: "Shakespeare has surface beneath surface, to an immeasurable depth. . . . There is no exhausting the various interpretation of his symbols."

[2] "Poe, Hawthorne, Melville: an Essay in Sociological Criticism," *Partisan Review,* Feb., 1949.

tion of the natural universe as an ordered unity which harmonizes with human ideals.[3]

It is precisely those problems, the relation of the individual to society, the way in which a distinctively American society developed and how it came to have a tradition of its own, the relation of the creative writer to the earlier nineteenth century American community, and his function and how he could contrive to exercise it—the exploration of these questions and the communication in literary art of his findings—that are his claim to importance. It is true that he is most successful in treating pre-Revolutionary America, but that, after all, is, as he saw it, the decisive period, and *The Blithedale Romance* is the finest test of his dictum in *Old News* that "All philosophy that would abstract mankind from the present is no more than words." As I see it, Hawthorne's sense of being part of the contemporary America could be expressed only in concern for its evolution—he needed to see how it had come about, and by discovering what America had, culturally speaking, started from and with, to find what choices had faced his countrymen and what they had had to sacrifice in order to create that distinctive "organic whole." He was very conscious of the nature of his work; he asserted that to be the function of every great writer, as when in *The Old Manse* he wrote: "A work of genius is but the newspaper of a century, or perchance of a hundred centuries." (Indeed, in some sketches, such as *Old News*, we can see the half-way stage between the newspapers and the work of genius; these sketches have a function like that of the *Letters* of Jane Austen in the evolution of her novels.) And he prepared himself for the task by study, though Providence had furnished him with an eminently usable private Past, in the history of his own family, which epitomized the earlier phases of New England history; this vividly stylized the social history of Colonial America, provided him with a personal mythology, and gave him an emotional stake in the past, a private key to tradition. We know that his first pieces which he later burned in despair of getting published were called *Seven Tales of My Native Land*. Though he was the very opposite of a Dreiser (whom Mr. Parkes backs in contrast) yet I should choose to describe Hawthorne as a sociological novelist in effect, employing a poetic technique which communicates instead of stating his findings. The just comparison with *The Scarlet Letter* is not *The Pilgrim's Progress* but *Anna Karenina*, which in theme and technique it seems to me astonishingly to resemble. This brings up again the objection cited above that

[3] This naïve demand should be measured against this passage from E. H. Davidson, *Hawthorne's Last Phase* (1949): "The rare springtime beauty of the English scene struck him more forcibly than it could the ordinary tourist, for it represented to him the perfect balance between man and nature. This balance was conspicuously absent in the untamed forests of the U. S., where man was busily engaged in subduing nature and dominating a continent. 'It is only an American who can feel it,' Hawthorne wrote."

"Remaining always aloof from the world around him, he was able to record what he felt with a remarkable balance and detachment, but lacked the compulsive drive of the writer who is himself the victim of conflict and must find a way of salvation." There is disguised here a romantic assumption about the Artist. We surely recognize, equally in the Shakespeare of the great tragedies and *Measure for Measure,* in Henry James in his novels and *nouvelles,* and in the Tolstoy of *Anna* (as opposed to the Tolstoy of *Resurrection*) that "remarkable balance and detachment" which is indispensable to the greatest achievement of literary art. Like these artists Hawthorne in his best work is offering in dramatic form an analysis of a complex situation in which he sides with no one party but is imaginatively present in each, having created each to represent a facet of the total experience he is concerned to communicate. The analysis and the synthesis help us to find our own "way of salvation" (not a form of words I should have chosen). Tolstoy *was* in many respects Levin, as we know, but *Anna Karenina* the novel is not presented through Levin's eyes, and could not have been written by Levin. To analyze the way in which Hawthorne actually works as a writer is the only safe way to come at the nature of his creation, to make sure we are taking what he has written and neither overlooking it nor fathering on the author some misreading of our own or of inert traditional acceptance. Until there is an established reading of the texts it is impossible to evaluate an author at all, and it is this, the very first business of the critic, that seems never to have been done for Hawthorne.

The Maypole of Merry Mount is an early work bearing obvious signs of immaturity but it also shows great originality, and it is a root work, proving that Hawthorne had laid the foundations of much later successes, notably *The Scarlet Letter* and *The Blithedale Romance,* in his beginnings almost. It proves also that he decided in his youth on his characteristic technique. We notice that it is essentially a poetic technique: the opening is almost too deliberately poetic in rhythm and word order. But once the convention has been established in the first two paragraphs, he relaxes and proceeds less artificially. We are, or should be, struck in this early piece by the mastery Hawthorne achieves in a new form of prose art, by the skill with which he manages to convey ironic inflexions and to control transitions from one layer of meaning to another, and by which he turns, as it was to become his great distinction to do, history into myth and anecdote into parable. The essential if not the greatest Hawthorne had so soon found himself.

The tale originally had a sub-title: "A Parable," and in a few prefatory sentences Hawthorne wrote that "the curious history of the early settlement of Mount Wollaston, or Merry Mount" furnishes "an admirable foundation for a philosophic romance"—we see his decision to take for his own from the start the associations of "romance" and not of "novel" or some such term suggesting a disingenuous connection between fiction and daily life. He continued: "In the slight sketch here attempted the facts, recorded on the grave pages of our New England annalists, have wrought themselves, almost spontaneously, into a sort of allegory." If an allegory (unfortunate word), it is a "sort" that no experience of *The Faerie Queen* and *The Pilgrim's Progress* can prepare us for. Its distinctive quality is its use of symbols to convey meaning, and a boldness of imagination and stylization which while drawing on life does not hesitate to rearrange facts and even violate history in that interest. The outline of the historically insignificant Merry Mount affair, whether as recorded by the Puritan historian Governor Bradford or so very differently by the protagonist Thomas Merton in his entertaining *New England Canaan*, was a godsend to Hawthorne, who saw in it a means of precipitating his own reactions to his forefathers' choice. While Hawthorne's imagination was historical in a large sense, he was never an imaginative recreator of the romantic past, a historical novelist: he had always from the first very clearly in view the *criticism* of the past. The past was his peculiar concern since it was the source of his present. He always works through the external forms of a society to its essence and its origin. He felt that the significance of early America lay in the conflict between the Puritans who became New England and thus America, and the non-Puritans who were, to him, merely the English in America and whom he partly with triumph but partly also with anguish sees as being cast out (here is a source of conflict). He saw this process as a symbolic recurring struggle, an endless drama that he recorded in a series of works—*The Maypole, My Kinsman Major Molineux, Endicott and the Red Cross, The Gray Champion, The Scarlet Letter, The Blithedale Romance*, among others—that together form something that it would not be fanciful to describe as a ritual drama reminding us of, for instance, the Norse Edda. If his artistic medium is primitive, his intention is not. It is a kind of spiritual and cultural casting up of accounts: what was lost and what gained, what sacrificed to create what? he is perpetually asking, and showing.

Perhaps the American Puritans, who must if so have had none of the humane qualities of Bunyan and his class that make *Pilgrim's Progress* so pleasing—perhaps those who emigrated were more intensively intolerant than those who remained at home, or perhaps the persecuting aspect of their way of life was peculiarly present to Hawthorne because of the witch-hanging judge and the Quaker-whipping Major among his ancestors. But the essential truth Hawthorne rightly seized on, that the decisive minority set themselves in absolute hostility to the immemorial culture of the English folk with its Catholic and ultimately pagan roots, preserved in song and dance, festivals and superstitions, and especially the rites and dramatic practices of which the May-Day ceremonies were the key. Morton did rear a Maypole at Merry Mount and the fanatic

Governor Endicott did indeed (but only after Morton had been seized and shipped home) visit the settlement and have the abominable tree cut down. Moreover the early theologians and historians had dramatized in their writings the elements of the scene in scriptural and theological terms. But this theological myth Hawthorne adapted to convey subtle and often ironic meanings, just as he freely adapts the historical facts. Morton was actually as well as ideally a High Churchman of good birth, a Royalist and deliberately anti-Puritan, but the object of his settlement was profitable trading with the Indians. Having none of the Puritans' conviction of the damned state of the savages, he made friends with them. Thus Hawthorne could make these settlers embody the old way of living as opposed to the new. He starts with the Maypole as the symbol of the pagan religion for "what chiefly characterized the colonists of Merry Mount was their veneration for the Maypole. It has made their true history a poet's tale." A living tree, "venerated" for it is the center of life and changes with the seasons, it is now on the festival of Midsummer's Eve hung with roses, "some that had been gathered in the sunniest spots of the forest and others, of still richer blush, which the colonists had reared from English seed." Here we have the earliest use of one of Hawthorne's chief symbols, the rose, and we notice that the native wild rose and the cultivated rose carried as seed from England (with generations of grafting and cultivation behind it) are in process of being mingled at Merry Mount. Round the tree the worshippers of the natural religion are figured with extraordinary vitality of imagination: "Gothic monsters, though perhaps of Grecian ancestry," the animal-masked figures of mythology and primitive art (man as wolf, bear, stag and he-goat); "And, almost as wondrous, stood a real bear of the dark forest, lending each of his fore-paws to the grasp of a human hand, and as ready for the dance as any in that circle. His inferior nature rose half-way to meet his companions as they stooped"; the Savage Man, well known in heraldry, hairy as a baboon and girdled with green leaves"; Indians real and counterfeit. The harmony between man and beast and nature that was once recognized by a religious ritual could hardly be more poetically conjured up. Then the youth and maiden who represent the May Lord and Lady are shown; they are about to be permanently as well as ritually married, by an English priest who wears also "a chaplet of the native vine-leaves." Later on he is named by Endicott as "Blackstone," though Hawthorne protects himself against the fact that the historic Blaxton had nothing to do with Merry Mount by an equivocal footnote: Blackstone here represents a poetic license which Hawthorne is perfectly justified in taking. Blackstone, who is similarly imported into *The Scarlet Letter* in a key passage, was actually not a High Churchman nor "a clerk of Oxford" as he declares in *The Maypole,* but like most New England divines a Cambridge man and anti-Episcopalian. But he must be of Oxford because Hawthorne needs him to represent Catholicism and Royal-ism, to complete the culture-complex of Merry Mount, which has been shown in every other respect to be ancient, harmonious and traditional, a chain of life from the dim past, from the tree and animal upwards, all tolerated and respected as part of the natural and right order. The reader is expected to take the reference to the historical Blaxton, who like Endicott and Anne Hutchinson, among others, become in Hawthorne's art cultural heroes. How eminently adapted for Hawthorne's purpose he was is seen in this account by the historian of *The Colonial Period of American History*:

> The Rev. William Blaxton, M.A. Emmanuel College, Cambridge, removed to the western slope of Shawmut peninsula [Beacon Hill] where, near an excellent spring, he built a house, planted an orchard, raised apples, and cultivated a vegetable garden. Leaving Boston in 1635, disillusioned because of the intolerance of the Puritan magistrates, he went southward saying as he departed, "I came from England because I did not like the Lord Bishops, but I cannot join with you because I would not be under the Lord Brethren." He too wanted to worship God in his own way.

He represents, among other things, the crowning, the un-Puritan virtue of tolerance, one of Hawthorne's main positives. Without what he stands for the dance and drama round the Maypole and the whole pagan year-cycle of "hereditary pastimes" would be negligible in comparison with the Christian culture even of the Puritans.

Meanwhile a band of Puritans in hiding are watching the scene. To them the masquers and their comrades are like "those devils and ruined souls with whom their superstitions peopled the black wilderness." For:

> Unfortunately there were men in the new world, of a sterner faith than these Maypole worshippers. Not far from Merry Mount was a settlement of Puritans, most dismal wretches, who said their prayers before daylight, and then wrought in the forest or the cornfield, till evening made it prayer time again.

This, to judge by the "most dismal wretches," is to be discounted by the reader as probably the prejudiced view of the Maypole worshippers, just as to the Puritans the others appear to be "the crew of Comus." But if so persuaded, we are brought up short by a characteristic taut statement about the Puritans, shocking both in its literal and allegorical implications, that immediately follows: "Their weapons were always at hand to shoot down the straggling savage." At Merry Mount we have seen a life where the "savage," without and within the human breast, is accepted as part of life. Hawthorne continues in the same tone:

> When they met in conclave, it was never to keep up the old English mirth, but to hear sermons three hours long, or to proclaim bounties on the heads of wolves and the scalps of Indians. Their festivals were fast

days, and their chief pastime the singing of psalms. Woe to the youth or maiden who did but dream of a dance! The selectman nodded to the constable; and there sat the light-heeled reprobate in the stock; or if he danced, it was round the whipping-post, which might be termed the Puritan Maypole.

The practices of the Puritan are described as being a horrible parody of those of the Maypole worshippers, a deliberate offense against the spirit of Life. The force of the cunning phrase "to proclaim bounties on the heads of wolves and the scalps of Indians," charged with a sense of the inhumanity that leveled the Indian with the wolf, should not be overlooked.

I need not continue to analyze and quote in detail, I hope, to demonstrate the success of the kind of literary art Hawthorne has here created, but I want to note a few more of his total effects, by way of prelude to his later work. We have seen and felt what the religion of the old order was. We find ourselves then inescapably faced by Hawthorne with the question: And what did the Puritans worship? We are left in no doubt as to Hawthorne's answer: Force. Hawthorne had realized that religion is a matter of symbols, and his choice of appropriate symbols is not at all simple-minded. The Maypole worshippers are not, it turns out, to be accepted without qualification. They have another symbolic quality attached to them, they are "silken"—"Sworn triflers of a life-time, they would not venture among the sober truths of life, not even to be truly blest." Everyone was "gay" at Merry Mount, but what really was "the quality of their mirth"? "Once, it is said, they were seen following a flower-decked corpse, with merriment and festive music, to his grave. But did the dead man laugh?" We have been rounded on as in the passage about the Puritans. Hawthorne is preparing a more complex whole for us, and preparing us to receive it. The term for the Puritans corresponding to "silken" for the settlers is "iron." We find it immediately after the passage quoted above where their practices are described as systematically inhumane. A party comes "toiling through the difficult woods, each with a horse-load of iron armour to burden his footsteps." A little later they are "men of iron," and when they surround and overpower the Maypole-worshippers their leader is revealed as iron all through: "So stern was the energy of his aspect, that the whole man, visage, frame and soul, seemed wrought of iron, gifted with life and thought, yet all of one substance with his headpiece and breastplate. It was the Puritan of Puritans; it was Endicott himself." He cuts down the Maypole with his sword, which he rests on while deciding the fate of the May Lord and Lady, and "with his own gauntleted hand" he finally crowns them with the wreath of mingled roses from the ruin of the Maypole. The associations of iron are all brought into play, suggesting the rigid system which burdens life, the metal that makes man militant and ultimately inhuman, and it is spiritually the sign of heaviness and gloom, opposed in every way to the associations of lightness—silken, sunny, gay and mirthful, used for the followers of the old way of life. The iron imagery is finally concentrated in the doom brought on New England by the Puritans' victory at Merry Mount: "It was a deed of prophecy. As the moral gloom of the world overpowers systematic gaiety. . . ." The armor in *Endicott and the Red Cross* and *The Scarlet Letter* has more extensive meanings too.

The Puritans' religion is expressed in their rites—acts of persecution, oppression and cruelty. Endicott and his followers pass sentence on "the heathen crew." Their tame bear is to be shot—"I suspect witchcraft in the beast," says the leader, and even the "long glossy curls" on the May Lord's head must be cut. "Crop it forthwith, and that in the true pump-kin-shell fashion"—the brutal denial of personal dignity and natural comeliness is indicated with striking economy. The language of Bunyan is made to sound very differently in these mouths; Hawthorne, a master of language, has many such resources at his command. But Hawthorne's total meaning is very complex and his last word is not by any means a simple condemnation. While the Merry Mount way of life embodies something essential that is lacking in the Puritans', making theirs appear ugly and inhuman, yet Hawthorne's point is that in the New World the old way could be only an imported artifice; New England, he deeply felt, could never be a mere reproduction of the Old. The fairies, as John Wilson says in *The Scarlet Letter,* were left behind in old England with Catholicism. And Hawthorne implies that the outlook of Merry Mount is not consonant with the realities of life in the New World, or the new phase of the world anywhere perhaps. The Puritans may be odious but they have a secret which is a better thing than the religion of nature and humanity. The May Lord and Lady, at Endicott's command, leave their Paradise—the reference to Adam and Eve driven from the Garden is un-mistakable, as others to Milton in this tale—and there is a general sug-gestion that the "choice" imposed on New England is like that made by Adam and Eve, they sacrifice bliss for something more arduous and bet-ter worth having. Hawthorne has no doubt that the May Lord and Lady enter into a finer bond in Christian marriage than they could otherwise have known as symbolic figures in a fertility rite. Nevertheless though their future is "blessed" it is not pleasant or gracious. Hawthorne felt acutely the wrong the Lord Brethren had done to the Blaxtons, typified by the doings of an Endicott. The close parallel between the Merry Mount drama and the corresponding conflict in Milton's poem between the Brothers and the followers of Comus must be intentional—there are explicit references—and intended by Hawthorne as a criticism of Milton's presentment of the case. Virtue and Vice are a simple-minded division in Milton's *Comus,* however his symbolism may be interpreted. In Haw-thorne's view that contest was quite other than a matter of Right and Wrong; his Puritans are an ironic comment on Milton's cause and case.

Hawthorne's rendering shows two partial truths or qualified goods set in regrettable opposition. What Hawthorne implies is that it was a disaster for New England that they could not be reconciled. Hawthorne is both subtler and wiser than Milton, and his poem, unlike Milton's, is really dramatic and embodies a genuine cultural and spiritual conflict. Milton is a Puritan and Hawthorne is not; to Hawthorne, Milton is a man of iron. Hawthorne is seen explicitly the unwilling heir of the Puritans, and their indignant critic, in a fine passage in *Main Street* which ends "Let us thank God for having given us such ancestors; and let each successive generation thank Him not less fervently, for being one step further from them in the march of ages."

Just as the rose, the flower that symbolizes human grace and whose beauty is essentially something cultivated, the product of long training —just as the rose is used from *The Maypole* onwards, so the concept of the iron man becomes basic thereafter. The meaning is expounded in a remarkable section of *Main Street* which concludes:

> All was well, so long as their lamps were freshly kindled at the heavenly flame. After a while, however, whether in their time or their children's, these lamps began to burn more dimly, or with a less genuine lustre; and then it might be seen how hard, cold and confined, was their system,—how like an iron cage was that which they called Liberty.

I believe the image was taken by Hawthorne, consciously or unconsciously, from Bunyan; it may be remembered that in the Interpreter's House Christian is shown a Man in an Iron Cage as an awful warning of what a true Christian should never be. Now Bunyan's Man in an Iron Cage exemplified Despair. I have mentioned also that "Blackstone" recurs in *The Scarlet Letter* in an almost mystically poetic context. In fact, these writings of Hawthorne's, to yield all they offer, must be studied as a whole, as a poet's works are, each illuminating and strengthening the rest. This is not the case with the fictions of any English nineteenth century novelist. Perhaps this makes my point that Hawthorne needs a quite other approach from the one we commonly make to a novelist. His recurrent drama is a poet's vision of the meaning of his world, and it is communicated by poetic means.

Young Goodman Brown, visibly a much later and more practiced work than the last, is also more powerful and more closely knit than anything else of Hawthorne's with the possible exception of the very complex and ambitious *Major Molineux*. It lends itself to much the same kind of analysis, that is, demands the same approach, as has been already outlined, and is even more unmistakably a prose poem. If its content has reminded literary critics of *Macbeth* and the Walpurgisnacht of *Faust*, that is unfortunate, for the relevant point is that Young Goodman Brown is Everyman in seventeenth century New England—the title as usual giving the clue. He is the son of the Old Goodman Brown, that is, the Old Adam (or Adam the First as he is called in Bunyan), and recently wedded to Faith. We must note that every word is significant in the opening sentence: "Young Goodman Brown came forth at sunset into the street of Salem Village; but put his head back, after crossing the threshold, to exchange a parting kiss with his young wife." She begs him to "put off his journey until sunrise," but he declares he cannot: "My journey, as thou callest it, forth and back again, must needs be done 'twixt now and sunrise." It is a journey he takes under compulsion, and it should not escape us that she tries to stop him because she is under a similar compulsion to go on a "journey" herself—"She talks of dreams, too," Young Goodman Brown reflects as he leaves her. The journey each must take alone, in dread, at night, is the journey away from home and the community, from conscious, everyday social life, to the wilderness where the hidden self satisfies, or is forced to realize, its subconscious fears and promptings in sleep. We take that journey with him into the awful forest. We note the division, which is to be the basis of *The Scarlet Letter,* between the town (where the minister rules) and the forest (where the Black Man reigns). From his pious home and Faith, Young Goodman Brown reluctantly wanders back into the desert, meeting as he expects one who "bears a considerable resemblance to him. They might have been taken for father and son." He resists as best he can until he is made to realize to his surprise and horror that his father had gone on that journey before him, and sees many respected neighbours indeed pass him to the trysting place. At first, confident in the appearance of virtue in the daily life of his fellows, he retorts indignantly: "My father never went into the woods on such an errand, nor his father before him. We have been a race of honest men and good Christians since the days of the martyrs." "We are a people of prayer, and good works to boot, and abide no such wickedness." The sinister likeness of his grandfather is able to convince him otherwise, though "the arguments seemed rather to spring up in the bosom of his auditor than to be suggested by" the Devil. We feel how an accumulation of unconscious doubts about the "saints" precipitates Young Goodman Brown's conviction of universal sinfulness. As he loses his belief in the reality of virtue in others the scene grows increasingly sinister until the road "vanished at length, leaving him in the heart of the dark wilderness, still rushing onward with the instinct that guides mortal man to evil. The whole forest was peopled with frightful sounds—the creaking of the trees, the howling of the wild beasts, and the yell of Indians." We see Hawthorne making timely use of the traditional Puritan association of trees, animals, and Indians as the hostile powers, allies of the fiend.

But he was himself the chief horror of the scene, and shrank not from its other horrors.

"Ha! ha! ha!" roared Goodman Brown when the wind laughed at him. "Let us hear which will laugh loudest. Think not to frighten me with your deviltry. Come witch, come wizard, come Indian pow-wow, come devil himself, and here comes Goodman Brown. You may as well fear him as he fear you."

In truth, all through the haunted forest there could be nothing more frightful than the figure of Goodman Brown.

The nightmare poetry gathers volume and power as he approaches the flaming center of the forest, but Hawthorne's poetic imagination is as different as possible from Poe's—there is no touch of the Gothic horrors one might anticipate. When Goodman Brown ends his journey he finds his whole world, even the elders and ministers, assembled to worship at the devil's altar; he and his Faith are only the latest to be received into the communion of the lost.

When Young Goodman Brown returns to Salem Village with the morning light, "staring around him like a bewildered man," his eyes have been opened to the true nature of his fellowmen, that is, human nature; he inescapably knows that what he suspected of himself is true of all men. He must live with that knowledge, and he is thenceforward a man of gloom, the Man in the Iron Cage, a Calvinist indeed. What Hawthorne has given us is not an allegory, and not an ambiguous problem-story (we are not to ask: Was it an actual Satanic experience or only a dream?). Hawthorne has made a dramatic poem of the Calvinist experience in New England. The unfailing tact with which the experience is evoked subjectively, in the most impressive concrete terms, is a subordinate proof of genius. I should prefer to stress the wonderful control of local and total rhythm, which never falters or slackens, and rises from the quiet but impressive opening to its poetic climax in the superb and moving finale, which I should have liked to quote in full. It ends "they carved no hopeful verse upon his tombstone; for his dying hour was gloom."

Hawthorne has imaginatively recreated for the reader that Calvinist sense of sin, that theory which did in actuality shape the early social and spiritual history of New England. But in Hawthorne, by a wonderful feat of transmutation, it has no religious significance, it is as a psychological state that it is explored. Young Goodman Brown's Faith is not faith in Christ but faith in human beings, and losing it he is doomed to isolation forever. *Young Goodman Brown* seems to me very much more impressive than the Walpurgisnacht scene in Joyce's *Ulysses,* which smells of the case-book and the midnight oil. If anyone is inclined to question its claim to be a dramatic poem he might be asked to examine along with it Cowper's acknowledged masterpiece *The Castaway,* comparable in theme but in every other respect so inferior. And I am tempted to ask what advantage has *The Castaway* or even *The Ancient Mariner* over

Young Goodman Brown by being in verse? In fact, the regularity of verse and stanzas is a disadvantage, imposing monotony and other limitations; either of these poems is less forceful, artistically serious and truly "poetic" than Hawthorne's prose poem. The alleged superiority of poetic form may be specious and there is in fact no sharp distinction between prose and poetry.

In this tale Hawthorne achieved a considerable contribution toward the comprehensive masterpiece he was to produce in *The Scarlet Letter,* for the tale is partially taken up into the later romance.

In his introduction to a volume of tales brought out in 1851 but mostly written much earlier Hawthorne, then in his prime as an artist, with *The Scarlet Letter* a year behind him, confessed that he was "disposed to quarrel with the earlier sketches," most of all "because they come so nearly up to the standard of the best that I can achieve now." As one of the earlier sketches in his collection was *My Kinsman Major Molineux* (1831), he might justly have felt that he was never to achieve anything better.

Ideally it should be preceded by a reading of the three studies collected under the title *Old News,* which give the historical background and are clearly the fruit of work preparatory for *Major Molineux.* This remarkable tale might have been less commonly overlooked or misunderstood if it had had a sub-title, such as Hawthorne often provided by way of a hint. It could do with some such explanatory sub-title as "America Comes of Age." But though if a naturalistic story is looked for the reader would be left merely puzzled, the tale lends itself readily to comprehension as a poetic parable in dramatic form, and the opening paragraph as usual clearly explains the situation and furnishes the required clue. We are in the age which was preparing the colonies for the War of Independence and we are made to take part in a dramatic precipitation of, or prophetic forecast of, the rejection of England that was to occur in fact much later.

The actual tale begins by describing a country-bred youth coming to town, starting with the significant sentence: "It was near nine o'clock of a moonlight evening, when a boat crossed the ferry with a single passenger." The sturdy pious youth Robin, the son of the typical farmer-clergyman, represents the young America; he has *left his home* in the village in the woods and crossing by the *ferry, alone, at nightfall,* reaches the little metropolis of a New England port—that is, the contemporary scene where the historic future will be decided. He arrives poor but hopeful, confidently anticipating help in making his fortune from "my kinsman Major Molineux," the reiteration of the phrase being an important contribution to the total effect. The kinsman is Hawthorne's and ours (if we are Americans) as well as Robin's, and his name suggests both his military and aristocratic status. Robin explains much later in the tale that his father and the Major are brothers' sons—that is, one brother had stayed in England and the other left to colonize New England. Their children, the next generation, represented by Robin's father and the Major, had kept on friendly terms and the rich Major, representative in New England of the British civil and military rule and keeping "great pomp," was in a position to patronize his poor country cousin. We do not get this straightforward account in the tale, of course, we have to unravel it for ourselves, for the presentation of the theme is entirely dramatic and we have to identify our consciousness with the protagonist Robin. The essential information is revealed only when we have ourselves experienced for some time the same bewilderment as poor Robin, who cannot understand why his request to be directed to the house of his kinsman is met by the various types of citizen with suspicion, with contempt, with anger, with disgust, with sneers, or with laughter. In fact, Robin has arrived at a critical moment in his kinsman's history. The colonists—with considerable skill and economy Hawthorne represents all ranks and classes of the states in this dream-town—have secretly planned to throw off British rule, or at any rate to rid themselves of Major Molineux, a symbolic action which, performed in the street outside the church at midnight and before the innocent eyes of the mystified youth, takes the form of something between a pageant and a ritual drama, disguised in the emotional logic of a dream. As a dream it has a far greater emotional pull than actuality could have. Hawthorne never anywhere surpassed this tale (written when he was not more than twenty-seven) in dramatic power, in control of tone, pace, and tension, and in something more wonderful, the creation of a suspension between the fullest consciousness of meaning and the emotional incoherence of dreaming. How this is achieved and for what purpose can be seen only by a careful examination of the last half of the tale, but I will quote as sparingly as possible.

Until this point, precisely the middle of the work, no departure from the everyday normal has been necessary, though we have been wrought to a state of exasperation which is ready for working on. And Hawthorne now introduces another note:

He now roamed desperately, and at random, through the town, almost ready to believe that a spell was on him, like that by which a wizard of his country had once kept three pursuers wandering, a whole winter night, within twenty paces of the cottage which they sought. The streets lay before him, strange and desolate, and the lights were extinguished in almost every house. Twice, however, little parties of men, among whom Robin distinguished individuals in outlandish attire, came hurrying along; but though on both occasions they paused to address him, such intercourse did not at all enlighten his perplexity. They did but utter a few words in some language of which Robin knew nothing, and perceiving his inability to answer, bestowed a curse upon him in plain English. and hastened away. Finally, the lad determined to knock at the door of every mansion, trusting that perseverance would overcome the fatality that had hitherto thwarted him. Firm in this resolve, he was passing beneath the walls of a church, which formed the corner of two streets, when, as he turned into the shade of its steeple, he encountered a bulky stranger, muffled in a cloak. The man was proceeding with the speed of earnest business, but Robin planted himself full before him, holding the oak cudgel with both hands across his body, as a bar to further passage.

"Halt, honest man, and answer me a question," said he, very resolutely. "Tell me, this instant, whereabouts is the dwelling of my kinsman, Major Molineux!"

. . . The stranger, instead of attempting to force his passage, stepped back into the moonlight, unmuffled his face, and stared full into that of Robin.

"Watch here an hour, and Major Molineux will pass by," said he.

Robin gazed with dismay and astonishment on the unprecedented physiognomy of the speaker. The forehead with its double prominence, the broad hooked nose, the shaggy eyebrow, and fiery eyes, were those which he had noticed at the inn, but the man's complexion had undergone a singular, or, more properly, a two-fold change. One side of the face blazed an intense red, while the other was black as midnight, the division line being in the broad bridge of the nose; and a mouth which seemed to extend from ear to ear was black or red, in contrast to the color of the cheek. The effect was as if two individual devils, a fiend of fire and a fiend of darkness, had united themselves to form this infernal visage. The stranger grinned in Robin's face, muffled his parti-colored features, and was out of sight in a moment.

The stranger, whose unearthly appearance we were prepared for by the "individuals in outlandish attire" speaking in a code—for as we realize later they were obviously conspirators demanding from Robin a password he could not furnish, but they help to increase the nightmare atmosphere—is shown by his face to be something more than a man in disguise. The tension is being screwed up to the pitch needed for the approaching climax of the drama: this is not a man like the others but a Janus-like fiend of fire and darkness, that is, we presently learn, "war personified" in its dual aspects of Death and Destruction. But it is not just a personification, it is a symbol with emotional repercussions which passes through a series of suggestive forms. The account of its features at first: "The forehead with its double prominence, the broad hooked nose" etc. suggests Punch and so also the grotesque associations of puppet-show farce. The division of the face into black and red implies the conventional get-up of the jester, and indeed he "grinned in Robin's face" before he "muffled his parti-colored features." At this point Robin, carrying the reader with him, having "consumed a few moments in philosophical speculation upon the species of man who had just left him," is able to "settle this point shrewdly, rationally and satisfactorily." He and we are of course deceived in our complacency. He falls into a drowse by sending his thoughts "to imagine how that evening of ambiguity and weariness had been spent in his father's household." This actually completes his bewilderment—"Am I here or there?" he cries, "But still his mind kept vibrating between fancy and reality."

Now, so prepared, we hear the murmur that becomes a confused medley of voices and shouts as it approaches, turning into "frequent bursts from many instruments of discord, and a wild and confused laughter filled up the intervals." "The antipodes of music" heralds "a mighty stream of people" led by a single horseman whom Robin recognizes as the eerie stranger in a fresh avatar. With the "rough music" that in Old England was traditionally used to drive undesirable characters out of the community, by the red glare of torches and with "War personified" as their leader, the citizens of America, with Indians in their train and cheered on by their women, are symbolically if proleptically casting out the English ruler. The nightmare impression reaches its climax: "In his train were wild figures in the Indian dress, and many fantastic shapes without a model, giving the whole march a visionary air, as if a dream had broken forth from some feverish brain, and were sweeping visibly through the midnight streets. . . . 'The double-faced fellow has his eye upon me' muttered Robin, with an indefinite but uncomfortable idea that he was himself to bear a part in the pageantry."

It seems indeed that the pageant has been brought to this place for Robin's benefit.

A moment more, and the leader thundered a command to halt: the trumpets vomited a horrid breath, and then held their peace; the shouts and laughter of the people died away, and there remained only a universal hum, allied to silence. Right before Robin's eyes was an uncovered cart. There the torches blazed the brightest, there the moon shone out like day, and there, in tar-and-feathery dignity, sat his kinsman Major Molineux!

He was an elderly man, of large and majestic person, and strong, square features, betokening a steady soul; but steady as it was, his enemies had found means to shake it. His face was pale as death, and far more ghastly; the broad forehead was contracted in his agony, so that his eyebrows formed one grizzled line; his eyes were red and wild, and the foam hung white upon his quivering lip. His whole frame was agitated by a quick and continual tremor, which his pride strove to quell, even in those circumstances of overwhelming humiliation. But perhaps the bitterest pang of all was when his eyes met those of Robin; for he evidently knew him on the instant, as the youth stood witnessing the foul disgrace of a head grown

gray in honor. They stared at each other in silence, and Robin's knees
shook, and his hair bristled, with a mixture of pity and terror.

The pageant is thus seen to represent a tragedy and is felt by us as
such; it arouses in Robin the appropriate blend of emotions—the classical "pity and terror." But Hawthorne has by some inspiration—for how
could he have known except intuitively of the origins of tragedy in ritual
drama?—gone back to the type of action that fathered Tragedy. Just
as the "War personified" suggests an idol or a human representive of the
god, so does the other terrible figure "in tar-and-feathery dignity" in the
cart. We seem to be spectators at that most primitive of all dramatic
representations, the conquest of the old king by the new.

If the story had ended here, on this note, it would have been remarkable enough, but Hawthorne has an almost incredible consummation to
follow. I mean incredible in being so subtly achieved with such mastery
of tone. From being a spectator at a tragedy, Robin has to fulfill his
premonitions of having "to bear a part in the pageantry" himself. He
is drawn into the emotional vortex and comes to share the reactions of
the participants. He has felt intimately the dreadful degradation of
his English kinsman, but now he is seized with the excitement of the
victors, his fellow-countrymen, and sees their triumph as his own—"a
perception of tremendous ridicule in the whole scene affected him with
a sort of mental inebriety." Drunk with success the whole town roars in
a frenzy of laughter, and Robin's shout joins theirs and is the loudest.
Then in a sudden calm that follows this orgy "the procession resumed
its march. On they went, like fiends that throng in mockery around some
dead potentate, mighty no more, but majestic still in his agony." We are
left in the silent street, brought back into the world of problems in which
the tale opened. Robin still has to settle with reality and decide his future, the future of his generation. He asks to be shown the way back
to the ferry: "I begin to grow weary of a town life" he says to the towns-
man who has stayed behind to note his reactions. But his new friend
replies: "Some few days hence, if you wish it, I will speed you on your
journey. Or, if you prefer to remain with us, perhaps, as you are a shrewd
youth, you may rise in the world without the help of your kinsman, Major Molineux."

Hawthorne has been blamed for failing to provide a "solution" and for
not being optimistic as a good American should be, but it seems to
me that here, as in *The Maypole*, he ends in reasonable, sober hopefulness for the future of life. Provided we recognize the facts and fully com-
prehend the position, we can cope with it, if not master it, he implies.
Declining to be, perhaps incapable of being, a naturalistic novelist, he
was true to his best perceptions of his genius when he did the work of
a dramatic poet, the interpreter and radical critic of the society which
had produced him and for whose benefit he expressed his insight in a
unique literature.

II

The Scarlet Letter has an unfortunate title, catchpenny in fact, which has some responsibility for the common mistake that the novel is "about adultery" or even about Sin. The stress falls where it always does in Hawthorne as can be seen in the lay-out, the dialogue, the characterization and a rather obtrusive "message" in the novel itself, which, incidentally, is described by its author as a "Romance." This term is strictly correct for both *The Scarlet Letter* and *The Blithedale Romance*; as Lord Raglan points out in his anthropological study *The Hero,* "romance is often myth in disguise." It is Hawthorne's distinction to have given artistic validity to the term Romance which he makes a serious vehicle. The kernel of this romance, and I believe the first form of it, is the rather crude story *Endicott and the Red Cross* (1837), and to examine that is to rescue the skeleton of *The Scarlet Letter* from the sentimental and moralistic misreadings that have given it a false appearance.

Endicott comes in historical time after *The Maypole* (which begins with the first settlers) and is contemporary with *The Scarlet Letter*. They are both supposed to occur in the reign of Charles I, the age when the colonists felt menaced by the threatened Romanization of England by Laud and the royal family. *Endicott* is followed by *The Gray Champion* which ends with the overthrow of James II and that in turn is followed by *Major Molineux,* the prophecy of the Revolution. Hawthorne completes his series with *The Blithedale Romance,* wherein the contemporary scene is typified. It will be noted that Hawthorne took upon himself, very suitably for the originator of a national literature, the work of the Edda-poets, of the makers of antique tragedy and of medieval drama; hence a good deal of his writings, his best creative work, is a damatization of the same theme, or portions of it. It must be something of this kind that James had in mind when he wrote of Hawthorne: "No one has had a literary form that more successfully expressed his vision. He was not a moralist, and he was not simply a poet."

The tale opens with Endicott mustering the Salem trainband in full armor—we recall that *The Maypole* ended with the triumph of the armored Puritans, and we are now to face the consequences of the victory over what Blackstone and Merry Mount stood for. The social-moral scene of the new order is described by the symbol of Endicott's breastplate; reflected in such a mirror the details are doubly suggestive—the wolf's head on the meeting-house door splashing "the sacred edifice" with blood is immediately understood like an image in a poem of Blake's.

> This piece of armor was so highly polished that the whole surrounding scene had its image in the glittering steel. The central object in the mirrored picture was an edifice of humble architecture with neither steeple nor bell to proclaim it the house of prayer. A token of the perils of the wilderness

was seen in the grim head of a wolf, which had just been slain within the precincts of the town, and according to the regular mode of claiming bounty, was nailed on the porch of the meeting-house. The blood was still plashing on the doorstep. There happened to be visible, at the same noontide hour, so many other characteristics of the time and manners of the Puritans, that we must endeavour to represent them in a sketch, though far less vividly than they were reflected in the polished breastplate of John Endicott.

A neatly symmetrical setting is staged for us thus. The grim meeting-house with "in close vicinity to the sacred edifice that important engine of Puritan authority, the whipping-post" and "at one corner of the meeting-house the pillory, and at the other the stocks." Now for the living wolves nailed to the meeting-house: in the pillory is a suspected Catholic, while a Royalist is confined in the stocks; on the meeting-house steps are exposed ignominiously a man and a woman who in different ways have voiced heterodox views, the man being labelled "A Wanton Gospeller." There are other victims of the harsh rule of the saints in the crowd, including most notably a beautiful young woman doomed to wear the "A" for adulteress on her gown. She has defiantly embroidered it in gold on scarlet cloth, but we hear no more of her now. Except for the malefactors, all the men are in the trainband, "iron-breasted." Gazing at them, armed with their superseded flint-headed arrows, are the ousted natives, "stately savages, in all the pomp and dignity of the primeval Indian"; they also have an ironic function. They suggest that their conquerors differ from them chiefly in having matchlocks and iron armor and that "pomp and dignity" are not proofs of civilization. They will recur in *The Scarlet Letter* in a more powerful context—the chapter there called "The New England Holiday" stresses the "Puritanic gloom" and slyly goes on to describe the party of Indian onlookers "with countenances of inflexible gravity, beyond what even the Puritan could attain," a comment on the theory that gravity is a sign of godliness.

This is the actual setting also of *The Scarlet Letter,* a simple, almost primitive, stage-setting to which the romance adds only scenes in the forest. We are reminded again of the childhood of the drama; it is a stage suitable for the enaction of a morality play or a mystery. The setting is inevitably typical of the moral action, but Hawthorne's stress is here seen to fall on the sociological and not the "moral" in the popular sense at all, since he is clearly demanding sympathy for the anti-social members of the community, victims of a theocratic society where "religion and law were almost identical." The only other actor is Roger Williams, the minister, who serves a similar function to Blackstone in *The Maypole.* "His aspect was perfectly that of a pilgrim," he comes onto the stage out of the wilderness, and his first act is to "drink at a bubbling fountain which gushed into the sunshine" near the corner of the meeting-house. Historically Williams was a Cambridge divine who emigrated in 1630 and became, in Cotton Mather's words, "the first rebel against the divine church-order established in the wilderness." He stood for tolerance and was finally obliged to fly to the wilderness and take refuge with the Indians, founding a liberal state on Rhode Island.

In the story, Endicott voices a characteristic tyranny which Williams endeavors to check without success; the culprits in durance make sardonic comments. Incensed at the news from England, Endicott demands: Why had they emigrated except for liberty to worship according to their conscience? " 'Call you this liberty of conscience?' interrupted the Wanton Gospeller. A sad and quiet smile flitted across the mild visage of Roger Williams. But Endicott shook his sword wrathfully at the culprit." Finally Endicott rends the Red Cross, as the symbol of Papacy and Royalty, from the ensign. " 'Sacrilegious wretch!' cried the high-churchman in the pillory, unable longer to restrain himself, 'thou has rejected the symbol of our holy religion!' " It is difficult to see how the last paragraph of the little drama can be anything but ironically intended.

Though *The Scarlet Letter* was not published till thirteen years later, its essence is still that of this story which Hawthorne must have been brooding over in the interval. The meeting-house as before dominates the square, with the same accompaniments. The scaffold of the pillory is the scene of the three main parts of the drama—the opening, the final act, and the chapter exactly half-way. At the close Hester expresses for us the reason for its omnipresence: "There was a sense within her—too ill-defined to be made a thought, but weighing heavily on her mind,— that her whole orb of life, both before and after, was connected with this spot, as with the one point that gave it unity." The iron-breasted Puritan is in control, the Indians and the wilderness surround the town which is open only on one side, to the seashore, where in turn all the chief actors have come from England and which offers the only way of escape. The chief difference is that the scarlet-lettered young woman has been brought into the center of the stage and her history used as a measure of the inhumanity of the society she is fixed in. Just as Tolstoy's novel is framed to evoke the response: This is the society that condemned Anna! so Hawthorne makes Hester the critic of the society that similarly rejects and victimizes her. And just as in *Anna* Tolstoy managed to find room for all his interests, experiences, and problems, so *The Scarlet Letter* has a richer life than any other of Hawthorne's works because it is the most inclusive. What he had worked on and crystallized out in *The Minister's Black Veil, Endicott and the Red Cross, Young Goodman Brown, Main Street, Rapaccini's Daughter,* and *The Maypole of Merry Mount* he swept into a finely organized whole, so that every portion is concentrated with meanings and associations and cross-references. Only something in the nature of a poetic *procédé* and technique could have coped with such an undertaking and that is what we have here as evidently as in such shorter pieces of work as *Young Goodman Brown.*

For example, instead of the briefly indicated layout of *Endicott and the Red Cross* there is to *The Scarlet Letter* an introductory chapter of two pages called "The Prison-Door" and which may be compared, for it is a prose poem, with Crabbe's introductory vision of *The Village* where there is a very similar mobilizing of symbols ("Lo! where the heath, with withering brake grown o'er. . . . There poppies nodding, mock the hope of toil. . . . O'er the young shoot the charlock throws a shade, And clasping tares cling round the sickly blade" etc.). It wonderfully concentrates the theme of the book. Hawthorne describes in one pregnant sentence a Puritan throng waiting outside a prison door, and we realize that that is an index of the nature of their life. He continues, with that disturbing likeness to Swift that shows another formative influence in his literary heredity:

> The founders of a new colony, whatever Utopia of human virtue and happiness they might officially project, have invariably recognized it among their earliest practical necessities to allot a portion of virgin soil as a cemetery, and another portion as the site of a prison.

The graveyard and the prison: the existence of Death and Sin as primary factors in that way of life, equally inescapable, have thus been indicated. To Hawthorne the Prison represents man's punishment for transgression by society, and that is one aspect of his theme. Between the prison and the street there is a grass plot overgrown with noxious weeds (like Crabbe's)

> which evidently found something congenial in the soil that had so early borne the black flower of civilized society, a prison. But on one side of the portal, and rooted almost at the threshold, was a wild rose-bush, covered, in this month of June, with its delicate gems, which might be imagined to offer their fragrance and fragile beauty to the prisoner as he went in, and to the condemned criminal as he came forth to his doom, in token that the deep heart of Nature could pity him.

We feel of course that the rose ought to be Divine Grace, but Hawthorne's use of this symbol is his own. It seems to stand for him for the indestructible humane impulse that survives somewhere in some people even in the most repressive social order, in the most unpromising natural conditions:

> This rose-bush, by a strange chance, has been kept alive in history; but whether it had merely survived out of the stern old wilderness, so long after the fall of the gigantic pines and oaks that originally over-shadowed it,—or whether, as there is fair authority for believing, it had sprung up under the footsteps of the sainted Anne Hutchinson as she entered the prison-door,—we shall not take it upon us to determine.

If we are—as Hawthorne assumes—acquainted with the history of Anne Hutchinson, we at once ask ourselves: Why sainted? and realize that she was a saint only in struggling for liberty of conscience against an intolerant church.[4] We now have an inkling of what the wild rose stands for in Hawthorne's symbolic structure. We remember its occurrence in *The Maypole* mingled with "others which the colonists had reared from English seed." Blackstone, Roger Williams, Anne Hutchinson, and Eliot "the holy Apostle of the Indians" (who figures in the same way in *The Blithedale Romance*) keep the rose alive, or tend and cultivate it to the finer flower of traditional humane civilization. Hawthorne ends his prologue by plucking one of the roses and presenting it to the reader.

Hawthorne's preoccupation with something that is at once the cultural and the psychological classes him with George Eliot and Tolstoy and Conrad. Hence probably the enigmatic final sentence of James's *Hawthorne*: "Man's conscience was his theme, but he saw it in the light of a creative fancy which added, out of its own substance, an interest and, I may almost say, an importance." His profound concern with the history of his local civilization and its importance for himself distinguishes him even among his kind there. Here is the point where Hawthorne, Henry James, and Melville meet. If James found in Hawthorne a pattern of the novelist as social critic of New England and the mother country, Melville saw the archetypal American poet in him, one of "the masters of the great Art of Telling the Truth" like Shakespeare—in fact, the American Shakespeare, "an unimitating and perhaps an inimitable man."[5] What is commonly considered as characteristic of Melville's mode of communicating his vision is often only a technique imitated from Hawthorne.

The scaffold for instance in *The Scarlet Letter* is the scene first of Hester's martyrdom before the throng and the temporal and spiritual rulers (after which she undergoes "a new birth" and so can be said to have symbolically died); then of Dimmesdale's Agony when in the central chapter he offers himself on the scaffold in a midnight vigil in expiation of his sin; finally of his death, after he has preached in the adjacent church the Election Sermon prophesying "a high and glorious destiny" for the chosen people of New England. Roger Chillingworth, the wronged husband whose passion for revenge has "transformed a wise and just man to a fiend," declares then: "there was no place so secret—no high place nor lowly place, where thou couldst have escaped me,—save on this very scaffold!" On her first exposure there Hester with her baby in her arms is likened (with reservations) to the Madonna and Child.

From this daring parallel with the symbolism of Christianity (the scaffold substituted for the cross), wherein Hawthorne's idea of the martyrdom of man at the hands of a theocratic society is pretty clearly

---

[4] She was banished from the colony of Massachusetts in 1638 for claiming that the superiority of personal revelation exempted her from the authority of the clergy.

[5] From a review of Hawthorne's *Mosses* in 1850, before he had met Hawthorne.

hinted, Melville must have taken the scheme of deliberately suggesting the crucifixion of Billy Budd with which that tale ends, and the symbolic history of Billy too. In *Israel Potter*, which Hawthorne admired, there is a marked imitation of Hawthorne in the fine opening and the poignant close. Israel's upbringing and history are described in impressive detail as the symbolic making of a nation until thus "unwittingly preparing himself for the Bunker Hill rifle" Israel takes up arms against the British and we realize that we have really been given a chart of "the temper of the men of the revolutionary era." But in between there is only an uneven picaresque eighteenth-century novel, and *Benito Cereno* is a worthier instance of Hawthorne's influence on the one side; James's early *nouvelle, The Europeans,* that masterly symbolic analysis of the New England mores in the Hawthorne age, is James's finest tribute on the other. Hawthorne's achievement is thus seen to have been decisive for the American novel.

What Hawthorne can do by concentration is best seen in the chapter "The Governor's Hall" which, with the next chapter "The Elf-Child and the Minister," is central to the "romance." The garden (New England) is seen from within the Hall, the account of the Governor, his Hall and clerical advisers and the portraits of the Governor's "lineage," forms the climax of the book on its sociological side as the last chapters do of the emotional interest. Endicott's *breastplate* has become a much more subtle and elaborately-reflecting *suit of mail.*[6] Hester draws Pearl away from it to look out of the window at the garden saying "It may be, we shall see flowers there; more beautiful than we find in the woods." But apart from "some rude and immature attempt at shrubbery," "the proprietor appeared already to have relinquished, as hopeless, the effort to perpetuate on this side of the Atlantic, in a hard soil and amid the close struggle for subsistence, the native English taste for ornamental gardening." The conditions of pioneering settlement favored both literally and socially "cabbages in plain sight" and no flowers—understandably; but Hawthorne continues:

> There were a few rose-bushes, however, and a number of apple-trees, probably the descendants of those planted by the Reverend Mr. Blackstone, the first settler of the peninsula; that half-mythological personage, who rides through our early annals, seated on the back of a bull.

The apple trees, like the rose bushes, represent the fruits of civilization. Blackstone brought them with him when he crossed the sea like Europa (hence "on the back of a bull"), who, thus taken from ancient Phoenicia, founded the civilization of Crete. As mother of Minos she was also connected with the Labyrinth, which probably also connected her with *The*

---

[6] The significance of the suit of armor is admirably explained by Mr. Yvor Winters in his essay on Hawthorne, "Maule's Curse" [reprinted in this volume—ED.].

Scarlet Letter in Hawthorne's mind where the Labyrinth is a recurrent image as will be seen. Blackstone is half mythological because his real history, like the existence of Merry Mount, furnished "facts [which] have wrought themselves almost spontaneously into a sort of allegory." Then the Governor appears. "The wide circumference of an elaborate ruff, beneath his gray beard, in the antiquated fashion of King James's reign, caused his head to look not a little like that of John the Baptist in a charger"—we have evoked the Puritan theory, put in practice as it were, of the opposition between soul and body in this description of a head cut off from the body by the ruff. This theory is hinted and next enlarged on, then it is explained that in practice the rejection of bodily comforts "or even luxury" was not acted on as it should in consistency have been; the deduction is that hypocrisy is the consequence of submitting to an inhuman theory—another underlining of the argument of *The Scarlet Letter*. The case of John Wilson is next opened, as proof of the inextinguishable humanity of man, in a passage of great beauty and which to me might have sooner been looked for in this form in T. F. Powys:

> This creed was never taught, for instance, by the venerable pastor, John Wilson, whose beard, white as a snowdrift, was seen over Governor Bellingham's shoulder; while its wearer suggested that pears and peaches might yet be naturalized in the New England climate, and that purple grapes might possibly be compelled to flourish, against the sunny garden-wall. The old clergyman, nurtured at the rich bosom of the English Church, had a long-established and legitimate taste for all good and comfortable things; and however stern he might show himself in the pulpit, or in his public reproof of such transgressions as that of Hester Prynne, still, the genial benevolence of his private life had won him warmer affection than was accorded to any of his professional contemporaries.

The imagery of the wall-fruit takes us back to the wider symbolism of the Garden that represents the cultural life of New England. The genial character of the English Church is delightfully evoked, contrasting with the Puritan government in the previous paragraph: "the impression made by his [Bellingham's] aspect, so rigid and severe, and frost-bitten with more than autumnal age." It is appropriately Wilson who asks Pearl "Art thou one of these naughty elfs or fairies, whom we thought to have left behind us, with other relics of Papistry, in merry old England?"

The veins represented by *The Minister's Black Veil* and *Young Goodman Brown* are united toward the end of the book. When Hester comes out of prison near the beginning, emerging from the grave (it is implied), she is Young Goodman Brown—she cannot escape recognizing the evil in the hearts of the townspeople who treat her as a leper ("such loss of faith is ever one of the saddest results of sin" Hawthorne ironically explains⁷). This is balanced by the chapter "The Minister in a Maze" toward the end, where after meeting Hester in the forest and agreeing to her plan of elopement Dimmesdale on returning to Boston has Young Goodman Brown's experience on returning to Salem but with this differ- ence, that the minister learns that in himself are all the evil impulses of other men. "Another man had returned out of the forest; a wiser one." "Nothing short of a total change of dynasty and moral code in that interior kingdom would account for it." As Hawthorne has just described the forest as "that wild, heathen Nature of the forest, never subjugated by human law, nor illumined by higher truth," it seems that he did not endorse the theological myth. Though the Puritans alleged the forest to be the domain of the Black Man, Hawthorne shows that in com- parison with the settlement the wilderness is a blissful place for the lovers. There they are able to assure each other that "What we did had a consecration of its own," and we recognize that the relation between them has been the only good human relation in the book. A proof of its validity is that it produced the child Pearl, who appears as the choice channel of Life and is contrasted with the horrible offspring of the Pilgrims (just as is the outcast Quaker child in *The Gentle Boy*). Pearl is created in terms that one would have looked for in D. H. Lawrence rather than in the Hawthorne of common esteem and she alone escapes the Puritan ethos, not by dying but by escaping to a fuller life in Europe. Hawthorne's undisguised "message" is that the evil lay in the conceal- ment—"Thou wast not bold, thou wast not true," Pearl accuses her father. The tragedy consists in the separation of the genuinely united couple by an inhuman society and originated in the false relation im- posed on a girl by an unlovable husband (as in *Anna*); Tolstoy shows in addition that even avoiding the evil of concealment and being bold and true cannot prevent disaster when people carry the world they were born into about with them. Hawthorne points his unorthodox position by ending, it may seem incongruously, with a regenerated Hester promising to other unhappy women a brighter future "when the world should have grown ripe for it" and "a new truth would be revealed" which will "establish the whole relation between man and woman on a surer ground of mutual happiness." Though prepared for by a good many "liberal" notes throughout the book, this, landing us with a bump in the era of Margaret Fuller, is a finally discordant note. But it is quite in keeping with the discussion in *The Blithedale Romance* between

---

⁷ The element of irony in Hawthorne has been even more overlooked than in James. Melville's intelligence made him inveigh against the "absurd misconception" of Haw- thorne as "a man who means no meanings," "a harmless man." Melville insists on the force of Hawthorne's intellect which implies what he calls "blackness," but concludes "Nor need you fix upon that blackness in him, if it suits you not. Nor, indeed, will all readers discern it; for it is, mostly, insinuated to those who may best understand it, and account for it."

the emancipated Zenobia and Hawthorne's mouthpiece Coverdale about Woman, Love, and Society. It is really a touching proof of Hawthorne's democratic optimism. Without it the drama would have been a watertight tragedy like Anna Karenina's or those created by George Eliot for her Gwendolen Harleth and Mrs. Transome. It is, like theirs, a perfect sociological tragedy—given this kind of society and this situation occurring in it, with principals of such a nature and so conditioned, only this can result, there is no escape but in death. And the theological disputation between Hester and her husband is genuinely distilled from the action and its religious environment, not, like Hardy's President of the Immortals finishing his sport with Tess, an imposed "philosophy":

> "Peace, Hester, peace" replied the old man, with gloomy sternness. "It is not granted me to pardon. I have no such power as thou tellest me of. My old faith, long forgotten, comes back to me, and explains all that we do, and all we suffer. By thy first step awry, thou didst plant the germ of evil; but since that moment, it has all been a dark necessity. Ye that have wronged me are not sinful, save in a kind of typical illusion; neither am I fiend-like, who have snatched a fiend's office from his hands. It is our fate. Let the black flower blossom as it may!"

"The black flower" is meant to connect with "the black flower of civilized society, a prison" in the prologue which there typifies the social condemnation of sin in contrast with the other flower, the rose. We may pause at the image in Hester's speech to him ("who are wandering here together in this gloomy maze of evil, and stumbling at every step, over the guilt wherewith we have strewn our path") which is picked up in a later chapter title "The Minister in a Maze," and connects with Hawthorne's frequent use in this work of "labyrinth"—"Hester wandered without a clue in the dark labyrinth of mind," Hester is in "a dismal labyrinth of doubt," Chillingworth is the monster who prevents the elopement from the labyrinth, whose action affects Hester as a "dark and grim countenance of an inevitable doom, which—at the moment when a passage seemed to open for the minister and herself out of their labyrinth of misery—showed itself, with an unrelenting smile, right in the midst of their path." Hawthorne was undoubtedly fertilized by his early classical studies as much as by his seventeenth-century reading. The myth of the labyrinth had obviously struck root in him, and it is characteristic of his genius that the use he makes of it is psychological and emotive. There is the remarkable sustained account of the psychological warfare Chillingworth wages on the unconscious—though intuitively self-protecting—minister, "working in the soil like a dark miner." Hawthorne can with justice declare of the resolution of his drama: "some deep life-matter was now to be laid open to them," when the way out of the Labyrinth was to be found. He has the right to such a vocabulary for he creates it in the concrete. His discovery of the need for creating such an idiom, at once poetic and psychological—and who beside Shakespeare could have helped him?—is one of his claims to rank with the most serious masters of the novel. He produced a very moderate number of volumes; and if even in that his creation was sometimes uneven, his experiments were not always successful and his search for "images which shall place themselves in picturesque correspondence with the spiritual facts with which he is concerned" sometimes ended in the trivial or the labored, that is to be expected of such a distinctly pioneering artist. Greatly as I admire *The Scarlet Letter* I can't agree with Mr. Winters that it is "faultless in detail," for the want of tact in handling the scarlet "A" and the brook in the forest, for instance, everyone must feel as strongly as Henry James did. When trying for an archaic diction he can be seen to write no language, though he is never unplausible like Scott and he can use Bunyan's speech-idiom, which his ear had thoroughly caught, with great skill for poetic and ironic purposes.

If *The House of the Seven Gables* has been consistently over-rated (it seems to me quite uninteresting, illogical in conception and frequently trivial in execution, proof of the mischief of the pressure that forced Hawthorne to try and write something like the popular idea of a novel), *The Blithedale Romance* has never as far as I can make out had justice done it. Its style is more consistently distinguished than that of *The Scarlet Letter,* its tone ranges with remarkable command from the dryly critical to the poetic. It is only apparently more personal than the other creative works I've discussed because the theme, still Hawthorne's great theme, is treated in the contemporary context and founded very slightly in an experience of Hawthorne's of ten years back, which he must have been adapting ever since to the artistic use he could have for it. (Like Shakespeare in Keats's letter, Hawthorne must have "led a life of Allegory —his works are the comments on it"; Hawthorne similarly wrote: "Nelson expressed his life in a kind of symbolic poetry.") In this romance Hawthorne features as a "half-mythological personage" himself, appearing as Miles Coverdale, though Miles, apart from obviously being a poet-novelist, is shown as the representative of his age. Instead of the country-bred Robin we have the spoiled city-bred young man about town with private means, an amateur of the arts and good living; there, Hawthorne saw, was now the decisive battle-ground of the future of American culture. Blithedale resembles Brook Farm only as Hawthorne's Merry Mount did Morton's, and Hawthorne tried to stave off the inevitable misreading of his work as a *roman à clef* by a warning in the Preface where he announces that "His whole treatment of the affair is altogether incidental to the main purpose of the romance." Blithedale is then the contemporary Merry Mount, the symbol of a life superior in the theory on which it is based and in the possibilities it offers to the form of life forced on one by the society in which one finds oneself by birth. Its existence represents the possibility of a choice—there is none in *The Scarlet Letter,* hence the Labyrinth is the comprehensive image used in that.

As always, we must pay the closest attention to the construction, to the form in which the story or plot is exposed to the reader, and to the associations of the characters and their attributes in order to grasp what Hawthorne is at. There are no irrelevancies in Hawthorne's best works and when we seem to find one it should be read with particular care as it will undoubtedly turn out to be structural. A first reading leaves most people bewildered, asking questions about the unresolved mysteries of the drama (was Westervelt Zenobia's husband or lover? why all this fuss about Old Moodie? what is the point of the Veiled Lady?), complaining of the long pauses holding up the action, of the disquieting way the plot skips about and of the apparent discontinuity. The stress seems to fall in the oddest places. A truly inward reading however sees how everything is part of a whole and in its appropriate place; the book is uncanny because unconventional, not incompetent, original as *Women in Love* or *Nostromo* had to be. For lack of space my account of it cannot be adequate but I can at least outline what it seems to me about and for.

The book seems as though it should start with the second chapter, "Blithedale," but like the brief first chapter of *The Scarlet Letter* the short first chapter called "Old Moodie" is indispensable. It puts us in possession of the personae and hints their relation: the bachelor "I" has just visited an exhibition of the Veiled Lady and tomorrow will go to join "the Blithedale enterprise" where he is to find the philanthropist Hollingsworth and a literary woman Zenobia. He is having an encounter toward midnight in the street (we recall the opening of *Major Molineux*) with an old man with a patch over one eye (suggesting Odin, a prime mover, who wears the patch because he sold his eye for knowledge) who tries ineffectually to tell Coverdale of a service connected with Blithedale and Zenobia that he wishes done. But something Coverdale says, connecting Zenobia and the Veiled Lady, in a simile, appears to seal the old man's lips.

Next day Coverdale leaves his comforts and "plunges into the pitiless snow-storm in quest of the better life." What this meant to him is conveyed finely in detail in the imagery of the journey as he travels in dead winter from the City to the Farm. The experiment is founded on ideals such as agriculture as the basis for the good life, no class distinctions, the equality of the sexes and the brotherhood of man. Disillusionment as the ideals are tested by the reality begins for Coverdale at once. The absence of class-consciousness proves theoretical rather than actually attainable. The presence of Zenobia, rich, luxuriantly beautiful, with a hothouse flower in her hair, "caused our heroic enterprise to show like an illusion, a masquerade, a counterfeit Arcadia. I tried to analyze this impression, but not with much success." More particularly, he notices from the start and in the next paragraph "that, as regarded society at large, we stood in the position of new hostility, rather than new brotherhood." They could support themselves in a competitive society only by "getting the advantage over the outside barbarians in their own field of labor." The connection with Zenobia of this "dawning idea, driven back into my inner conciousness by her entrance," is very real though not immediately apparent: Zenobia is a luxury product. Her beauty, which is a matter of "bloom, health and vigor," of always having had all that money can buy, her self-confidence and freedom and cultivation, all depend on her being a wealthy woman. She always wears an exotic flower in her hair, fresh daily; and on Coverdale's arrival at Blithedale the costly flower, flung to the ground because it has withered, affects him immediately, and so the reader: "The action seemed proper to her character. Nevertheless, it was a singular but irresistible effect; the presence of Zenobia caused our heroic enterprise to show like an illusion." We have just registered this when Hollingsworth breaks in carrying an unknown young girl. She is revealed as the very opposite of Zenobia, poorly dressed, physically blighted. She is the Little Dorrit of the New England city, the working-girl of the industrial age, the seamstress or mill-hand, and Hawthorne's concern for this typical product of his civilization is touchingly conveyed:

> . . . her face was of a wan, almost sickly hue, betokening habitual seclusion from the sun and free atmosphere, like a flower-shrub that has done its best to blossom in too scanty light. . . . In short, there has seldom been so depressed and sad a figure as this young girl's; and it was hardly possible to help being angry with her, from mere despair of doing anything for her comfort.

Later on he says Priscilla "reminded me of plants that one sometimes observes doing their best to vegetate among the bricks of an enclosed court, where there is scanty soil, and never any sunshine."

Her presence and her behaviour there are equally mysterious.

> She stood near the door, fixing a pair of large, brown, melancholy eyes upon Zenobia,—only upon Zenobia!—she evidently saw nothing else in the room but that bright, fair, rosy, beautiful woman. It was the strangest look I ever witnessed; long a mystery to me, and forever a memory. . . . I never thoroughly forgave Zenobia for her conduct on this occasion.

She begs Zenobia to shelter her and let her be always near her, but Zenobia is unresponsive. The scene is precisely that of a morality play and offers the clearest indications that it is to be understood as such. Only in this ideal community, of course, can the two sisters, one the daughter of Poverty and the other of Wealth, live together (we learn later that Zenobia and Priscilla are daughters of the same father by different mothers, though only Priscilla is aware of it). Hollingsworth the philanthropist makes a high-minded appeal to Zenobia and the community to receive Priscilla, warning them: "As we do by this friendless girl, so shall we prosper." But the right unaffectedly human note is struck only by the genuine farmer, their host Silas Foster. Silas's contribution to the whole theme should not be overlooked. He is a touchstone of reality, explicitly so in the later chapter "The Masqueraders" where we are told:

> But Silas Foster, who leaned against a tree near by, in his customary blue frock, and smoking a short pipe, did more to disenchant the scene, with his look of shrewd, acrid, Yankee observation, than twenty witches and necromancers could have done in the way of rendering it weird and fantastic.

Hollingsworth can tell them only that Priscilla was handed over to him by an old man who begged him to convey her to Blithedale.

Thus a number of flaws in the actuality of Blithedale have been insinuated into our consciousness before Coverdale goes shivering to bed with ominous anticipations fulfilled in "half-waking dreams" all night. The chapter ends: "Starting up in bed at length I saw the moon was shining on the snowy landscape, which looked like a lifeless copy of the world in marble. How cold an Arcadia was this!"

It is natural that the next chapter finds Coverdale too ill to rise. He has a delirious fever in which he virtually dies, seeing his previous existence as worthless. While thus out of life, as it were, in a state of clairvoyance or morbid sensitiveness he has an intuitive knowledge of the relation between Priscilla and Zenobia, of what each is, and of the true character of the others at Blithedale. His sense of values has been refined. He can now perceive that Hollingsworth's philanthropy is a terrible form of egotism, his benevolence not human tenderness but a disguise for the need to dominate others. Hollingsworth was formerly a *blacksmith,* that is, as Westervelt observes later on, "a man of iron in more senses than one"— he is the Endicott of Hawthorne's age.

When Coverdale gets up again it is May Day, he is reborn with the coming of Spring (the symbolism is conscious, for we are told it is not the calendar but the seasonal May Day, and we are to recall the year-cycle celebrated in *The Maypole,* for Zenobia is celebrating with Priscilla). I cannot omit singling out the remarkable passage in which he explains this experience, of his reconcilement with Nature "whose laws I had broken in various artificial ways."

> I was now on my legs again. My fit of illness had been an avenue between two existences; the low-arched and darksome doorway, through which I had crept out of a life of old conventionalisms, on my hands and knees, as it were, and gained admittance into the freer regions that lay beyond. In this respect, it was like death. And, as with death, too, it was good to have gone through it. No otherwise could I have rid myself of a thousand follies, fripperies, prejudices, habits, and other such worldly dust as inevitably settles upon the crowd along the broad highway, giving them all one sordid

aspect before noon-time, however freshly they may have begun their
pilgrimage in the dewy morning. The very substance upon my bones had
not been fit to live with in any better, truer, or more energetic mode than
that to which I was accustomed. So it was taken off me and flung aside,
like any other worn-out or unseasonable garment; and, after shivering a
little while in my skeleton, I began to be clothed anew, and much more
satisfactorily than in my previous suit. In literal and physical truth, I was
quite another man. I had a lively sense of the exultation with which the
spirit will enter on the next stage of its eternal progress, after leaving the
heavy burthen of its mortality in an earthly grave, with as little concern
for what may become of it as now affected me for the flesh which I had lost.

In this chapter, ironically called "A Modern Arcadia," the new Coverdale sees the reality of the society for which he has abandoned (in every
sense) the city. He perceives that those attracted to Blithedale were inevitably social misfits: "Our bond, it seems to me, was not affirmative, but
negative"—that is, it could not be a true community. What his fellow-
members had joined Blithedale for is conveyed in a digression, reminiscent of Swift, on old clothes. But even in spite of themselves the idealists
acquire a schooling in reality and Coverdale can still believe in Blithedale
in a disenchanted way: "My hope was, that, between theory and practice,
a true and available mode of life might be struck out." And one of the
positives of the Blithedale life is that Priscilla benefits from it.

Now the scene is set, Old Moodie appears again, "A Visitor from
Town." Unaccountably interesting to Coverdale, as he says, and mysteriously connected with both women, he has come to see whether Zenobia
and Priscilla are really equals here. But he is not satisfied, seeing they are
still as mistress and servant, and he leaves a curse on the farmhouse. The
following chapter begins with a visitor from the opposite direction who
comes to fulfill Old Moodie's prediction. Coverdale has sought "The
Wood-Path"; being the artist whose function is "to distill in his long-
brooding thought the whole morality of the performance" (a clue for the
reader), he needs at times to retire from the settlement to renew his inner
life in the solitude of the forest. But a sinister figure who haunts the
woods unknown to him takes him by surprise. There is no poverty in the
imagination of evil in Hawthorne, and the evocation of it in this chapter
is one of the most astonishing feats in his works. To Young Goodman
Brown the devil came in the sober likeness of his grandfather, distinguish-
able only by his serpent staff, and to Miles Coverdale he appears in an
equally appropriate form, as a finished man of the world though still with
a serpent-headed cane and the aura of scepticism. The nineteenth century Black Man is insufferably familiar in manner and still more insufferable to Coverdale because his tone and appearance are a caricature of
what Coverdale was in his former city existence. "I detested this kind of
man; and all the more because a part of my own nature showed itself

responsive to him." Later his "dislike for this man" is rendered in physical terms as "nothing less than a creeping of the flesh, as when, feeling about in a dark place, one touches something cold and slimy, and questions what the secret hatefulness may be." No quotation can convey the psychological subtlety of the scene between the two, which is excellent "novel" as well, but it is notable that Westervelt is introduced by association with "the salvage man of antiquity, hirsute and cinctured with a leafy girdle." There is something underlying his good looks which gives him away: "there was in his eyes (although they might have artifice enough of another sort) the naked exposure of something that ought not to be left prominent"; and when he laughs, he

> disclosed a gold band around the upper part of his teeth, thereby making it apparent that every one of his brilliant grinders and incisors was a sham. This discovery affected me very oddly. I felt as if the whole man were a moral and physical humbug; his wonderful beauty of face, for aught I knew, might be removable like a mask.

He also it appears has come to look up Zenobia, Priscilla, and Hollingsworth, with whose affairs he is intimately acquainted. Asked for his credentials:

> He offered me a card, with "Professor Westervelt" engraved on it. At the same time, as if to vindicate his claim to the professional dignity, so often assumed on very questionable grounds, he put on a pair of spectacles, which so altered the character of his face that I hardly knew him again.

He is also the lecture-hall quack of Hawthorne's day, appropriately symbolized as a mesmerist (the name Westervelt is a happy stroke). Coverdale in his reborn phase reacts against Westervelt's personality and refuses to assist him, so the Professor, ceremoniously raising his hat, departs. Coverdale then climbs up into his secret "hermitage," a green eyrie in a mass of vine foliage up a pine tree; he looks forward in autumn to surprising the Community with the fruits of the vine. The imagery of the fruit is as always in Hawthorne cultural in significance, and toward the end of the romance he finds on his return from the city that the grapes in his hermitage have ripened:

> In abundant clusters of the deepest purple, deliciously sweet to the taste, and, though wild, yet free from that ungentle flavor which distinguishes nearly all our native and uncultivated grapes. Methought a wine might be pressed out of them possessing a passionate zest, and endowed with a new kind of intoxicating quality, attended with such bacchanalian ecstasies as the tamer grapes of Madeira, France and the Rhine, are inadequate to produce.

He seems to have agreed with Melville that he had originated a literature and of a different kind than any Europe could show.

Coverdale is next found with his three associates spending Sunday afternoon by a rock in the forest known as Eliot's Pulpit. The passage describing its situation suggests a duality of significance, and Hollingsworth the professed philanthropist (but actually the modern Endicott) preaching there is implicitly contrasted with the real philanthropist "the holy Apostle Eliot" who had traditionally preached there to the Indians two centuries earlier. There follows a considerable discussion about the position of women and their relation to men, enabling Coverdale to exercise some irony and psychological insight in making his point that "the intensity of masculine egotism" represented by Hollingsworth was more acceptable than his own offer of equal fellowship, to both the poor girl and the pseudo-emancipated woman because both were "the result of ages of compelled degradation." Both women love Hollingsworth, now seen to be the Victorian dominant male. Then we have a painful psychological battle between the two men when Hollingsworth is forced to admit that he will suffer no freedom of thought and allow no one individual rights; they are forever sundered.

Sickened by these revelations Coverdale is now as stifled by the farm as he was formerly by the city, he feels he must return to "the settled system of things, to correct himself by a new observation from that old stand-point." After taking leave of the socialists he has an impulse he cannot explain to take leave of the pigs. Their unselfconscious contentment is a satisfying contrast to the quarrelsome idealists. It is a touch of Hawthorne's genius which is as rightly executed as prompted. Only the inhabitants of the pig-sty have come to terms successfully with life— a criticism of the teaching that preached a return to nature.

The action takes a long pause in the next chapters, "The Hotel" and "The Boarding-House" which form the dead center of the romance and repay close consideration. Here, passively gazing out of the hotel window, Coverdale takes stock of his experience of Blithedale and formulates his now maturer attitude to "city" life. Slowly he identifies himself with the life of the city again, the general culture of his age. The passage beginning

> Whatever had been my taste for solitude and natural scenery, yet the thick, foggy, stifled element of cities, the entangled life of many men together, sordid as it was, and empty of the beautiful, took quite as strenuous a hold upon my mind. I felt as if there could never be enough of it.

is endorsed in minute particulars and he concludes: "All this was just as valuable, in its way, as the sighing of the breeze among the birch-trees that over-shadowed Eliot's Pulpit." There is an unexpected wisdom in this part of the book. Hawthorne understood the shallowness of complaining of a "general sameness" in the houses in city streets and of concluding "It seemed hardly worth while for more than one of those families to be in existence." On examining even the one establishment opposite his window he finds it to be a boarding-house with an intriguing variety of forms of life (the opposite in fact of the "lifeless copy of the world in marble"). To complete the discomfiture of his old assumptions, it turns out also to house Priscilla, Zenobia, and Westervelt. When he calls on Zenobia there he finds her in her town aspect, fashionably gowned and in her mid-nineteenth century setting of dazzling chandeliers, baroque furnishings, and all the vulgar opulence that Henry James reproduced in *The Wings of the Dove* for Aunt Maud's London drawing-room. Hawthorne expresses here a genuine personal disgust for the social life of the rich and the interiors of the purse-proud; his integrity was more than artistic. In return for his contempt Zenobia twits him, enabling him to note the American class-consciousness based on money ("In society indeed, a genuine American never dreams of stepping across the inappreciable air-line which separates one class from another. But what was rank to the colonists of Blithedale?"). It seems to me that in spite of Mr. Parkes's denial, in this book alone Hawthorne enlarges our understanding of the society in which he lived.

Coverdale then hunts up Old Moodie in a saloon, an aspect of the city thoroughly brought into focus. He coaxes out at last for us, at the most telling moment, as in *Major Molineux,* the clue to the plot. It might be called The Parable of The American. Originally Fauntleroy, he was princely in his wealth, living in a "palace" in New York (one thinks of Henry James's millionaire-princes typifying America) and the daughter of his first marriage is an American princess Zenobia (her name suggesting Eastern opulence and royal state). Losing his wealth and position he sets up in another incarnation as "Old Moodie," in New England, among the poverty-sticken inhabitants of "a squalid court" which originally was "a stately habitation" built by a colonial governor whose aristocratic residence had become by the evolution of history a slum tenement. Here his second marriage to Poverty in the person of "a forlorn, mean-spirited, feeble young woman, a seamstress" leaves him with Priscilla who "like his elder one, might be considered as the true offspring of both parents, and as the reflection of their state." This is the life of the masses, the Priscilla described earlier by Coverdale as one "whose impalpable grace lay so singularly between disease and beauty," and of whom he added, "if any mortal really cares for her, it is myself; and not even I for her realities . . . but for the fancy-work with which I have idly decked her out." Thus Hawthorne already in 1852 had anticipated Dos Passos's discovery of the Two Nations, symbolized at the end of *U.S.A.* in a neat parable but compared with Hawthorne's artistically barbarous.

The last section of New England to be mapped is covered in the next chapter, "A Village Hall"—an occasion for a "sociological" note on village life not unrelated to the Blithedale venture. Coverdale observes the farmers, the black-coated workers, the women and girls, and finds all but the old farmers "looking rather suburban than rural. In these days, there

is absolutely no rusticity, except when the actual labor of the soil leaves
its earth-mould on the person." He tells us that Puritanism "however
diversified with later patchwork, still gives its prevailing tint to New England character." And here he naturally finds Hollingsworth. Westervelt
in his role of quack produces Priscilla, the Veiled Lady, as his medium;
we are back where the romance began. She is rescued by Hollingsworth
and the scene instantly shifts to Blithedale, where there is a Masquerade,
similar in intention to the scene in *The Maypole,* to suggest the artifici-
ality of the Blithedale communal life. Escaping this, Coverdale comes on
a movingly dramatic scene at Eliot's Pulpit between the other three, "at
some acme of their passion that puts them into a sphere of their own,
where no other spirit can pretend to stand on equal ground with them."
It is evident that some vital decision has been taken: the iron man, rejecting Zenobia and thus rejecting vitality, intelligence and passion
chooses instead in Priscilla the fate we see him subject to in the last
chapter. We have in *Blithedale* even more than in the other works I've
discussed the disproof of the fallacious current account of Hawthorne.
The true artist, he has the indispensable genius for knowing, and communicating, where life flows and wherein lies its value and health. He
has consistently shown Zenobia as a creature radiant with life, the splendid human animal, but the stress falls on "human"; she is not only contrasted with the run of New England women who lacked sensual experience, she is also characterized by her "noble and beautiful motion" and
we are told of her then: "Natural movement is the result and expression
of the whole being, and cannot be well and nobly performed, unless responsive to something in the character." Her death by drowning is the
most poignant of all Hawthorne's writing. Even after she has left the
scene for ever Coverdale feels "It was as if the vivid coloring of her character had left a brilliant stain upon the air," and the memory of her loss
blights Coverdale's life. The meditation by her grave is outstanding too.

Hawthorne's sense of the truly human included intellectual freedom,
passion and tenderness and he can thus bring home to us in the concrete
the tragedy for New England life of the Puritan's rejection of the human
possibilities represented by Zenobia who is drowned, Hester who is starved
and outlawed, and the Maypole which is cut down, all by the death-
dealing Puritan judge (Hollingsworth rejecting Zenobia seemed to Coverdale "the grim portrait of a Puritan magistrate holding inquest of life
and death in a case of witchcraft"). Hawthorne, we see, required man to
be humane, and his ideal opposite he represents by the image of the iron
man, whether it takes the form of Endicott, or Governor Bellingham
with his head separated from his body, or "that steel engine of the devil's
contrivance, a philanthropist." The very antithesis of the better form of
social life he tried to indicate in his writings is represented by the Shaker
community, used by him in *The Canterbury Pilgrims* and *The Shaker
Bridal.* In the latter the very title is an irony, for the relation imposed on

the betrothed couple by the Shaker system is the antithesis of marriage—death in life, ending with the woman "like a corpse in its burial clothes." With his usual genius for imagery Hawthorne concentrates the sense of life-hatred in the castration image of the "awful" old man, Father Ephraim, their dying leader; "Tradition whispered, that Mother Ann had been compelled to sear his heart of flesh with a red-hot iron, before it could be purified from earthly passions." Hester Prynne's nature in afflicted households "showed itself warm and rich, a well-spring of tenderness."

Hawthorne's moral sense is not something in conflict with these instinctive preferences, it is a corresponding form of sensitiveness. He believed —the proof is in his art—that human beings have no right to take up attitudes of rejection and condemnation toward life. The Prison is Hawthorne's symbol of the society that condemns and punishes, and his heroes and heroines are its victims. The eternal pattern that he saw behind all social life in his America from the beginning has in *Blithedale* been traced in the nineteenth century too: the ideal community is disintegrated for the Puritan and hence the Devil cannot be kept out; the separation of rich and poor is insuperable in this age; the Puritan always masters the scene, and as always he rejects Zenobia for Priscilla and what Zenobia stands for is destroyed and lost to society. Coverdale relapses again, having no choice, into a self-indulgent man-about-town, for life. The Blithedale experiment has failed. "Alas, what faith is requisite to bear up against such results of generous effort!" Those are almost Coverdale's last words, but his actual last are a positive affirmation of faith.

Not unrelated to Hawthorne's recurrent theme, but more directly personal, is the class of stories to which *The Snow Image* belongs, which includes *The Devil in Manuscript* and *The Artist of the Beautiful,* the equivalents of Henry James's stories about writers. Their theme is equally the problem of the artist in a society in which, as James wrote, "the interest in literature is of the smallest." James continued: "Poor Hawthorne, beginning to write subtle short stories at Salem, was empirical enough." The finest of these, *The Snow Image*—significantly sub-titled "A Childish Miracle"—at first sight might seem merely a translation into the New England idiom of a Hans Anderson story. But it is not playful nor a fairy-tale, it is an exposition of Hawthorne's predicament as an artist in an entirely bourgeois society such as he found himself doomed to write for. Though Poe and Melville wrote admiring reviews of his stories, they otherwise fell flat until *The Scarlet Letter* made him known at the age of forty-six. "Snow-images" occurs in the introduction to *The Scarlet Letter* as symbolic of what the artist makes—"the forms which fancy summons up" and which, if "a heart and sensibilities of human tenderness" are communicated to them, are "converted from snow-images into men and women." Literature needs collaboration; the Snow-

Image is the creation of the artist's imagination but it is only by sympathetic participation, by an imaginative sharing of the whole community (the father and mother in the story, as well as the children) that it can continue to be kept alive or valid. It is destroyed by the uncomprehending spirit that has no belief in anything but the materially profitable. *The Artist of the Beautiful* puts the same case rather differently. Hawthorne was then forty, and we find him concluding that "It is requisite for the ideal artist to possess a force of character that seems hardly compatible with its delicacy; he must keep his faith in himself while the incredulous world assails him with its utter disbelief." Hawthorne had a good deal of experience of that, as the Preface to the *Twice-Told Tales* shows. He is the classic case of the artist foiled by his inability to find an intelligent public, and it is a proof of his genius that he managed to carry on so long without co-operation—like Blake, Melville, D. H. Lawrence, Conrad, Henry James, with whom he is entitled to stand. There are few things more impressive in the history of the novel than the determination of the first great American novelists to find a non-naturalistic form for their work and to reject the English novelists' tradition of social comedy and melodrama, derived from the theater. Hawthorne was truly "empirical." He can be seen consciously trying, or somehow discovering for himself, the various possible techniques for his purpose: the märchen (*Young Goodman Brown*), the allegory of Bunyan (*The Celestial Railroad*), of Spenser and Milton, the romance, the morality play, the legend (*The Gray Champion* follows the widespread Holgar the Dane pattern), the myth, the masque, drama of various kinds in the light of Shakespeare, the panorama (*Main Street*), the pageant, the fable, the parable. As became a pioneer, Hawthorne instinctively kept close to the sources of literature. His stage is the platform stage of early drama, his settings of the traditional sort such as are provided for by a tree, an archway, a street, a public square, a forest clearing, the outside of a church, a fountain or well or pool. His stage noticeably differs from his equally dramatic successor's—in comparison, James's is seen to be the modern three-sided box. James took Hawthorne's drama indoors, or if not always into the drawing-room then onto the lawn or terrace of the country-house. Though both are equally concerned with the problems of a social life, they work at different levels. Over against Hawthorne's symbol of Young Goodman Brown James has, among many such, Pandora Day, a name so happily symbolic as to need no commentary. His American Artist is Roderick Hudson, his Old Moodie is Christopher Newman, he turns Westervelt (as Mr. Bewley has shown in *Scrutiny*) into Selah Tarrant. Instead of the problem of the Snow-Image we have to decide what is the Lesson of the Master. In sum, James's symbols belong to a later stage of civilization, but greater sophistication is not necessarily a proof of superiority in literature. It would have been impossible for James to create Hawthorne's rose-bush and fruit and scaffold symbols, or to seize on Hawthorne's Maypole as the appropriate symbol for describing the conflict between the cultures of the old world and the new. James's drama has become secular, whereas Hawthorne's concern for his culture is positively religious and never gets out of touch with the sources of a religious drama. His use of a folklore element is always notably more serious than Scott's, though he has nothing so picturesque as *Wandering Willie's Tale* and many of his attempts to write American folk-story are failures (like *Mr. Higginbotham's Catastrophe*) from poverty of the raw material. The apparent oddities of his writings are not due to incompetence but are inherent in their nature; he is fragmentary as are Shakespeare's *Winter's Tale* and the old Ballads.

This is the case it seems to me to urge against the argument that genius must be bulky and that Hawthorne did not write enough to be a major novelist. Hawthorne's claim does rest on a small body of work, but even ignoring his importance as a trail-blazer, an infector and literary ancestor, that work is sufficient. It is slight only in being tense, sensitive, elegant as a mathematical proof, sinewy, concentrated as a poem and incorruptibly relevant. Economy in art is not only a means but a test, a condition of significance. *The Europeans* has been dismissed as "slight," "a water-color" and insignificant because it is brief, but it is none the less demonstrably a major work of art and profoundly significant;[8] whereas the bulkiness of a Dreiser or a Thomas Wolfe is positively against him. As in *The Europeans* there is always in Hawthorne's best writings the sense of a deeply significant public drama being enacted behind the deceptively simple apparent story. Looking back on his work, one's eye is inevitably caught and held by *The Scarlet Letter* with its structural symbols of the Scaffold and the Labyrinth, the Rose and the Black Flower, and one recalls Mrs. C. N. Deedes's conclusion in her essay on that most ancient structure "The Labyrinth":

> The Labyrinth was the centre of all the strongest emotions of the people —joy, fear and grief were there given the most intense forms of expression. These emotions were directed into certain channels, producing ritual and the earliest forms of art. The Labyrinth, as tomb and temple, fostered the development of all art and literature, activities which in those days possessed a religious and life-giving significance.

[8] F. R. Leavis, "*The Europeans,*" *Scrutiny,* Summer 1948.

Hawthorne as Symbolist

by Charles Feidelson, Jr.

> I remember them with the sunlight breaking through overshadowing branches, and they appearing and disappearing confusedly . . . as if the every day laws of Nature were suspended for this particular occasion.
>
> Hawthorne, *The American Notebooks*

Hawthorne had enormous respect for the material world and for common-sense reality; he admired the novels of Trollope, "solid and substantial, . . . and just as real as if some giant had hewn a great lump out of the earth." Even in his own writings, as he pointed out, the style is public. There is "none of the abstruseness of idea, or obscurity of expression, which mark the written communications of a solitary mind with itself. . . . It is, in fact, the style of a man of society." Yet this devotee of Trollope began his literary career by a ten years' retreat, and his books are precisely the expression of the solitary and the mental. Or, rather, they might be considered the resultant of the two quite opposite forces within Hawthorne; they establish "a neutral territory, somewhere between the real world and fairy-land, where the Actual and the Imaginary may meet, and each imbue itself with the nature of the other." Unable to feel any confidence in the reality of the subjective, and unable, despite the long effort of his notebooks, to come to grips with the solid earth, Hawthorne evolved his conception of the "romance." Whereas the novelist was limited to "the probable and ordinary course of man's experience," the romancer tried to create a realm midway between private thought and the objective world. This doctrine, which is the burden of the prefaces to *The House of the Seven Gables, The Blithedale Romance,* and *The Marble Faun,* betrayed an intellectual as well as a literary problem. Hawthorne was anxious not merely to draw the literary distinction between the novel and the romance, and to enter apologies for the latter, but also, and more fundamentally, to fix the status of the romance in an

"Hawthorne as Symbolist." From *Symbolism and American Literature* by Charles Feidelson, Jr. (Chicago, University of Chicago Press, 1953). Copyright 1953 by the University of Chicago. Reprinted by permission of the University of Chicago Press and Charles Feidelson, Jr. The pages reprinted here are a part of the chapter entitled "Four American Symbolists."

almost metaphysical sense. While he was granting or even insisting that "reality" belonged to Trollope, he was trying, in effect, to say what kind of reality his own work had. For the fact is that what seems at first a wholly personal problem, resulting from Hawthorne's peculiar temperament, turns out to be a reflection of the problem of the times. The Actual and the Imaginary can meet only in a theory or habit of perception. Hawthorne's comment on *Twice-Told Tales* is true of all his books: they were "attempts, and very imperfectly successful ones, to open an intercourse with the world."

The imperfect success may be attributed at least partially to the way he put the question. Hawthorne, who was contemptuous of abstract speculation, was caught willy-nilly in a speculative dilemma, and his approach to it was oversimplified. He believed that he had only to discover suitable materials: he chose Brook Farm as the subject of *The Blithedale Romance* because that social experiment in itself had been "essentially a day-dream, and yet a fact, . . . thus offering an available foothold between fiction and reality." But the problem before him actually involved the relationship of the imagination to *any* fact, and it could be solved only by a fundamental adjustment of the mind and things, not by seeking out ready-made solutions. It was inevitable that Hawthorne should find, as he complained in preface after preface, that materials with the proper "atmosphere" were hard to come by. This faulty conception of his problem was complicated by his prejudice in favor of the physical and the rational, a bias which, if followed through, would have made any valid union of the Actual and the Imaginary not only impossible but undesirable. While he stated clearly enough that he sought to mediate between the private vision and the common-sense objective world, he was likely at the same time, adopting an apologetic tone, to speak of his work as "fancy-pictures" and "castles in the air," as though his aim were simply the amusement of cutting himself loose from any reality.

The natural outcome of this theoretical indecisiveness was Hawthorne's allegorical method; by this means, consciously or not, he evaded the issue with which he was confronted. For it is in the nature of allegory, as opposed to symbolism, to beg the question of absolute reality. The allegorist avails himself of a formal correspondence between "ideas" and "things," both of which he assumes as given; he need not inquire whether either sphere is "real" or whether, in the final analysis, reality consists in their interaction. Hawthorne's initial notes for his tales are for the most part abstract formulas, equally remote from the subjective and the objective world: "Personify the Century—talk of its present middle-age—of its youth, and its adventures—of its prospects." Such schemata point to a parallelism between the two worlds, but hardly would lead to richness either of imagination or of physical substance, and certainly would never produce a meeting in which each might "imbue itself with the nature of the other." If Hawthorne's writings tend to be thin in both respects, it is because he never fully faced the problem of knowledge which his own situation raised.

Yet his underlying purpose was always "to open an intercourse with the world," and out of this purpose arose not allegory but symbolism. The "Custom House" essay, introductory to *The Scarlet Letter,* is a portrait of the artist as symbolist in spite of himself. Of course Hawthorne indulges in his usual *peccavi:* "It was a folly, with the materiality of this daily life pressing so intrusively upon me, to attempt to fling myself back into another age; or to insist on creating the semblance of a world out of airy matter. . . . The fault was mine." But this reverence for the material present and trivial view of the imagination do not obscure the central theme of the sketch—the theme implicit in the vignette of Hawthorne poring over the scarlet letter. That self-portrait—which, be it noted, is a self-projection, since Hawthorne in point of fact came upon his subject quite otherwise—amounts to a dramatic definition of the following "romance" and of the author's relation to it. The author's *donnée,* as James would call it, is neither Imagination nor Actuality per se but a symbol whose inherent meaning is *The Scarlet Letter.* The world that the writer seeks is generated by contemplation of the symbol, not by the external yoking-together of two realms which by definition are different in kind. This integral act of perception effectually "opens" an imaginative reality. That it is not the material reality of nineteenth century Salem becomes wholly irrelevant, since the meaning of the symbol, accreted by generations who have lived with it and in it, is continuous in time.

Such would seem to be the implication of the essay as a whole. The Custom House itself, with Hawthorne as Surveyor of the Customs, is the stage for potential commerce or "intercourse with the world." The Custom House is at once the Surveyor's ally and his enemy. As enemy, it destroys his creative power by involving him in material commerce, in weighing and gauging, in all the mechanistic ways of thinking which, as Melville said, make "the round world itself but an empty cipher, except to sell by the cartload." On the other hand, business at the Salem wharf is virtually at a standstill, and the Custom House actually imposes very few practical duties on the Surveyor. As his ally, it embodies, like its aged inhabitants, the residue of past experience; it is the analogue of the Surveyor's own consciousness, in which, though a mere "writer of storybooks," he feels a continuity with his Puritan and seafaring ancestors. Thus the Custom House makes possible another kind of commerce and another kind of revenue: a traffic with the world by means of the significance vested in a traditional symbol. The discovery of the scarlet letter amid the old documents of the Customs—lists of wrecked or rotten ships and dead merchants—signalizes not a retreat into the past but a penetration into persistent meaning.

In this way "The Custom House" throws light on a theme in *The Scarlet Letter* which is easily overlooked amid the ethical concerns of the book. Every character, in effect, re-enacts the "Custom House" scene in which Hawthorne himself contemplated the letter, so that the entire "romance" becomes a kind of exposition of the nature of symbolic perception. Hawthorne's subject is not only the meaning of adultery but also meaning in general; not only *what* the focal symbol means but also *how* it gains significance. This aspect of the book is emphasized by Hawthorne's pointed use of the most problematic kind of symbol, a letter, and by his method of circling interpretation through the minds of various characters. In the opening chapters the scarlet "A" is the object of hundreds of eyes; Hester is not the only one who wears the symbol, if "wearing" it is synonymous with discovery and absorption of its meaning. As Mr. Wilson delivers his "discourse on sin . . . with continual reference to the ignominious letter," the minds of the populace are confirmed in the mold of Puritan thought, and the real Hester for them is the Adulteress. Hester, standing before them, is caught in their vision of the world. Looking down at the letter on her bosom and touching it with her finger, she feels that this hostile society and its judgment upon her are "her realities." Yet, at the same time, "the scaffold of the pillory was a point of view," and one wholly different from that of her judges. Although the pageant of her past life which presents itself before her cannot withstand the pressure of the surrounding Puritan vision, the independent view that she will later attain is foreshadowed by this "mass of imperfectly shaped and spectral images." As the years pass, the symbol has a "powerful and peculiar" effect upon her being; Hester escapes the Puritan world by taking the letter to herself, extending the "lawlessness" of adultery into all her habits of thought, and reshaping conventional values into her own reality. "The world's law was no law for her mind. . . . She assumed a freedom of speculation . . . which our forefathers, had they known it, would have held to be a deadlier crime than that stigmatized by the scarlet letter." For all her seeming compliance with the doctrines of the Puritans, the symbol has rendered to her, and she inhabits, a realm quite different from theirs.

More important than this divergence, however, is the fundamentally similar process by which Hester and the Puritan populace come to terms with the symbol of adultery. In both cases the "A" is psychophysical, entering into and shaping the perceiving mind and the objective scene. This notion is applied with variations to the other principal characters. Pearl, as Hawthorne reiterates at tiresome length, *is* the scarlet letter both physically and mentally. Her function in the book is more than to symbolize the union of Hester and Dimmesdale; she is actually a kind of commentary on the symbol itself. As "the scarlet letter in another form" she reveals what the letter is—the psychophysical presence of "adultery," whatever meaning that word may take. In Dimmesdale the symbol is diverted from its normal course and emerges obliquely as the psychosomatic mark on his breast. Dimmesdale is constrained from accepting either the popular version of adultery or Hester's. He cannot believe for long that what they did "had a consecration of its own," but he cannot repent and thereby take his destined place in the world projected by the Puritans. Thus his agony is not only moral but intellectual. As he tells Hester, he is cut off from any reality, conventional or otherwise. The "strange sympathy betwixt soul and body" which characterizes his disease is the indirect satisfaction of his frustrated yearning for "substance."

Chillingworth, who discovers the psychosomatic malady of Dimmesdale, is himself afflicted in the same way: his aspect changes, just as his mind is transformed, from the scholar to the devil. But in his case the effect of the symbol on body and mind is complete, because Chillingworth has totally submerged himself in a symbolic role. His interpretation of the letter is a heterodox Calvinism: embarking on his obsessive quest for the "A" in Dimmesdale, he is unconsciously throwing himself into the character of Satan in the Puritan myth of the Fall. Naturally enough, after he becomes aware of what has happened to him, he turns to Calvinism for comfort, asserting that "a dark necessity" beyond the human will has determined the whole action: "Ye that have wronged me are not sinful, save in a kind of typical illusion; neither am I fiend-like, who have snatched a fiend's office from his hands. It is our fate." Again, however, his view is heretical, since it denies moral responsibility, and his statement actually has a rather aesthetic turn. Chillingworth holds that he and the others are committed to roles in a symbolic drama, the "typical illusion" of which he speaks; in effect, their lives, both mental and physical, are a function of the meaning of the scarlet letter, which alone remains real amid the appearances that it generates. While Hawthorne obviously regards this speech as the misguided speculation of a lost soul, the unusual vigor of the language indicates the appeal which he found in these ideas. With the reservation that human lives do not become illusory, but gain reality, through the operation of the symbol, he himself could have subscribed to the sweeping theory of Chillingworth. Something like it is implicit in the tableau of Hester, Dimmesdale, and Pearl on the scaffold, with the immense letter "A" shining above them in the sky. The celestial letter transmutes the everyday objects of the scene: "All were visible, but with a singularity of aspect that seemed to give another moral interpretation to the things of this world than they had ever borne before." The world thus illuminated is at once physical and ideal. At its center are human beings who perceive the world by wearing the symbol in mind and body:

And there stood the minister, with his hand over his heart; and Hester Prynne, with the embroidered letter glimmering on her bosom; and little Pearl, herself a symbol, and the connecting link between those two.

With respect to symbolism, as in every other way, *The Scarlet Letter* is a special case among Hawthorne's works. Here, since the very focus of the book is a written sign, he has no difficulty in securing a symbolistic status for his material. The symbolistic method is inherent in the subject, just as the subject of symbolism is inherent in the method. This is only partially true of the other romances. In *The House of the Seven Gables, The Blithedale Romance,* and *The Marble Faun,* Hawthorne's effort to establish a symbolistic standpoint has an air of contrivance; he falls back on *ad hoc* devices. Donatello in *The Marble Faun,* for example, is associated with the Faun of Praxiteles, and he is apprehended by Miriam, Hilda, and Kenyon in much the same way as they perceive a work of art. The imputed identity of the man and the statue serves to abstract Donatello from any objective existence and, without relegating him to the realm of sheer fancy, to locate him in the middle ground that Hawthorne wanted. Similarly, the "sylvan dance" of Miriam and Donatello is treated as "the realization of one of those bas-reliefs where a dance of nymphs, satyrs, or bacchanals is twined around the circle of an antique vase." Although Hawthorne's judgments on statuary and painting are crude and often amount to no more than sheer padding, the constant allusion to these arts in *The Marble Faun* has an overall function. Hawthorne is trying to suggest a situation in which everything perceived has the symbolic status of an aesthetic object. "The Bronze Pontiff's Benediction," conferred on the three friends in the market place at Perugia, is typical of a mode of perception that recurs throughout the book. The statue of the Pope seems "endowed with spiritual life" because all things can become significant in the "unexpected glimpse" which removes them from the customary world:

> There is a singular effect oftentimes when, out of the midst of engrossing thought and deep absorption, we suddenly look up, and catch a glimpse of external objects. We seem at such moments to look farther and deeper into them, than by any premeditated observation; it is as if they met our eyes alive, and with all their hidden meaning on the surface, but grew again inanimate and inscrutable the instant that they became aware of our glances.

In *The Blithedale Romance* Hawthorne makes use of another expedient. Miles Coverdale, the ill-natured aesthete who serves as narrator, views the entire action as a kind of play enacted before him. For him, the three leading figures—Hollingsworth, Zenobia, and Priscilla—form a "knot of characters, whom a real intricacy of events, greatly assisted by my method of insulating them from other relations, . . . kept . . . upon my mental stage, as actors in a drama." Again Hawthorne's purpose is to place the story in terms of aesthetic perception. But neither the imagination of Coverdale nor the artistic analogy of *The Marble Faun* can actually carry that weight, since neither is maintained fully and consistently enough. In both cases the net effect is one of coy excuse; Hawthorne is not sure of his own stand. Perhaps his books are to claim an aesthetic reality; perhaps they merely constitute an "unreal" opposite of the physical world; perhaps they must take refuge in a noncommittal parallelism between Imagination and Actuality. He himself was well aware of one aspect of this indecision—the split within him between the man of "fancy" and the admirer of Trollope. He did not see so clearly that this opposition was transected by another, more debilitating conflict—between the symbolist and the allegorist.

The truth is that symbolism at once fascinated and horrified him. While it spoke to his "sensibilities," it evaded "the analysis of [his] mind." On the one hand, the symbol was valuable precisely because it transcended analytic thought; on the other hand, that very transcendence, with its suggestion of the unconventional, the novel, the disorderly, was potentially dangerous. The letter had "deep meaning," but the letter was scarlet, and Pearl, its embodiment, had no "principle of being" save "the freedom of a broken law." Hawthorne dwells on the elusiveness, the rationally indefinable quality of Pearl, who "could not be made amenable to rules, . . . whose elements were perhaps beautiful and brilliant, but all in disorder; or with an order peculiar to themselves, amidst which the point of variety and arrangement was difficult or impossible to be discovered." Allegory was the brake that Hawthorne applied to his sensibility. For allegory *was* analytic: allegory was safe because it preserved the conventional distinction between thought and things and because it depended on a conventional order whose point of arrangement was easily defined. The symbolistic and the allegorical patterns in Hawthorne's books reach quite different conclusions; or, rather, the symbolism leads to an inconclusive luxuriance of meaning, while allegory imposes the pat moral and the simplified character. This predicament comes to the surface in an absurd conversation between Kenyon and Miriam toward the end of *The Marble Faun*. Since Donatello has been symbolically identified with the statue of the Faun, in which "the characteristics of the brute creation meet and combine with those of humanity," his crime, from this point of view, is a necessary step in his attainment of fully human qualities. At the same time, Donatello has been associated with Adam, and his crime with the Fall of Man. The combination of these two meanings in the one character forces a reinterpretation of orthodox Evil. "Was the crime," Miriam asks, "in which he and I were wedded—was it a blessing, in that strange disguise?" This is more than Kenyon can stomach: "You stir up deep and perilous matter, Miriam. . . . I dare not follow you into the unfathomable abysses whither you are tending. . . . It is too dangerous." And Hawthorne himself repudiates "these meditations, which the sculptor rightly felt to be so perilous." He falls back on the simple morality of

Hilda, a purely allegorical creature equipped with white robe, tower, lamp, and doves.

Yet there can be no doubt that Hawthorne experienced the attraction of inverted values—the extreme form of that anticonventional impulse which is inherent in symbolism. In the Roman Eden, he ventures to say, "the final charm is bestowed by the malaria. . . . For if you come hither in summer, and stray through these glades in the golden sunset, fever walks arm in arm with you, and death awaits you at the end of the dim vista." The "piercing, thrilling, delicious kind of regret" which these thoughts arouse in him points in an obvious direction: "Aux objets répugnants nous trouvons des appas." Baudelaire stood at the end of the dim vista. If Hawthorne was unduly anxious about the freedom of symbolic meaning, it may be to his credit that he had some inkling of how far that method could go.

The Return into Time: Hawthorne

by R. W. B. Lewis

> Adam saw it in a brighter sunshine, but never knew the shade
> of pensive beauty which Eden won from his expulsion.
> HAWTHORNE, *The Marble Faun*

Hawthorne was perhaps the first American writer to detect the inevitable doubleness in the tribal promise. For he was able by temperament to give full and fair play to both parties in the *agon:* to the hero
and to the tribe as well. And, having done so, he penetrated to the pattern
of action—a pattern of escape and return, at once tragic and hopeful—
which was likely to flow from the situation as given. In addition, Hawthorne felt very deeply the intimacy between experience and art, and
he enacted a change as well in the resources and methods of the narrative
art: something which mirrored, even while it articulated, his heroes' and
heroines' adventures. Finally, it was Hawthorne who saw in American
experience the re-creation of the story of Adam and who, more than any
other contemporary, exploited the active metaphor of the American as
Adam—before and during and after the Fall. These are the three aspects
of Hawthorne that I shall consider.

I

The opening scene of *The Scarlet Letter* is the paradigm dramatic
image in American literature. With that scene and that novel, New
World fiction arrived at its first fulfillment, and Hawthorne at his. And
with that scene, all that was dark and treacherous in the American situation became exposed. Hawthorne said later that the writing of *The
Scarlet Letter* had been oddly simple, since all he had to do was to get
his "pitch" and then to let it carry him along. He found his pitch in
an opening tableau fairly humming with tension—with coiled and

"The Return into Time: Hawthorne." From *The American Adam: Innocence, Tragedy,
and Tradition in the Nineteenth Century* by R. W. B. Lewis (Chicago, University of
Chicago Press, 1955). Copyright © 1955 by the University of Chicago. Reprinted by
permission of the University of Chicago Press and R. W. B. Lewis. The opening transitional paragraphs of the chapter have been omitted with the author's permission.

covert relationships that contained a force perfectly calculated to propel the action thereafter in a direct line to its tragic climax.

It was the tableau of the solitary figure set over against the inimical society, in a village which hovers on the edge of the inviting and perilous wilderness; a handsome young woman standing on a raised platform, confronting in silence and pride a hostile crowd whose menace is deepened by its order and dignity; a young woman who has come alone to the New World, where circumstances have divided her from the community now gathered to oppose her; standing alone, but vitally aware of the private enemy and the private lover—one on the far verges of the crowd, one at the place of honor within it, and neither conscious of the other—who must affect her destiny and who will assist at each other's destruction. Here the situation inherent in the American scene was seized entire and without damage to it by an imagination both moral and visual of the highest quality: seized and located, not any longer on the margins of the plot, but at its very center.

The conflict is central because it is total; because Hawthorne makes us respect each element in it. Hawthorne felt, as Brown and Cooper and Bird had felt, that the stuff of narrative (in so far as it was drawn from local experience) consisted in the imaginable brushes between the deracinated and solitary individual and the society or world awaiting him. But Hawthorne had learned the lesson only fitfully apprehended by Cooper. In *The Scarlet Letter* not only do the individual and the world, the conduct and the institutions, measure each other: the measurement and its consequences are precisely and centrally what the novel is about. Hester Prynne has been wounded by an unfriendly world; but the society facing her is invested by Hawthorne with assurance and authority, its opposition is defensible and even valid. Hester's misdeed appears as a disturbance of the moral structure of the universe; and the society continues to insist in its joyless way that certain acts deserve the honor of punishment. But if Hester has sinned, she has done so as an affirmation of life, and her sin is the source of life; she incarnates those rights of personality that society is inclined to trample upon. The action of the novel springs from the enormous but improbable suggestion that the society's estimate of the moral structure of the universe may be tested and found inaccurate.

The Scarlet Letter, like all very great fiction, is the product of a controlled division of sympathies; and we must avoid the temptation to read it heretically. It has always been possible to remark, about Hawthorne, his fondness for the dusky places, his images of the slow movement of sad, shut-in souls in the half-light. But it has also been possible to read *The Scarlet Letter* (not to mention "The New Adam and Eve" and "Earth's Holocaust") as an endorsement of hopefulness: to read it as a hopeful critic named Loring read it (writing for Theodore Parker's forward-looking *Massachusetts Quarterly Review*) as a party plea for

self-reliance and an attack upon the sterile conventions of institutional-
ized society. One version of him would align Hawthorne with the
secular residue of Jonathan Edwards; the other would bring him closer
to Emerson. But Hawthorne was neither Emersonian nor Edwardsean;
or rather he was both. The characteristic situation in his fiction is that of
the Emersonian figure, the man of hope, who by some frightful mis-
chance has stumbled into the time-burdened world of Jonathan Edwards.
And this grim picture is given us by a writer who was skeptically cordial
toward Emerson, but for whom the vision of Edwards, filtered through a
haze of hope, remained a wonderfully useful metaphor.[1] The situation.
in the form which Hawthorne's ambivalence gave it, regularly led in his
fiction to a moment of crucial choice: an invitation to the lost Emersonian, the thunder-struck Adam, to make up his mind—whether to
accept the world he had fallen into, or whether to flee it, taking his
chances in the allegedly free wilderness to the west. It is a decision about
ethical reality, and most of Hawthorne's heroes and heroines eventually
have to confront it.

That is why we have the frantic shuttling, in novel after novel, between the village and the forest, the city and the country; for these
are the symbols between which the choice must be made and the means
by which moral inference is converted into dramatic action. Unlike
Thoreau or Cooper, Hawthorne never suggested that the choice was an
easy one. Even Arthur Mervyn had been made to reflect on "the contrariety that exists between the city and the country"; in the age of hope
the contrariety was taken more or less simply to lie between the restraints
of custom and the fresh expansiveness of freedom. Hawthorne perceived
greater complexities. He acknowledged the dependence of the individual,
for nourishment, upon organized society (the city), and he believed that
it was imperative "to open an intercourse with the world." But he knew
that the city could destroy as well as nourish and was apt to destroy the
person most in need of nourishment. And while he was responsive to
the attractions of the open air and to the appeal of the forest, he also
understood the grounds for the Puritan distrust of the forest. He
retained that distrust as a part of the symbol. In the forest, possibility
was unbounded; but just because of that, evil inclination was unchecked,
and witches could flourish there.

For Hawthorne, the forest was neither the proper home of the admirable Adam, as with Cooper; nor was it the hideout of the malevolent
adversary, as with Bird. It was the ambiguous setting of moral choice,
the scene of reversal and discovery in his characteristic tragic drama.

[1] Cf. the fine observation and the accompanying discussion of Mark Van Doren, in
Nathaniel Hawthorne (1949), p. 162: "Hawthorne did not need to believe in Puritanism
in order to write a great novel about it. He had only to understand it, which for a man
of his time was harder." [See p. 137 below—ED.]

The forest was the pivot in Hawthorne's grand recurring pattern of escape and return.

It is in the forest, for example, that *The Scarlet Letter* version of the pattern begins to disclose itself: in the forest meeting between Hester and Dimmesdale, their first private meeting in seven years. During those years, Hester has been living "on the outskirts of the town," attempting to cling to the community by performing small services for it, though there had been nothing "in all her intercourse with society . . . that made her feel as if she belonged to it." And the minister has been contemplating the death of his innocence in a house fronting the village graveyard. The two meet now to join in an exertion of the will and the passion for freedom. They very nearly persuade themselves that they can escape along the forest track, which, though in one direction it goes "backward to the settlement," in another goes onward—"deeper it goes, and deeper into the wilderness, until . . . the yellow leaves will show no vestiges of the white man's tread." But the energy aroused by their encounter drives them back instead, at the end, to the heart of the society, to the penitential platform which is also the heart of the book's structure.

In no other novel is the *agon* so sharp, the agony so intense. But the pattern is there again in *The Marble Faun,* as Miriam and Donatello flee separately from the city to the wooded Apennines to waste their illicit exultation in the discovery that they must return to Rome and the responsibility for their crime. It is true that Zenobia, in *The Blithedale Romance,* never does return from her flight, because her escape consummates itself in suicide, and she drowns in the river running through the woods near the utopian colony. Zenobia, who is often associated in the narrator's fancy with the figure of Eve, is too much of an Eve to survive her private calamity. The more usual outcome—more usual, that is, with Hawthorne—is realized in a sort of tremulous parody by the abortive train ride of Hepzibah and Clifford Pyncheon in *The House of the Seven Gables*—"the flight of the two owls," who get only a station or so along the line into the country before limping back to town to confess to a crime which has not after all been committed.

It is poor Clifford who most blatantly gives voice to the contemporary aspirations imitated in these journeys, as he babbles on in an echo of the hopeful language he must have heard from Holgrave, the daguerreotypist. Homelessness, he explains to an embarrassed fellow-passenger, is the best of conditions; "the soul needs air: a wide sweep and a frequent change of it." He sees "the world and my best days before me" and is sure the flight has restored him to "the very heyday of my youth." These exclamations comprise the first principles of Adamism; Clifford trembles in the untenable belief that he has fulfilled the action attributed (by Lawrence) to Copper's Hawkeye—the motion "backwards from old age to golden youth." The ironic context for his babbling and the total collapse that it rapidly leads to reveal that here, for the first time in American fiction, the story of Adam has become an element of the story actually being narrated—and so begins to suffer serious modification. Clifford, too, wants to make that leap from memory to hope; his Adamic ambition is an ingredient in the novel; but his leap is Icarian.

Many things are being *tested* as well as exemplified in these circular journeys, in the pattern of escape and return. Among them, the doctrine inherited from Edwards that "an evil taint, in consequence of a crime committed twenty or forty years ago, remain[s] still, and even to the end of the world and forever." Among them, too, the proposition, implicit in much American writing from Poe and Cooper to Anderson and Hemingway, that the valid rite of initiation for the individual in the new world is not an initiation *into* society, but, given the character of society, an initiation *away from it:* something I wish it were legitimate to call "*de*nitiation." The true nature of human wickedness is also in question. Hawthorne's heroes and heroines are almost always criminals, according to the positive laws of the land, but Hawthorne presumed all men and women to be somehow criminals, and himself not the least so. The elder James reported to Emerson how Hawthorne had looked to him at a Saturday Club meeting in Boston: "like a rogue who finds himself in the company of detectives"; we can imagine him there: furtive, uneasy, out of place, half-guilty and half-defiant, poised for instant flight. No doubt it was because he appraised his personal condition this way that Hawthorne so frequently put his characters in the same dilemma: James's comment is a droll version of the opening glimpse of Hester Prynne. And no doubt also this was why Hawthorne so obviously sympathized with what he nevertheless regarded as an impossible enterprise—the effort to escape.

But if he customarily brought his sufferers back *into* the community; if he submitted most of his rogues to ultimate arrest; if the "evil taint" does turn out to be ineradicable, it was not because Hawthorne yielded in the end to the gloomy doctrine of Edwards. It was much rather because, for all his ambivalence, Hawthorne had made a daring guess about the entire rhythm of experience and so was willing to risk the whole of it. His qualifications as a novelist were at stake; for if the guess had been less comprehensive, he would have been a novelist of a very different kind: an inferior Melville, perhaps, exhausting himself in an excess of response to every tragic, new, unguessed-at collision. But if the guess had been any more certain, he might scarcely have been a novelist at all, but some sort of imperturbable tractarian. As it was, he could share some part of the hope motivating the flight; he could always see beyond the hope to the inevitable return; and he could even see a little distance beyond the outcome of surrender to the light and strength it perhaps assured.

Beneath the sunshine that illuminates the soul's surface, he once wrote, there is a region of horror that seems, to the inward traveler, "like hell itself," and through which the self wanders without hope; but deeper still there is a place of perfect beauty. He was not often so certain, but that was the substance of his guess about experience. And this is why there is always more to the world in which Hawthorne's characters move than any one of them can see at a glance. There is more than the surface sunshine covering the whole horizon of the hopeful of his day or his fiction —his "new Adam and Eve," the comfortable customers of his "Celestial Railroad," in their untested faith in human purity and in a new world all the braver because it had stamped out the past. But there is more too, much more, than the darkness, the monsters, and the diverse shapes which tormented the souls of the lost and the guilty—Mr. Hooper behind his black veil, Reuben Bourne of "Roger Melvin's Burial," young Goodman Brown. There was still some fulfillment of the spirit, some realization of the entire self which it was worth losing one's self to find; only the lost, indeed, were likely to find it on their return journey, though a soul might shrivel, like young Brown's, in the process.

II

The nature and prerequisites of the achievement Hawthorne envisaged are best illustrated by *The Marble Faun*—though that novel sometimes gains its clarity at the expense of its poetry. The achievement in question was, of course, a kind of salvation: Hawthorne's kind. And his kind seemed to depend upon an individual perception which was in great part artistic. *The Marble Faun* is a novel explicitly about the hero as Adam; but it is no less a novel about the heroine as artist. In it, Hawthorne's sense of the analogy between human creativity and human conduct— so evident elsewhere in his fiction—receives its most thorough and complex expression. The artistic dimension of *The Marble Faun* is neither secondary nor peripheral; it is precisely the dimension in which the story's chief "epiphany" is clinched.

There is, for example, a moment in the novel when the pattern of escape and return is conducted entirely in terms of artistic creation. Miriam, the dark-haired heroine of the book and the spokesman for both ethical *and* creative freedom from the past, discovers that her self-portrait is a very recognizable, though unconscious, copy of a stylized portrait of the sixteenth century. The shock of that recognition sets off a chain reaction. Miriam's acknowledgment of the resemblance between her own portrait and that of a long dead lady helps her later to perceive the resemblance between the action she has shared with Donatello and the adventure of a long dead pair—of Adam and Eve, in fact. It is a saving shock, for salvation by recognition is the heart of the book's epiphany. It is the kind of

perception, Hawthorne suggests, which restores the self to its right relation with the world; it is the great means of control both in art and in
life.

Here, as in a number of his other writings, Hawthorne presents a
judgment about Adam as artist (the hopeful ideal) which spilled over
into a judgment of Adam as moral agent. He always had a good deal to
say about the problems of the artist in America; and as to the available
materials for literature, he shared the misgivings of Channing and Cooper
about their meagerness. In the little notes with which he took to intro-
ducing his novels—as though bracing himself in advance for a poor recep-
tion—Hawthorne contended that human relations cast too slight a shadow
in America for the artist's purpose; that there was too little texture in
American life; and that, besides, the temper of his countrymen contained
too little tragic expectancy. Those were his discursive pronouncements;
but Hawthorne delivered his most cogent opinions and his principal
doubts by the more artful means of stories about writers and artists.

There are a surprising number of the latter; and, indeed, in Hawthorne's tales and novels the moral agents—persons of no stated vocation
who are simply vessels of ambition or guilt or wayward desire—seem almost to alternate as main characters with those who are artists by profession: the unnamed painter of "The Prophetic Pictures"; Drowne, the
carver of the wooden image; Owen Warland, the goldsmith in "The
Artist of the Beautiful"; Kenyon, the sculptor, and Miriam and Hilda,
painters, in *The Marble Faun*; Coverdale, the poet in *The Blithedale
Romance*; Holgrave, the daguerreotypist in *The House of the Seven
Gables*. The number of them testifies to the curious significance that
Hawthorne attributed to his own profession; and the alternation testifies
to his deep sense of the analogy.

Something further was probably at work in the bundle of artistic anec-
dotes: namely, a certain perplexity on Hawthorne's part, prompted by the
same misgivings he spoke of in the Preface. In more recent fiction the
ubiquity of the artist as hero has meant one of two things: that the writer
(like Joyce) has hit upon the artist as the representative figure in the modern world or that the writer (like Gide) has found it so difficult to cope
with the shadowless fragmentations of the immediate scene that he is
forced to take that difficulty as the only subject he can bear living witness
to. In the latter case, one is presented less with the imitation of an action
than with the trials of the imitator; the artist in the work is not so much
a hero as an apology for the absence of a hero; literature doubles back
on itself and becomes obsessed with the task of exploiting its own tribulations.

A century ago, the American scene—not because it was falling apart,
but inversely because it had not yet come together—gave some warrant
to the self-consuming anxiety which issued in poetry about poetry and
the troubled self-portrait. Hawthorne exhibited an uneasy awareness of

the almost willful contemporary impoverishment of artistic resources; perhaps this accounts for the proportion of artists among the characters he invented—or at least for the proportion of frustrated artists, like Miriam and Owen Warland and Coverdale. Hawthorne's anxiety was increased by his conviction that creativity was an analogous, possibly even an alternate, route to salvation. For Hawthorne could neither share the belief of his Puritan ancestors that the artistic enterprise was at best a mere trope for the really impressive work of the rescue of the human soul; nor could he arrive at the later romantic avowal that what had formerly been described as the rescue of the soul was in reality a concealed metaphor for the greatest human accomplishment—that is, for art.

It was a matter, for Hawthorne, of an analogy almost amounting to an equivalence—and, on the whole, an equivalence of difficulty and frustration. Thus, in "The Artist of the Beautiful" (1943), Owen Warland is willing to seek fulfillment either in "life" (via love and marriage and acceptance within the village community) or in the making of beautiful objects. Frustrated in life, he turns to art; and when he has fashioned an object of supreme beauty, it is destroyed by the clumsy hands of those same persons who had previously rejected him. The story closes with a reflection much admired by Melville and seeming to point to a resolution: "When an artist rises high enough to achieve the beautiful, the symbol by which he made it perceptible to mortal sense became of little value in his eyes, while his spirit possessed itself in the enjoyment of the reality." But I think we should take this as ironic, since the story it concludes is itself a perceptible symbol and indestructible; the conclusion is, in fact, a knowing description of the habitual recourse of the thwarted transcendentalizing imagination.

The hopeful, and especially the transcendental, critic pinned his faith on the Now, as the subject of fiction and poetry: the Now purged of accretions from the past. Hawthorne remarked, in another but relevant context, that the "visionary and impalpable Now . . . if you once look closely at it, is nothing." And, indeed, the stuff of the Now did tend to evaporate, under artistic scrutiny. Yet the hopeful critic continued to insist that the Now was the only portion of *time* important to the writer, because if the immediate could be jostled long enough, beams of the Eternal would begin to show up in it; and it was with the Eternal that poetry had to deal. This was the tactic of writers like Emerson and Thoreau, and occasionally even of Herman Melville: they manipulated the concrete and transient to the point where, in the climaxes of paragraphs, they could set off metaphysical skyrockets. And the creative spirit thereupon possessed itself in the enjoyment of the higher "reality." This was the procedure proper to what Allen Tate has called the "angelic imagination": the imagination prompted by the assumption that humans, like angels, can have direct perception of timeless essences. Now if anyone was certain that men were not in any respect like angels, it was Nathaniel

Hawthorne; though he was restless and heretical enough to wish some-times that they were and to tell, as in the tale of Owen Warland or of Aylmer in "The Birthmark," the sad story of someone who thought so. Given his conviction, however, Hawthorne could never rest in Owen Warland's complacency; he had to do what, according to Mr. Tate, "the symbolic imagination" always had to do: "to return to the order of tem-poral sequence—to *action*."

Hawthorne returned to "the order of temporal sequence" for the pur-pose of getting beyond it. He wanted to be in touch with the eternal as much as did the transcendentalists; but he suspected that men, imperfect animals that they were, saw *through* time rather than over it or around it. When he forgot this suspicion, he tended to indulge in those *concetti* which Henry James rightly regarded as his greatest weakness.[2] When he remembered, he enlisted his language on the side of the actual in such a way that he was able to look within occurrences for signs of *re*-currence, to probe the action for what it *re*-enacted. He listened for echoes. For Hawthorne at his best, it was a question of the right quotation: a very hard question in an age which thought it slavish to quote. The moral and artistic awareness Hawthorne was struggling to realize has been ex-pressed in our generation by Thomas Mann: "Life so to speak in quo-tation is a kind of celebration, in that it is a making present of the past." But the awareness urged upon Hawthorne's generation was indicated in Emerson's abrupt little sentence: "I hate quotations. Tell me what you know." This was a painful utterance for anyone who felt that telling what he knew was precisely what quotations were good for. It was just that contempt for the past—as the source of symbols explanatory of the present—which led to Hawthorne's anxiety about the profession he had chosen; his anxiety was damatized in his stories about artists. But in *The Marble Faun*, Hawthorne tackled the job of exploiting even the anxiety: of finding the right quotation for the hatred or ignorance of quotation itself.

III

The Marble Faun describes a double or perhaps a triple return into time: the return of art itself as expressed by analogy in the enforced and tragic return of the hero and the hero's artist-lover. On the literal level there is simply the return of a young man to the city of Rome to sur-render himself to justice. The vibrations of that return bear testimony to Hawthorne's expert sense of the right relation between character and setting. Cooper was right to place his Adamic hero, at the moment of his rebirth, in the benign and timeless forest beyond the frontier. Hawthorne

[2] In a little known essay on Hawthorne, contained in *Library of the World's Best Literature*, edited by Charles Dudley Warner (New York, 1897), XII, 7055.

was no less astute to lead his own Adam to his transfiguring experience in an environment dense with the linked histories of several scores of generations. Donatello in *The Marble Faun* is the most innocent person and the figure least conscious of the force and challenge of time in nine-teenth century American literature, with the exception of Billy Budd. And he is introduced in the midst of an immeasurable and continuously influential antiquity—an antiquity which touches him not at all, until he has sinned.

The novel's plot verges more than once on incoherence and wanders somewhat helplessly for about a dozen chapters, while we wonder whether Hawthorne will find the sustaining power to finish it. *The Marble Faun* is not the best and probably not even the second-best of Hawthorne's novels; but its deficiencies are deficiencies of talent rather than of genius. The incoherence, that is, remains for the most part superficial and in the execution; it only slightly impairs our view of the classical design of the action. With an eye on the action, we may reduce the plot to the following incidents:

> Donatello, a young Italian nobleman of great simplicity and charm, en-counters in Rome a group of visiting artists: two Americans, Kenyon and Hilda, and a beautiful dark-haired Anglo-Jewish woman, Miriam. Falling in love with Miriam, Donatello becomes aware of some mysterious event in her early private history, and of the continuing pressure exerted by a Capuchin monk, evidently a participant in the event, who now lurks menacingly on the periphery of Miriam's new life.
>
> Incited by Miriam's fear of the Capuchin, her violent desire to be free of him, and perhaps an actual gesture of encouragement, Donatello murders him. Donatello flees Rome to his country estate at Monte Beni in the Apen-nines, to brood on the meaning of his act and upon his own muddled re-sponses to it. Miriam follows him. They meet and agree that neither of them may escape the consequences of the crime. Donatello returns to Rome and gives himself up; he is last heard of in the depths of a civil prison. But the experience has transformed him into a man.
>
> Miriam returns to give *her*self up to a life of penance, entering upon a pilgrimage to last as long as Donatello's imprisonment, which may be life-long. Their friends, Kenyon and Hilda, having in some degree shared in the tragedy, are its survivors; and the gloom of the conclusion is faintly lit by the subdued joy of their discovery of each other and their belief—however fal-tering—in the value of the adventure they have all of them shared.

Thus the plot: an assortment of rather melodramatic incidents with those Mysteries-of-Udolpho overtones later complained of by Eliot. Donatello's resemblance to the marble faun of Praxiteles gave the novel its American title. *The Marble Faun* is apt enough as regards the plot; but *Transformation,* the title supplied by the English publishers, is a better index to the action; and it may be because Hawthorne knew that action only becomes realized in plot that he referred to the English publishers as pigheaded. That action is the transformation of the soul in its journey from innocence to conscience: the soul's realization of itself under the impact of and by engagement with evil—the tragic rise born of the fortunate fall. It is a New World action—my supposition is that it is *the* New World action, the tragic remainder of what Lawrence called the myth of America. It is what has to happen to "golden youth" if it is to mature; and the novel is the kind of novel which had to be written if the young literature was to mature. Donatello, though purportedly an Italian aristocrat, is nonetheless the hero of the hopeful, seen in a tragic perspective: the figure who, in approaching experience, comes up against the social world under the great, appealing illusion that (in the words of Horace Bushnell) he is "a free person [who has] just begun to be."

The outline of Donatello's personality is made known to us through the recurring imagery of Eden: imagery employed in the beginning only by Hawthorne; then, after the "Fall," by Kenyon and Hilda; and only at the last by Miriam. This progression of insight and recognition is the core of the story. To Miriam, stifled by her own enveloping history, Donatello appears as "a creature in a state of development less than what mankind has attained"; less than mankind, yet oddly more perfect; a "creature of simple elements," part animal and part child, manifesting a kinship to "that wild, sweet, playful, rustic creature" whose marble image he resembled, and manifesting, too, the unreasoning variability of animals—the docility of the pet spaniel, the tenacity of the bulldog. The action of *The Marble Faun* is the assumption of total manhood by this child-animal. The young innocent becomes entangled (in the way Bushnell predicted that, given the world, he would have to be) with the net of preexisting relationships—involvements which, like those between Miriam and the Capuchin, the hero's very character makes it impossible for him to intuit or guard himself against. The action concludes not only with the hero's assumption of manhood but with the imaginative grasp by Miriam and more uneasily by Kenyon of the meaning and the value of the sin and suffering which manhood requires.

The action has to do with the discovery of *time* as a metaphor of the experience of evil. Rome is thus the best imaginable setting; nothing in the New World could match it. What was wanted, for the maximum effect, was maximum antiquity—a symbol coexistent, if possible, with the temporal order itself; and Rome is identified in the story as "the city of all time." The seven-gabled home of the Pyncheons had reached back a century or so to the Puritan period, and Hawthorne did all he could with it. But Rome, Hawthorne remarks on the opening page of *The Marble Faun,* reaches back through a "threefold antiquity"—Christian, Roman, Etruscan. And it is in dramatic contrast to such massive age that the hero is then promptly introduced as an "Arcadian simpleton." The tension between the simpleton unconscious of time and the infinitely history-laden environment parallels the introductory tension of *The Scarlet Letter* between

Hester Prynne and the hostile community. The action in *The Scarlet Letter*, discharged by that opening tableau, follows Hester's effort to escape from the community and her eventual return into it, to spend her life there as an increasingly revered member. In *The Marble Faun* the action unfolds from its starting point, in terms of Donatello's consciousness of the quality, the content, the pressures of time. It is thus only *after* the sin and the flight that Donatello seems to grow aware of his own ancestry—explaining to Kenyon, at Monte Beni, that his family history goes back beyond the Middle Ages to earliest Christendom and perhaps to a time before that. Donatello's family, like the city of Rome, has a multiple antiquity; and his acceptance of the burden of inheritance may be his way of coming to terms with all that Rome represents in the novel: with the world.

The degree of actual tension in *The Marble Faun* is the degree of Hawthorne's divided sympathies toward the contending factors. And he was not less ambivalent toward time than he had been toward the Puritan community. His involvement with time, always profound, had always been notably ambiguous. It was not a metaphysical interest; Hawthorne had been concerned not with the ontological status of time, but with its contents and effects: not with time as a concept, but with the coloration it lent to the things it perpetuated and with the value or the misfortune of sustained temporal relations. He had a passion for sources and beginnings, for traditions and continuities, and resented in America the scantiness of histories. Though Tocqueville was unduly impressed by the claims of the hopeful and had doubted that American poetry would "be fed with legends or the memorials of old traditions," Hawthorne never seemed able to get hold of legends and traditions enough. He wore out the few he could find; and it may have been to refurbish his stock that in 1853 he consented to go to Europe as his government's representative. In Europe, where he tripped over unchanging traditions and customs in appalling abundance, his resentment veered around toward the ancient.

"At home," Henry James remarked (1895), "he had fingered the musty; but abroad he seemed to pine for freshness." Both sides of the observation can be matched by its opposite. Even in the American days, the musty needed the fresh in the shaping of rewarding experience: this is the very formula that somewhat tamely concludes *The House of the Seven Gables*. And while, in England, Hawthorne consigned to the flames the accumulated treasures ("rubbish") of the British Museum and wondered how human aspiration could tolerate English social immobility, nonetheless in Paris he lamented fluidity and thought that nothing worth while could take root there.

Hawthorne himself had identified his generation's major ideal in the image of Adam, and he both celebrated and deplored it. The individual divorced from his racial or family past seemed to Hawthorne at once a liberated person and a lost son: an orphan, as he also had been. Such an ambivalence, the very stuff of drama, stayed with Hawthorne to the end;

even in the inchoate and unfinished *Dr. Grimshawe's Secret* (posthumous, 1883), the hero, Redclyffe, is an orphan cast afloat in the American world, who travels to England, motivated by "a great deal of foolish yearning for a connection with the past." Redclyffe's nostalgia is for the kind of "density" he finds in the atmosphere of an English country estate: a thickening of life and character caused by the hidden vitality of the past. In such a place, Redclyffe supposes, "the life of each successive dweller was eked out with the lives of all who had hitherto lived there . . . so that there was a rare and successful contrivance for giving length, fullness, body, substance, to this thin frail matter of human life." Yet Redclyffe stubbornly votes for America and returns there; America's homes were mere "tents of a day, inns of a night"; but, though its atmosphere was much thinner, it was also much freer. That was Hawthorne's personal conclusion, too, after a comparable meditation in Florence.

The Marble Faun was a dramatization on a large scale of these many fertile contradictions. The question of density was as relevant to art as to life. Fullness and substance for his thin, frail materials was just what the American artist needed, according to Hawthorne; and Rome offered the narrative artist every contrivance for giving such substance to the events recounted. Rome's "very dust . . . is historic," it is noted; and every fragment of church or temple is "a great solid fact out of the past." Hawthorne extended himself to exploit each indication of the past as the source of life in the present: newly built houses are "perched on the lofty delapidations of a tomb"; the Capuchin, for a Gothic moment, is confused with a legendary Wandering Pagan, lost in the Catacombs for fifteen hundred years; life feeds on death; Christianity is bolstered by paganism; the past is everywhere the exemplar or the substructure of the present. But the cumulative force of those associations, strained as some of them may be, is precisely to give maximum meaning to Miriam's cry of desperate and ebbing hope: "Is the past so indestructible, the future so immitigable?" The tension of the novel is provided by the vigor of Miriam's effort to escape the consequences of her private past and the solidity of the "fact" of the past in general.

The tension is illuminated by analogous oppositions within the field of artistic creation. Hilda, after a brief attempt at original creation, yields entirely to the work of copying the old masters; but her honesty and her heightened enjoyment of the beauty contrived by others are contrasted with the pretenses of an English sculptor who cooks up lifeless imitations of the antique and is an effete slave (Kenyon thinks) to something "whose business or efficacy in our present world, it would be exceedingly difficult to define." Miriam turns her back altogether on the art of the past, claiming to paint wholly from the self and about the self; and her self-portrait becomes an unconscious imitation of the very painting—the "Beatrice" of Guido—which Hilda is currently engaged in copying. This is one of the major "epiphanies" in the book—one of the major moments of reversal and recognition—and a crucial event in Miriam's education. It makes possible a recognition by her of the mythic model for the adventure she has shared with Donatello; and *that* recognition is the means of accepting it, appraising the experience, and knowing what to do about it. It is Donatello who acts and is acted upon, but it is Miriam who is gifted with the perception that controls the action at last and rounds out the novel. *"The story of the fall of man! Is it not repeated in our romance of Monte Beni?"*

The value of the identification is a sudden tremendous deepening of insight. Miriam explores the analogy further: the authentic manliness of the former child-animal Donatello may, she believes, offer a clue to an ancient mystery. "Was that very sin—into which Adam preciptated himself and all his race—was it the destined means by which, over a long pathway of toil and sorrow, we are to attain a higher, brighter, and profounder happiness, than our lost birthright gave?" If the Fall was, after all, immensely fortunate, so then was Donatello's reenactment of the Fall. Miriam is saved by the analogy, by her grasp of the analogy.

And so, perhaps, is Kenyon. A little later, he confronts Hilda with the novel's concluding ambiguity: that the adventure has proved life too "deadly serious" for anyone, like Donatello, "compounded especially for happiness"; or that Donatello's adventure illustrates the fact that "Adam fell that we might ultimately rise to a far loftier paradise than his." Hilda is far too "hopeful and happy-natured" to settle for either. A small shudder runs through the final pages at the suggestion of a fortunate fall; yet the lingering, uneasy impression remains that there has been demonstrated in action what the elder James had argued in theory. Hilda, and all the world, may call Donatello's action a crime or a sin. But his fall was in many serious respects an upward step—an entrance into that true reality which, for Hawthorne, is measured by time.

Wandering through the vineyards near Donatello's country estate, Kenyon speculates on Donatello's action and the astonishing mental and moral maturity it has bred in him. In the physical scenery about him Kenyon senses an answer by metaphor to the speculations that trouble him. He looks upon the setting "with somewhat the sensations of an adventurer who should find his way to the site of ancient Eden, and behold its loveliness through the transparency of gloom which has been brooding over those haunts of innocence ever since the fall." The gloom is there, but perhaps it has a greater beauty than the original. "Adam," reflects Kenyon, "saw it in a brighter sunshine, but never knew the shade of pensive beauty which Eden won from his expulsion." The language and the response suggest that here is an adjustment to time which offers a control for life. To the eye of the artist, the color of time was very much richer than the blankness of the original sunshine. For such was the nature of man.

How Ambiguous Is Hawthorne?

by H. J. Lang

I

Criticism of Hawthorne seems to me rather poor in general, substituting, as it often does, an infernal cliché, even a platitude—"man's dual nature," "man's radically mixed, his good-and-evil being" (one of the great metaphysical discoveries of the New Critics)—for the urgent philosophical problems of Hawthorne's own times, the problem of knowledge, e.g., the suspicion that all our insights into nature and human nature are likely to be subjective and unreliable. It may have been the shadow of Kant as much as that of Jonathan Edwards which fell across the path of Hawthorne's pilgrim's progress. This is simply a guess, so far, and I should like you to forget it when we now try to interpret five of Hawthorne's short stories. Four of them are central in every attempt to understand Hawthorne; they form a quartet of complex interrelationships. I mean "Young Goodman Brown" (1835), "The Minister's Black Veil" (1835), "The Birthmark" (1843), and "Rappaccini's Daughter" (1844). The first two were written before Hawthorne met Sophia Peabody, the other two when they were newly married. The first two deal with Puritan New England, the other two are vague in either time or place: "The Birthmark" is late eighteenth century, but not localized; "Rappaccini's Daughter" has its scene laid in Italy, but in an unspecified century, "very long ago." We might say that both stories are Gothic in theme and atmosphere. To these four stories we add, as a kind of prologue, "The Wives of the Dead" (1831).

In trying to measure the extent of their ambiguity we must say what we mean by that word. Roughly, there are three sorts of ambiguity relevant to our theme: first, there is the ambiguity inherent in language, especially language used for poetic purposes; second, there is the ambiguity of human conduct, or, rather, the inescapable doubt we encounter once we try to get beneath the surface of the obvious in motivations. Both sorts of ambiguities are very important for Hawthorne—we might say that the theme of at least one of our stories is ambiguity of the second sort—but they are very general, if not universal, in serious literature. More specific and, accordingly, more important for our inquiry is the third sort, which we might call ambiguity of external action. External action is paradoxically ambiguous only, since it should not give rise to real doubt at all, as far as essentials are concerned. It should be "the literal level," the secure basis for our more daring flights of interpretation. But there is room for doubt when we try to say what happens in "Young Goodman Brown" or "The Turn of the Screw"; a simple narration of what happens, in James's story, depends on our overall interpretation.

II

"The Wives of the Dead," a masterly but somewhat neglected tale, is a good example of an ambiguity of the third sort. As it is less well known, we must summarize it. It is introduced as a story "the simple and domestic incidents of which may be deemed scarcely worth relating." Two widows—"they were the recent brides of two brothers, a sailor and a landsman, and two successive days had brought tidings of the death of each, by the chances of Canadian warfare and the tempestuous Atlantic"—prepare to retire for the night. Mary is the more resigned; Margaret has "a lively and irritable temperament." Mary sleeps quietly, while Margaret becomes "more disturbed and feverish, in proportion as the night advanced with its deepest and stillest hours." She hears a knocking at the door and after some hesitation opens a window. A messenger has come to tell her that her husband is still alive. Margaret flies to her sister's bed with her good news, but hesitates to wake her, "to feel her sorrow sharpened by my happiness." Instead, she retires to her own room and falls asleep. Now Mary awakes "with a sudden start. A vivid dream had latterly involved her in its unreal life, of which, however, she could only remember that it had been broken in upon at the most interesting point." She listens to some rapping at the door, answers the summons and hears from a former suitor that her husband is alive. "He hurried away, while Mary watched him with a doubt of waking reality, that seemed stronger or weaker as he alternately entered the shade of the houses, or emerged into the broad streaks of moonlight. Gradually, however, a blessed flood of conviction swelled into her heart. . . ." She has the same impulse, but also the same scruple, as her sister-in-law has had, thinking that Margaret, who smiles in her sleep, "will waken too soon from that happy dream." Therefore, "before retiring, she set down the lamp, and endeavored to arrange the bedclothes so that the chill air might not do harm to the feverish slumberer. But her hand trembled against Margaret's neck, a tear also fell upon her cheek, and she suddenly awoke."

This is the end, and this is all. Let us hear a few typical comments.

Arlin Turner summarizes the "slight" story as showing "the response of each [sister] when she receives her own good news while believing her sister remains bereaved." Mark Van Doren finds it "one of Hawthorne's most attractive tales. Its atmosphere is the atmosphere of sadness and death, but its outcome—though the full effect of it upon the principals is withheld from us at the end—is in some rich, strange way happy and reassuring." For these and other critics the story is slight, plain, realistic and uncomplicated. In all the extensive literature on Hawthorne I have been able to find only two critics who read the story as, in my opinion, it must be read, as a dream of the widows. " 'The Wives of the Dead,' " H. Levin says, quoting the title, which alone should be sufficient, "dream vainly of their husbands' return."

Let us look at the last sentence carefully: is it believable that such a careful and unhurried writer as Hawthorne wrote an ambiguous sentence at the end of a story without meaning it to be ambiguous? If the last "she" refers to Margaret, awakened by Mary, the two sisters are now awake, and their husbands alive. This, as Mark Van Doren said, is deeply reassuring, but is it true? Syntactically, the "she" should refer to Mary; if it referred to Margaret, it would be a very clumsy sentence on top of being unintentionally ambiguous. But if it refers to Mary, it was all a dream, and the husbands are dead. It is a story with a surprise ending, only so few readers and critics were surprised. What the reader should get is a doubt and then a shock of recognition: the happy return was only a dream; reality is as terrible as it is. Here is a paradox: if we read the story on the realistic level, it is somewhat improbable (two simultaneous resurrections after two simultaneous deaths); read as a dream, it is perfectly natural: the widows would dream of their husbands' return. And another paradox: in order to convey the widows' sorrow to the reader, to make it really felt, the author has to break down the distinction between reality and unreality: a real emotion is conveyed by shocking the reader with this movement of the story from sorrow to joy and back to sorrow. Can it be proved that the story should be read as a dream? Reread on the realistic level, it does not lend itself to a construction of events as another of Hawthorne's stories does, "Mr. Higginbotham's Catastrophe," in which "ambiguous circumstances" and seemingly supernatural events receive a neat natural explanation at the end. Details such as a window left unhasped and a door closed rather force us to read the story as reality. But there is another reading altogether. The story's "miracles of lighting" have been admired, but there is more in it than that. Mary receives her good news in the light of the chaste moon, Margaret, sexually disturbed by her widowhood, by a lantern "reddening the front of the house." Excellent as these symbolic differentiations are, they do not yet lead into the center of the story's symbolism, which is the lamp. The widows retire "after heaping ashes upon the dying embers of their fire, and placing a lighted lamp upon the hearth." When Margaret hears the knocking, she seizes the lamp, hears the good news and "joy flashed into her heart, and lighted it up at once." Mary, too, takes the lamp from the hearth, hears her good news, goes to her sister's chamber, where she sets it down—and soon awakes. The lamp is a lamp left burning for those who might return late in the night, and in this story it is a symbol of hope. It is in the light of this lamp that the two women receive their good news—literally and symbolically.

My guess is that Hawthorne would not have minded people reading the story as reality. It is somewhat pointless then, true, but again, it is so reassuring. Read as a dream, it has a point, a sharp point which "stabs us from behind with the thought of annihilation," to quote one of the better critics of Hawthorne, the author of *Moby Dick*. In their commentary to that work, chapter XLII, "The Whiteness of the Whale," Mansfield and Vincent quote from an article on "The Doctrine of Colors," published in *The American Magazine of Useful and Entertaining Knowledge,* then edited by Hawthorne: "The gay coloring in which the Almighty has decked the pale marble of nature, is not the result of any quality inherent in the colored body, or in the particles by which it may be tinged, but is merely a property of the light in which they happen to be placed." This will be a main clue for the interpretation of Hawthorne's stories: the light in which the events happen to be placed. The matter is so simple that one hesitates to talk about symbolism. Taking Webster's Dictionary, College Edition, we read under *light,* item 11: "the way in which something is seen; appearance due to what is presented to view; aspect: as, he put the matter in an unfavorable *light*." This is what the hero of our next story does: Young Goodman Brown.

III

This is the most difficult of our stories, though, on the other hand, there is a large area of agreement among critics. G. E. Woodberry said the theme is "the secrecy of men's bosoms"; A. Warren said it is about "the devastating effects of moral scepticism." One of the best expositions of the problem is by Mark Van Doren. Evil, in the nightly experience of Brown in the wood,

> becomes a monster with which he cannot cope. But it is perhaps a monster of his own making—Hawthorne, always a master of such ambiguities, leaves it uncertain whether this was precisely so—and to that extent it wrecks him, as doubtless it wrecks his future happiness with Faith . . . As a good Puritan he had known that evil was real; but as a man he had not suspected it was this real. Yet is it real? Has he not imagined it? . . . It is not knowledge of evil he has now, but doubts and despairs. He is not made wiser by his experience; he is only made sadder. He is, indeed, made cynical; and Faith will be the chief sufferer by that.

This is excellent, and, indeed, the main point of the story is difficult to miss. But it has some elusive qualities nevertheless. Leaving aside the vexing questions of its biographic relevance and its historical truth as a picture of the Puritan mind, there is the basic problem of the innocence or guilt of the people Brown meets or thinks he meets at night. R. R. Male does not doubt that Faith is present at the witch meeting. He finds "the ambiguity of womanhood" in the story: "For Faith and her pink ribbon, so pure in the sunlight, are fiendish at night." And Harry Levin says that "The pharisaical elders, . . . meeting in 'the benighted wilderness,' are doing the devil's work while professing righteousness." But here is a dilemma: if even Faith is "under a similar compulsion to go on a 'journey' herself," as Mrs. Q. D. Leavis thinks, and if the elders are hypocritical, how can we, as we should, condemn Brown's cynicism? We are forced to ask the question which Hawthorne does not invite us to ask: whether it was all a dream or not. The author only points out the result: Brown's becoming "A stern, a sad, a darkly meditative, a distrustful, if not a desperate man" whose "dying hour was gloom." These questions send us back to the text, and a "close reading" is certainly one of the most interesting of literary exercises. But I submit that a full understanding of the story is possible only after some acquaintance with its sources. As long ago as 1934 F. N. Cherry discovered a source in one of Cervantes' *Novelas ejemplares,* "The Colloquy of the Dogs," which contains all the important motifs of Hawthorne's tale. It is the life history of the dog Berganza, who is young and inexperienced at first, but gains insight into appearance and reality, hypocrisy and righteousness, trying hard, at the same time, not to become cynical, though, as a dog, he has every right to be. The climax of his story is the meeting with an old witch, who explains to him the mysteries of witchcraft, as far as she understands them herself. She characterizes Satan as the prince of lies: "There is no use asking him anything, since with one truth he mingles a thousand lies." As to the reality of participation in a witch meeting, she has this to say:

> There is a prevalent belief that we attend these meetings only in our imagination and that the devil merely pictures for us all those things that we afterwards relate as having happened to us. Others take the contrary view and maintain that we really do go, in body and soul. As for myself, I hold that both opinions are true, and that we do not know when we go in one way or the other, for the reason that everything that takes place in our imaginations happens so intensely that it is impossible for us to distinguish between the imaginary and the real.

This should take care of the question of the "reality" of Brown's participation, and even more of other people's presence there. It was an intense experience for Brown, so intense that it colors his whole subsequent life's outlook, but it was his experience only, and we must be wary to accept anything as objective, as verifiable. If we are sane, we do not hold our neighbors responsible for what they do in our dreams. It is ironic that the discoverer of Hawthorne's source does not seem to get this vital point and falls into the usual infernal cliché when she writes:

> The conception of a Witches' Sabbath composed of the good and the wicked on equal terms is, I imagine, original with Hawthorne; but the idea for such an association was no doubt suggested to him by the dual nature of the witches in "El Colloquio," who, in the manner of Goodman Brown's townsmen, are respected citizens by day but who by night, or in consequence of an application of a magic ointment, assume the character of witches. Hawthorne's characters by their actions reveal their propensity for doing good as well as evil, though it is not clear that they seem conscious of the incongruity of their nature.

What F. N. Cherry failed to take into account is Salem Witchcraft itself, with which Hawthorne was not only acquainted very well, but for which he cared a good deal, one of his ancestors being a judge of the witches. It is important that in our story a few of the twenty victims of Salem witchcraft are introduced by name. They turn up as witches here, an ironic or playful inversion Hawthorne used in other stories as well. Some critics are very careless in this matter and quietly proceed to hang those victims once again. But David Levin, who edited historical and literary documents in his book *What Happened in Salem?* ("Young Goodman Brown" among them), very clearly saw that the devil in Hawthorne's story "amasses spectral evidence for the credulous goodman." On spectral evidence most of the victims of Salem witchcraft were hanged, on spectral evidence alone could we condemn Faith or the Reverend Elders. Though the temptation to pronounce these Elders hypocrites may be overwhelming (as overwhelming as for some critics to pronounce Hawthorne's women ambiguous), we have really nothing to go upon. To say that Faith is fiendish at night is to claim an acquaintance with her we cannot pretend to, really. This is not to say that the sexual theme is absent in our story. But it is kept in its place. The theme of the story is, simply, going to the devil. What for? For lust, certainly, but more for knowledge. When Brown returns, he is gloomy (because he believes it is really his— as the Devil had promised—"to penetrate, in every bosom, the deep mystery of sin"); we do not hear that he is dissolute. Brown is mistaken in this assumption that he can penetrate the deep mystery of sin, just as the witch judges were mistaken. Both were lacking in charity. The Puritans thought that they hanged witches, whereas they hanged Puritans. They acted according to their lights, and so did Brown. But the light in which he sees mankind is lurid, is the light of the hellish torches of the nightly witch meeting. The question of the real presence of persons at this witch communion (which is not consummated anyway) is less urgent once we get this point. Even a real person, in this light, would be no better than an apparition. If the theme of the story, as we said, is going to the devil for knowledge of human nature, Gordon and Tate give a twist to Hawthorne's meaning when they say that "Young Goodman Brown" deals with his favorite theme: "the unhappiness which the human heart suffers as the result of its innate depravity." The story is not about being evil, but believing our neighbor to be evil.

The next story is a companion piece, because it is about a man who sees evil in himself. "The Minister's Black Veil" raised more doubts as to its meaning than "Young Goodman Brown." Typical is Mark Van Doren's complaint that the moral is somewhat vague: "The veil 'obscurely typifies' some mystery, he [Hawthorne] lets Mr. Hooper say. Obscurely, yes. But even the mystery is obscure"—which should not surprise us. Hawthorne called the story a parable and put an unexceptionable moral into the dying minister's mouth: that there is a black veil on every face, so why tremble at him alone? But Hooper is more specific when Elizabeth, his betrothed, asks him to lift the veil, which he had suddenly taken one day, never to lift it in this world: "If I hide my face for sorrow, there is cause enough . . . and if I cover it for secret sin, what mortal might not do the same?" It is the reader's task to resolve this "ambiguity of sin or sorrow" if he can do it. For Harry Levin, though, the story is only a "rarefied apologue," but the inventor of the detective story looked out for the story behind the story. In his famous critique, E. A. Poe wrote:

> "The minister's Black Veil" is a masterly composition of which the sole defect is that to the rabble its exquisite skill will be *caviare*. The obvious meaning of this article will be found to smother its insinuated one. The moral put into the mouth of the dying minister will be supposed to convey the true import of the narrative; and that a crime of dark dye (having reference to the "young lady") has been committed, is a point which only minds congenial with that of the author will perceive.

Poe defined Hawthorne's method perfectly, but all the same his was not a congenial mind. There is an insinuation, there is an ambiguity in this story between the general and the specific: the impenetrability of every heart, the sinfulness, probably, of every heart; emblematically, the veil on every face. But why does Hooper take the veil? Hawthorne's insinuations make it abundantly clear where to look for a sin: in the sexual sphere. Poe is also correct in connecting Hooper's veil with the young lady who is buried the same day the minister first appears with the veil on his face. Theoretically, the reader's imagination may range over the whole moral spectrum from the lightest gray to the blackest black, from a mere passing sinful thought to a seduction or sexual murder. He may fill in the "blank," to use an expression of Henry James à propos "The Turn of the Screw." But in our story, he is actually less free, confined by what we learn of the minister's character, who erred, if at all, "by so painful a degree of self-distrust, that even the mildest censure would lead him to consider an indifferent action as a crime." If we take the wildest hint of the story, the superstitious old woman's allegation that the corpse of the young girl slightly shuddered when the veil hung straight down from the minister's face when he bent over the body, "so that, if her eyelids had not been closed forever, the dead maiden might have seen his face"—what does it tell us except that there *was* a revelation for the maiden, meaning that, if he had loved her, he had loved her without her knowledge. As he was engaged to marry Elizabeth, this love was sinful. But his conscience was over-tender and his penitence excessive. He is a sinner, but more a saint.

What about the symbolism of the story? The veil, as a mere piece of cloth, "probably did not intercept his sight, further than to give a darkened aspect to all living and inanimate things." We have here our inversion: "the gentle gloom" of Hooper's temperament makes him take the veil rather than that the veil makes his outlook gloomy. G. E. Woodberry gets only half of the story when he remarks that the relation of the image (the veil) to the idea (the secrecy of men's bosoms) is obvious and that "there is no true fusion of the two, but each is kept clearly apart." For him:

> The veil is "allegorical," and "stands for" the impenetrable curtain of the human breast. But Hawthorne's tale is more delicately told than these words imply. The veil, the physical object, is moralized and becomes a type, the universal garment of secrecy, and the particular minister himself, whatever his story, fades into a class of men; both veil and minister have entered into the intellectual world.

This is one way of reading the story, certainly. But this generalizing does not get the true impact of the veil, which then remains "allegorical." It is not a story about wearing a veil (as, emblematically, everybody does), but about taking the veil, as only a few religious persons do. The veil is not merely an emblem of the secrecy of men's bosoms, but also a symbol for the obfuscation of Hooper's view. The ambiguity of sin or sorrow can be resolved: it is sorrow for the lost maiden (we are tempted to give her a name: whom the angels name Lenore) and penitence for his sin, though he might have "argued the matter with Conscience." The veil is to Hooper what the Raven is to Poe's hero and the whale to Ahab. Harry Levin is right in his surmise that Ishmael's whiteness, "by virtue of a culminating paradox, is blackness in perversely baffling disguise."

IV

"The Birthmark" is the story of a scientist who discovers soon after his marriage that a tiny birthmark on his wife's cheek detracts from her otherwise perfect beauty. He begins to be fretful and dreams of removing the birthmark with a knife, following it down to his wife's very heart. The wife, made very unhappy by her husband's affliction and suffering from what Sartre calls "le regard d'autrui," the withering stare of the other person, not only consents to but wishes for an operation. She is less sanguine than her husband as to its outcome, and she dies. The birthmark is removed by alchemical fluids, she is perfect but dead. These are the bare outlines of the story which, by the excellence of the central symbol, might easily have become Hawthorne's best, though it only became one of his most interesting. Georgiana, when he first mentions the matter, is surprised at her husband's worrying about the birthmark, since "it has been so often called a charm that I was simple enough to imagine it might be so," as she tells him. But to Aylmer, the husband (what ails him?), the birthmark is not charming, but shocking. For him it is the "fatal flaw of humanity which Nature, in one shape or another, stamps ineffaceably on all her productions, either to imply that they are temporary and finite, or that their perfection must be wrought by toil and pain." In itself, the birthmark is nothing, only on her left cheek "a singular mark" which, "In the usual state of her complexion—a healthy though delicate bloom— . . . wore a tint of deeper crimson, which imperfectly defined its shape amid the surrounding rosiness. When she blushed it gradually became more indistinct, and finally vanished amid the triumphant rush of blood that bathed the whole cheek with its brilliant glow. But if any shifting emotion caused her to turn pale there was the mark again, a crimson stain upon the snow, in what Aylmer sometimes deemed an almost fearful distinctness. Its shape bore not a little similarity to the human hand, though of the smallest pygmy size." But, "selecting it as the symbol of his wife's liability to sin, sorrow, decay, and death, Aylmer's sombre imagination was not long in rendering the birthmark a frightful object, causing him more trouble and horror than ever Georgiana's beauty, whether of soul or sense, had given him delight." We miss the story's point if we connect the hand (if it is a hand at all) with the grip death has on everybody. Important is not the general liability to death and sin, which the woman happens to exemplify with her birthmark, but the special grip in which she suffers her fate: it is the husband's hand which kills her. This becomes quite clear when at the crisis of his preparations for the removal of the birthmark he "seized her arm with a gripe that left the print of his fingers upon it." Instead of keeping her in good health and spirits (then the birthmark would be faint and vague), he releases a vicious circle: he is unhappy and makes her unhappy and pale, which makes the birthmark come out distinctly, which makes him more unhappy, and so forth. He develops what the psychologists of the time called a monomania, the same mental aberration, of course, from which Captain Ahab suffered, for whom the white whale is the birthmark of the universe.

The symbol and the delicate way of handling it are masterful. But for once, and perhaps once only, Hawthorne was not a good moralist, I fear. The story itself has a birthmark, as we can see from two notebook entries. The first, dating from 1837, reads: "A person to be in the possession of something as perfect as mortal man has a right to demand; he tries to make it better, and ruins it entirely." The second entry of 1839 reads: "A person to be the death of his beloved in trying to raise her to more than mortal perfection; yet this should be a comfort to him for having aimed so highly and holily." The second consideration complicates the matter; we have an ethical ambiguity now. Aylmer is an idealist, and he is absolved by the dying woman: " . . . you have aimed loftily; you have done nobly. Do not repent that with so high and pure a feeling, you have rejected the best the earth could offer." This cannot be the last word, though; it might induce people to improve their wives by surgery, at whatever risk. So we get the author's final comment that Aylmer had not reached a profounder wisdom: "The momentary circumstance was too strong for him; he failed to look beyond the shadowy scope of time, and, living once for all in eternity, to find the perfect future in the present." It is a condemnation, but a mild and reluctant one. This had to happen as soon as Hawthorne made Aylmer represent the spiritual man and his assistant Aminadab the physical man, whose common-sense view of the matter—"If she were my wife, I'd never part with that birthmark"—does not save him from the author's disdain. To improve a woman is a very strange conceit, and Aylmer is self-deceived when he does not see that he uses her as a means and not as an end. He operates on her in artificial light; the light of the natural day discovers the dying woman. "The fatal hand had grappled with the mystery of life, and was the bond by which an angelic spirit kept itself in union with a mortal frame." Why angelic? Because she had submitted to her husband's misguided idealism? We had better postpone the question until we have made the acquaintance of another angelic spirit, Rappaccini's Daughter.

E. H. Rosenberry has called the story "one of the major unsolved enigmas in Hawthorne's work." It is an enigma entirely of the critics' own making, who have lately discovered "the ambiguity of Beatrice." It is the story of a girl who lives in a poisoned garden made by her father, who is a scientist, if not a magician. Beatrice is brought up on poison, which is innocuous to her, but she is poisonous to others, killing insects with her breath. A young medical student, Giovanni, comes to Padua, happens to rent rooms above the garden, is admitted to it, discourses with Beatrice and finds himself poisoned after a while, which makes him desperate. It had been Dr. Rappaccini's idea to get his isolated daughter a mate. She is innocent of this stratagem, and when it is discovered to her, she willingly swallows the antidote given to her by Giovanni, who got it from Dr. Baglioni, Rappaccini's rival. She dies—as she knows she will —"the poor victim of man's ingenuity and of thwarted nature, and of the fatality that attends all such efforts of perverted wisdom."

Where is the ambiguity? G. E. Woodberry thought the moral intention left vague. Mark Van Doren believes it to be "one of the richest of
his tales, even though it may not convince us that the poison in Beatrice's
body, . . . is understood in its true relation—if any relation exists at
all—to the quality and condition of her soul. Weak at the center, the
tale is nevertheless potent in the extremities"—whatever that may mean.
A. Warren is more positive and thinks the symbolism false because the
physical and the psychic do not correspond. "Though no other story has
excited more comment, most of the treatments of it are not very helpful,
and some of them are positively misleading," says H. H. Waggoner, and
he is certainly right, only we must include his own interpretation among
those positively misleading. It is H. H. Waggoner and R. R. Male, following him, who stress "the dual nature of humanity," "man's radically
mixed, his good-and-evil being" as the story's theme, pronouncements
that remind us of what has been said about the children in "The Turn
of the Screw," who are in Beatrice's position in the garden at Bly. The
critics, I believe, are victims of a verbal ambiguity which amounts to
muddleheadedness in ethics. If they would close their Freud and open
Webster's Dictionary, College Edition, they would find under *evil:* "1.
morally bad or wrong; wicked, depraved. 2. causing pain or trouble;
harmful, injurious." Beatrice is "evil" in the second sense only, and not
even that when approached in the right, that is, spiritual way. We have
the usual inversion. Beatrice is poisoned, Giovanni is poisonous, though
at first it seems to be all the other way round. The clue, of course, is the
speech of the dying girl: "Farewell, Giovanni! Thy words of hatred are
like lead within my heart; but they, too, will fall away as I ascend. Oh,
was there not, from the first, more poison in thy nature than in mine?"
If we want to be flippant, we could say it is a case of lead poisoning
(only to make it quite clear who poisons whom).

We can ask at long last: what does the poison symbolize? After the
minister's black veil, which has two different imports according to
whether you see it on another's face or see through it having it on your
own (and a third import symbolizing the difficulties of communication),
after the birthmark, which is on the wife's cheek but is the man's problem, we shall not be surprised to find a multiplicity of meanings here
too. As concerns Dr. Rappaccini, the poison is a symbol of his "perverted
wisdom," a moral evil; as far as his daughter is concerned, it merely
symbolizes, or rather is, physical evil, harmfulness; it is moral evil again
as concerns Giovanni; and concerning the whole situation, it symbolizes
what comes between persons in this world.

Beatrice Rappaccini is not ambiguous, she is ambivalent. Her name is
ambiguous: she could be a Beatice Cenci or Dante's Beatrice. There is
little doubt which in this, a story of a young man finding his Beatrice
but being less than a Dante. It is deeply ironic that Giovanni, when he
first overlooks the garden, says that it "would serve . . . as a symbolic

language to keep him in communion with Nature." He cannot read the garden's symbolic language, nor can most critics do it, victims, as they are, of a verbal ambiguity and a cliché. There is a circumstance which extenuates critical ineptitudes. Julian Hawthorne relates an anecdote about the story in the making. Hawthorne's wife asked him how it would end, whether Beatrice was to be a demon or an angel? " 'I have no idea!' was Hawthorne's reply, spoken with some emotion." In his facetious preface to the story, in which he criticizes his writings under the French translation of his name, M. de l'Aubépine, our story turns up as "Beatrice; ou la Belle Empoisonneuse." Julian would have preferred the French version, and so do many critics, but it so happened that Hawthorne wrote the Italian (Dantesque) version, though another Italian story, that of Beatrice Cenci, must have been in his mind all the time.

Hawthorne, in the two last stories, was feeling his way toward greater complexity, but for that very reason he was more cautious and so explicit as to be really didactic; he was certainly less ambiguous. Ethical ambiguity comes back to his fiction with the dark ladies of his novels.

V

We must try to summarize our quartet of stories. We have two average men, Young Goodman Brown and Giovanni (Giovanni—*il giovane?*), and two exceptional men, Hooper and Aylmer. Brown distrusts everybody, including Faith, Giovanni distrusts Beatrice. The exceptional men suffer from a sombre imagination as well, but are redeemed by their holiness (Hooper) or their striving for perfection (Aylmer). The women's role is passive. Brown, as the average man, has an average wife, presumably; Hooper probably has a remarkable fiancée; she turns up as a nurse when he dies. Perhaps she should have accepted Hooper with the veil—he asks her to—perhaps he should have lifted it for her once—she asks him to—but whatever their mistakes, they pay for it with a whole lifetime. Aylmer and Giovanni have or meet angels, but do not know how to live with them. Giovanni mistakes the physical for the spiritual, Aylmer is spiritual but fails to acknowledge physical imperfection for what it is, inescapable. Aylmer and Hooper are the doers, Brown and Giovanni the drifters. The upshot of their doings and driftings is two ruined marriages, two ruined engagements; in two cases the women have to die, in two they lead a life of frustration. Brown's gloomy vision sees sin as universal; Hooper's gloomy vision sees sin in himself (out of proportion); Giovanni sees sin where it is not, and does not see it where it is (in himself); Aylmer sees a symbol of sin and death in a mere birthmark, thinking he can remove it and thereby making it to be more than a mere symbol. The vision of the world is colored for each of the four heroes: the hellish torches, the veil, the artificial light of Aylmer's laboratory, the peculiar atmosphere of Rappaccini's garden, symbolize gloom (from hell or a darkened heaven), self-delusion, physical involvement. Going to the devil for knowledge, taking the veil, not letting well enough alone and doubting an angel are the basic situations. It is always the heroes who have the privilege of making a mess of things. The women are passive, but coming to the foreground in the later two stories, pronouncing judgments on the men, absolving one, condemning the other; also expatiating on their own worth and becoming slightly insufferable thereby.

There is no time to go into Hawthorne's influence on Melville and Henry James, but a last word on "The Turn of the Screw" will make my point clearer. The children are innocent, just as Hawthorne's women are in our four stories. The governess has a gloomy vision, such as Hawthorne's heroes have; but James does not let her down. It is a story about "seeing ghosts"—and going to them for knowledge. The stumbling block so far, to the interpretations of H. C. Goddard, E. Wilson and others, the identification of Quint by Mrs. Grose, will bother us less once we know how Hawthorne, too, e.g. in "The Wives of the Dead," made it impossible to separate the artfully mixed planes of reality and dream. These stories are not detective stories; the physical detail may deceive. Who objects to that as trickery, should leave such stories alone. James called "The Turn of the Screw" an "irresponsible little fiction" just for that. He had possibly reread Hawthorne when he wrote "The Turn of the Screw," anyway, he had just published an essay on Hawthone in 1897, and in his later preface he said his demons were "as loosely constructed as those of the old trials for witchcraft." From the traumatic experience of the witchcraft trials in 1692 over the witch-judge's descendant to James's "irresponsible little fiction" there is a chain of events and causations no link of which can be neglected. Of the three—the trials, Hawthorne and James—Hawthorne, with his firm sense of values, was the least ambiguous.

"The Artist of the Beautiful"

by Richard Harter Fogle

One is tempted to describe "The Artist of the Beautiful" as an aesthetic *Pilgrim's Progress,* in which the artist journeys his difficult road toward salvation, struggling through his Slough of Despond, combating his Giant Despair, overcoming his fiend Apollyon, until after many days he reaches the Heavenly City prepared for him. Owen Warland, the artist, is a watchmaker who strives to embody the pure idea of the beautiful in the form of a marvelously wrought artificial butterfly, a "spiritualized mechanism" strangely imbued by his imagination with a mysterious life of its own. Before he succeeds in consummating his imaginative conception he is forced to do battle with the mass of his society, which not only misunderstands but even actively condemns his purposes. This society is represented by three persons: Peter Hovenden, his old master; Hovenden's daughter Annie, whom Warland loves; and Robert Danforth, a herculean blacksmith, who wins Annie when Warland fails. The plot of "The Artist of the Beautiful" is the artist's struggle with these three friendly enemies, each of whom seeks to turn him from his purpose.

This plot consists of a series of oppositions. The broadest and simplest of these is Warland's disinterested search for the beautiful against the criteria of utility and self-interest assumed by his society. He has always been "remarkable for a delicate ingenuity. . . . But it was always for purposes of grace, and never with any mockery of the useful." Society has attempted without success to assimilate this rebel from its laws. "The boy's relatives saw nothing to be done—as perhaps there was not—than to bind him apprentice to a watchmaker, hoping that his strange ingenuity might thus be regulated and put to utilitarian purposes." Society's verdict on his art is uttered by the blacksmith Danforth, who is naïvely definitive. In the concluding scene of the story Annie inquires whether Warland's marvelous butterfly is actually alive, so perfect an imitation is it of life. "Alive? To be sure it is," answers Danforth. "Do you suppose any mortal has skill enough to make a butterfly, or would put himself to the trouble of making one, when any child may catch a score of them in a summer's afternoon?"

The second opposition devolves from the contrast of Warland's idealism with society's materialism—the latter appearing in different aspects in the various characters of Hovenden, Danforth, and Annie. Warland is a highly transcendental artist, who seeks to embody "the beautiful idea" in his butterfly. Peter Hovenden is a cold materialist, whose mere presence is blighting to Warland's imagination. "There was nothing so antipodal to his nature as this man's cold, unimaginative sagacity, by contact with which everything was converted into a dream except the densest matter of the physical world." Danforth represents another, more innocent aspect of materialism; whereas Hovenden is keen enough to hate (he has "just enough of penetration to torture Owen's soul with the bitterness of worldly criticism"), Danforth is merely puzzled and amused by the artist's aspirations. His spiritual impact on the sensitive artist is hardly less damaging, however, than the effect of Hovenden. A "man of main strength," he is intolerable to the delicate organization of Warland. " 'He would drive me mad were I to meet him often. His hard, brute force darkens and confuses the spiritual element within me. . . .' " The case of Annie Hovenden is more difficult to define. Possessing sufficient insight to delude Warland into believing her a kindred spirit, she yet lacks the talisman which would admit her to his inmost thought. With much kindliness, she feels a veiled contempt for Warland and his unreal quest for ideal beauty. Her marriage to Danforth, the man of earth and iron, is perhaps sufficient to account for her.

From this general antithesis of ideal and material arise three other oppositions in "The Artist of the Beautiful," each with its special emphasis and importance: time and eternity, understanding and imagination, and mechanism and organism. All of these concern primarily the relationship between Warland and Peter Hovenden.

In the opening scene of the story we are shown Warland's shop window. A number of watches are displayed within, "all with their faces turned from the streets, as if churlishly disinclined to inform the wayfarers what o'clock it was." This is a fitting introduction to the rebel watchmaker, of whose ingenuity Hovenden scornfully exclaims, " 'All the effect that ever I knew of it was to spoil the accuracy of some of the best watches in my shop.' " Warland, in fact, behaves toward Time with a levity which his society finds intolerable:

> . . . When his apprenticeship was served out, and he had taken the little shop which Peter Hovenden's failing eyesight compelled him to relinquish, then did people recognize how unfit a person was Owen Warland to lead old blind Father Time along his daily course. One of his most rational projects was to connect a musical operation with the machinery of his watches,

so that all the harsh dissonances of life might be rendered tuneful, and each flitting moment fall into the abyss of the past in golden drops of harmony. . . . Several freaks of this kind quite destroyed the young watchmaker's credit with that steady and matter-of-fact class of people who hold the opinion that time is not to be trifled with. . . .

When through the agency of Hovenden the artist temporarily loses his creative power, the loss manifests itself in a sudden devotion to the task of the watchmaker: "It was marvellous to witness the obtuse gravity with which he would inspect the wheels of a great old silver watch." So closely does Warland apply himself to business that at length he is invited by general consent to regulate the clock in the church steeple, a commission which he executes to perfection. To the mind of Hovenden, Time's devotee, the change is wholly for the better. He even proposes to Warland that he should " 'doctor this precious old watch of mine; though, except my daughter Annie, I have nothing else so valuable in the world.' " On Warland's disclaiming his worthiness, Hovenden replies with a strange ambiguity. " 'In time,' said the latter,—'in time, you will be capable of it.' " If Warland had consented to undertake this crucial task, one must suppose that his subjection to the tyranny of Time would have been irremediable; but he refuses and leaves a way open to freedom.

Warland the idealist and artist is a symbol of imagination, Hovenden the materialist a symbol of understanding, or analytical reason. The opposition is explicit and is clearly perceived by the sensitive Warland. "Owen never met this man without a shrinking of the heart. Of all the world he was most terrible, by reason of a keen understanding which saw so distinctly what it did see, and disbelieved so uncompromisingly in what it could not see." Amid the various tribulations which beset him, Owen for a time himself declines into the mental state of Hovenden. He loses his "faith in the invisible" and falls so far as to pride himself in his skepticism. "This," says Hawthorne, "is the calamity of men whose spiritual part dies out of them and leaves the grosser understanding to assimilate them more and more to the things of which it alone can take cognizance. . . ." In Warland, however, this state is a sleep from which he awakens, to become once more a "being of thought, imagination, and keenest sensibility."

In the conclusion of "The Artist of the Beautiful" the conflict between understanding and imagination is crucial. Warland, successful in embodying his imaginative vision in the miraculous butterfly, brings it as a gift to Annie, now long a matron. Hovenden is present at the scene, together with Annie and Danforth and their infant child. The insect, mysteriously alive, flutters from one person to another at the command of the artist. It is immediately clear that Hovenden is inimical to its being; his mocking unbelief is subtly destructive.

"Let us see," said Peter Hovenden, rising from his chair, with a sneer upon his face that always made people doubt, as he himself did, in everything but a material existence. "Here is my finger for it to alight upon. *I shall understand it better when once I have touched it.*"

At his touch the insect droops and instantly loses its luminous vitality. Warland calmly explains this phenomenon: " 'In an atmosphere of doubt and mockery its exquisite susceptibility suffers torture, as does the soul of him who instilled his own life into it.' "

And indeed, understanding succeeds in destroying the creature of imagination, though imagination itself emerges unscathed and triumphant. In an attempt to repair the effects of its contact with Hovenden, Annie delivers the butterfly over to its worst enemy—her child. This child, still a baby, is yet a reincarnation of the spirit of Hovenden and is all the more destructive because as yet he is unrestrained by social decency. Warland recognizes him at first sight: ". . . the artist was disturbed by the child's look, as imagining a resemblance between it and Peter Hovenden's habitual expression." The child seizes the butterfly and crushes it in his fingers. Understanding has taken its due tribute; what is subject to the senses it must command. But nevertheless, victory lies with Warland and imagination. "He had caught a far other butterfly than this. When the artist rose high enough to achieve the beautiful, the symbol by which he made it perceptible to mortal senses became of little value in his eyes while his spirit possessed itself in the enjoyment of the reality."

Warland's creation, although a mechanism, transcends the merely mechanical to become a living organism. The artist of the beautiful is a consummate mechanic who is yet unsatisfied with the purposes of mechanism. Danforth's blundering suggestion that he must be " 'trying to discover the perpetual motion' " merely disgusts Warland. Perpetual motion, he replies, is " 'a dream that may delude men whose brains are mystified with matter, but not me.' " Decisively he disposes of the question: " 'I am not ambitious to be honored with the paternity of a new kind of cotton machine.' " His real purpose is divined in part by a momentary insight on the part of Annie Hovenden: Owen is " 'taken up with the notion of putting spirit into machinery.' " Later the artist enlarges upon this hint. In his thought life, beauty, and ideality are one. He has considered it "possible, in a certain sense, to spiritualize machinery, and to combine with the new species of life and motion thus produced a beauty that should attain to the ideal which Nature has proposed to herself in all her ceatures but has never taken pains to realize."

This aspiration Warland successfully embodies in *his* creature: "Nature's ideal butterfly was here realized in all its perfection." It is organic, mysteriously vitalized. "The rich down was visible upon its wings; the lustre of its eyes seemed instinct with spirit." It glistens with a radiance of its own. Annie, now married to Danforth, asks the crucial question, which poses the whole problem of "organic unity" and the "life" of a work of art. " 'Tell me if it be alive,' " she demands, " 'or whether you created it.' " The artist's answer, though paradoxical, is also inevitable.

". . . It may well be said to possess life, for it has absorbed my own being into itself; and in the secret of that butterfly, and in its beauty,—which is not merely outward, but deep as its whole system,—is represented the intellect, the imagination, the sensibility, the soul of an Artist of the Beautiful!"

In "The Artist of the Beautiful" Hawthorne expounds the fundamental ethic, metaphysic, psychology, and aesthetic of English Romanticism. The antitheses of ideal-material, time-eternity, understanding-imagination, and mechanism-organism are pervasively present in all the great Romantic poets. Most fully and philosophically developed in Coleridge, they are also to be found in different degrees and various interpretations in Wordsworth, Shelley, Keats, and even Byron. The germ of Romantic doctrine is transcendental idealism and the Platonic belief in the ultimate identity of Goodness, Truth, and Beauty. This doctrine in its Romantic form is calculated to glorify the artist as the moral sage of all men and as the repositor and revealer of Beauty and Truth. Conversely but logically enough it tends also to isolate the artist by his very possession of a perception so largely unknown and uncredited by the mass of mankind that their attitude towards him is likely to be an odd and complex mixture of reverence, distrust, scorn, and amusement. And since his values, based as they are upon the unseen ideal, are largely a reversal of the utilitarian values of everyday existence, he will be despised by the insensitive in almost direct ratio to his real merits.

The relation of these remarks to "The Artist of the Beautiful" is evident. Understanding is the faculty by which we perceive the world as Material—utilitaian, abstractive, and divisive, understanding is indispensable but incomplete. Through it alone, the world is essentially dead and meaningless; and the mass of men view reality with the aid of understanding only. Imagination, on the other hand, perceives the ideal, which is the innate reality and truth of things. Imagination endows the world with life and unity, and consequently with meaning. Understanding permits only

> . . . that inanimate cold world allowed
> To the poor loveless ever-anxious crowd,

while through imagination we see "into the life of things," beholding

> A motion and a spirit that impels
> All thinking things, all objects of all thought,
> And rolls through all things.

The mechanical is the unfortunate result of applying the unaided understanding to the creation of art. Understanding, which imitates the
inadequate reality to which it is confined, produces a merely mechanical
work, an uninspired arrangement of inert and predetermined materials.
In the context of "The Artist of the Beautiful" the mechanical is the art
of the watchmaker who, unlike Warland, sticks to his trade. The imagination, perceiving in reality the ideal, the basic life principle, and unity,
reproduces them in art, endowing the individual work with such life
and organic unity as is possible and appropriate to it. It follows, then,
that the imaginative work of art will be a living organism with a
development and an individuality appropriate to the laws inherent in
itself and in its kind. Natural, yet superior to Nature in that it embodies
Nature's essence, it magically combines the ideal with the particular.
Such a work is the butterfly of Owen Warland.

"The Artist of the Beautiful" is a Romantic affirmation of the value
of art and of the spiritual preeminence of the artist's imagination,
which intuitively penetrates to highest Goodness, Truth, and Beauty.
In this story belief, idealism, and love of beauty are exalted by being
contrasted with materialist skepticism and mere utility. Let us now shift
the focus of the narrative to describe these oppositions in different terms,
this time emphasizing the artist's dedicated effort to carry out his task.
From this point of view the basic symbol is an exquisite mechanism,
almost tragically susceptible to the slightest jar. This "delicate piece of
mechanism" is immediately set before us in the opening scene, in which
Hovenden and his daughter watch Warland through the shop window
as he bends earnestly over his creation. Warland's mechanism represents
the problem of the work of art, and the movement of the story is the
movement of its fortunes. It stands also for Warland himself, and both
must surmount the hostility of the world, which is represented to us in
the figures of Hovenden, Danforth, and Annie.

The mere perception of Annie's presence is sufficient to banish the
poise of the artist. " 'I shall scarcely,' " says Warland, " 'be able to work
again on this exquisite mechanism tonight.' " The rude strength of
Danforth has a more violent influence. The uproar of his laughter causes
Owen and the bell glasses on his cupboard (also symbols of fragile organization and balance) to quiver in unison, and when the artist returns
to his work his first stroke ruins the mechanism and nullifies the labor
of many months. " 'The vapor, the influence of that brute force,—it has
bewildered me and obscured my perception.' " In his next trial Peter
Hovenden threatens to destroy the mechanism—" 'See! with one pinch
of my finger and thumb I am going to deliver you from all future peril' "
—and so agitates Warland as to stop the work once more. Annie Hovenden attacks him more subtly, and more successfully because of her partial
insight into his purposes. Warland is on the point of confiding in her
when she destroys everything by carelessly toying with the vital mecha-

nism. She gives it but "the slightest possible touch, with the point of a needle," but it is sufficient. She has trifled frivolously with his deepest yet most vulnerable sensibilities. And Annie has one more blow to strike, the heaviest of all. At Hovenden's announcement of her engagement to Danforth the artist seems unmoved, but

> one slight outbreak, however, imperceptible to the old watchmaker, he allowed himself. Raising the instrument with which he was about to begin his work, he let it fall upon the little system of machinery that had, anew, cost him months of thought and toil. It was shattered by the stroke!

The framework of Hawthorne's fiction is customarily a doctrine, a belief, or a moral proposition which he proceeds to test by using his imagination. The theme of *The Scarlet Letter* is the damage to the soul from sin, but the theme itself is tried to the utmost and is exposed to unrelenting scrutiny. The characters have leave to range; no possibility of escape from the grim prison of the sin is left unexplored; no evidence, though contrary to the novel's thesis, is slighted or suppressed. It is even suggested that sin itself is illusory and that the adultery of Hester and Dimmesdale has brought forth good instead of evil: doctrines which are to be taken as quite contrary to the book's true purport. *The Marble Faun* is another case in point. Its narrative is solidly based upon the doctrine of the fall of man. Miriam and Donatello have sinned and must pay the penalty morally, psychologically, and socially. Yet Hawthorne in one crucial instance casts doubt on the reality of free will and personal responsibility and in another seems to argue strongly that the ultimate consequences of Donatello's crime must actually be beneficial.

So Hawthorne also tests the theme of "The Artist of the Beautiful" and furnishes material for other interpretations than his own. His characters may and should be read allegorically both as types and as ideas, but they become complex human beings as well, creatures of mingled strength and weakness, good and evil. The four figures of the tale can be labeled as types. Warland is the artist, Hovenden the businessman, Danforth the common man, and Annie—shall we say—the domestic woman. Or they may be considered as abstract ideas, so that Warland now becomes the quest for the ideal, Hovenden cynicism or materialism (in Hawthorne much the same thing), Danforth physical strength, and Annie the world's temptations. But they are also men and women, appealing and repellent alike, good often and bad as well. Their conflicts and relationships, however clear the ultimate verdict, are frequently complex and ambivalent.

Of Warland's three antagonists Peter Hovenden is plainly the least amiable and the worst, a soul-blighting cynic and materialist; and yet his nature has a commonsense centrality which is worthy of respect. In his character is a tenacious clutch upon a harsh reality, a steady grasp upon the doom of Adam. "'. . . give me the worker in iron after all is

said and done,'" says he. "'He spends his labor upon a reality.'"
Toward Warland he feels "the mixture of contempt and indignation
which mankind, of whom he was partly a representative, deem themselves
entitled to feel towards all simpletons who seek other prizes than the
dusty one along the highway." Seen from Hovenden's point of view the
idealist Warland seems weak and frail, his vision of reality a deluded
optimism, his delicate intuition a reaching among shadows.

We may get at the quality of Hovenden by placing him among his
fictional family, a group of characters present throughout Hawthorne's
work. He closely resembles the nameless Cynic of "The Great Carbuncle,"
who "was chiefly distinguished by a sneer that always contorted his thin
visage, and by a prodigious pair of spectacles, which were supposed to
deform and discolor the whole face of nature, to this gentleman's perception." The Cynic is almost wholly bad and comes to a very bad end.
Doffing his spectacles in scornful skepticism, he looks full upon the Great
Carbuncle and is blasted by its light. "So long accustomed to view all
objects through a medium that deprived them of every glimpse of
brightness, a single flash of so glorious a phenomenon, striking upon his
naked vision, had blinded him forever." Hovenden likewise bears a family
resemblance to Westervelt, the mesmerist villain of *The Blithedale
Romance,* whose evil lies in no positive trait or spiritual bent, but
simply in an all-embracing materialism which negates all moral meaning.
The suicide of the brilliant and passionate Zenobia, the keystone of the
action, he views with contemptuous regret as "'a mere woman's whim.'"
Hawthorne's final word on Westervelt would well fit Hovenden: "He
was altogether earthly, worldly, made for time and its gross objects, and
incapable—except by a sort of dim reflection caught from other minds—
of so much as one spiritual idea."

Hovenden is also comparable, however, to more worthy characters. He
has a tinge of the earthly honesty of "stout Silas Foster," the farmer of
Blithedale, whose practicality is a good corrective of the soaring utopian-
ism of the colonists. Like Westervelt, Foster is unable to perceive any
but the grossest meaning, but his materialism takes a far more amiable
form. Faced with the problem of the ethereal and mysterious Priscilla,
whose enigma arouses in others the most romantic speculations, his estimate of her case within its limits is definitive: "'give the girl a hot cup
of tea, and a thick slice of this first-rate bacon,' said Silas, like a sensible
man as he was. 'That's what she wants.'" The truth that man does not
live by bread alone is beyond his understanding, but he thoroughly knows
the truth that without bread man does not live at all. Hovenden, like
Foster, possesses a certain solid virtue. So far as he sees what good is, he
wishes Warland nothing but good. He loves his daughter even better
than he loves his watch, and as grandfather he shares the real amenities
of Robert Danforth's "fireside circle," from which the artist is forever
exiled.

The materialism of the blacksmith Danforth is of a more innocent kind, although its effects upon Warland are almost equally destructive. Danforth has the sturdy integrity of a lower organism perfectly adjusted to its environment and immune from the ills, aberrations, and temptations of a higher and more delicate nature. The blacksmith had best be seen at his forge:

> Within was seen the forge, now blazing up and illuminating the high and dusky roof, and now confining its lustre to a narrow precinct of the coal-strewn floor, according as the breath of the bellows was puffed forth or again inhaled into its vast leathern lungs. In the intervals of brightness it was easy to distinguish objects in remote corners of the shop and the horseshoes that hung upon the wall; in the momentary gloom the fire seemed to be glimmering amidst the vagueness of unenclosed space. Moving about in this red glare and alternate dusk was the figure of the blacksmith, well worthy to be viewed in so picturesque an aspect of light and shade, where the bright blaze struggled with the black night, as if each would have snatched his comely strength from the other. Anon he drew a white-hot bar of iron from the coals, laid it on the anvil, uplifted his arm of might, and was soon enveloped in the myriads of sparks which the strokes of his hammer scattered into the surrounding gloom.
>
> "Now, that is a pleasant sight," said the old watchmaker. "I know what it is to work in gold; but give me the worker in iron after all is said and done. He spends his labor upon a reality."

Danforth is a "man of main strength," a "worker in iron." His physical force is pitted against the delicacy and physical weakness of Warland; the spiritual power of Warland thus implies a corresponding spiritual lack in the blacksmith, who is a kind of earth spirit and honest Vulcan, with the same incompleteness as is symbolized by the bodily defect of the Limping God. The dark-and-blazing imagery of his forge hints at once of hell-fire and of the warmth of the hearth, while in general the picture suggests the power, the spaciousness, and the mystery of a huge subterranean cavern containing unknown potentialities both for good and for evil. His shop is for Hawthorne the symbol of the heart, which we may call the unconscious, if we choose. Danforth is a creature of the bowels of the earth, in direct contrast to the artist, whose airy ethereality is fitly symbolized by the butterfly. Danforth represents the primitive power and centrality of the human spirit, Antaeus-like bound to the earth and susceptible neither to the glory nor to the danger of the soaring Warland. Superlatively central and safe, couched on the bedrock of actuality, he is one of the crowd, that great conservative in Hawthorne; one of the people of the heart. He dwells in the bosom of human society; his successful marriage to Annie is the logical consummation of his qualities, which might else be perverted to evil; and his domestic fireside, the counterpart of the forge, is the essence of social virtue. Warland, "seeking admittance to Danforth's fireside circle" (the artist, forever an outsider, can only visit), finds there "the man of iron, with his massive substance thoroughly warmed and attempered by domestic influences."

Danforth has many relatives in Hawthorne's pages, among them the earth-fiend Aminadab, the assistant of the scientist Aylmer, whose hoarse, chuckling laugh is to be heard exulting over the tragic failure of his master's aspirations. "Thus," says Hawthorne, "ever does the gross fatality of earth exult in its invariable triumph over the immortal essence. . . ." Another of these characters is the brutish Bartram, the lime-burner of "Ethan Brand," who is heavy earth set against the alienating fire of Brand's Unpardonable Sin. Here it is a question of extremes: the perverted heart against the perverse intellect, Bartram's brutality against the oversubtlety of Brand. Danforth is saved as these men are damned, for while he is capable of friendship and love, they are capable only of sullen rage or brutal mockery. They are exiled from society by their debasement as is Warland by his elevation. Danforth is far above them, as he is perhaps below Robert Hagburn, the foil to Septimius Felton, or Dr. Baglioni, the moral censor of Rappaccini.

Annie is a feminine and more refined Danforth, the embodiment of woman as social conservator, her unamiable common sense tempered and enlivened by a sensitivity which is tacitly understood to be feminine. The sympathy and the sisterly indulgence which she feels for Warland are mingled with a mocking contempt. She is, after all, Annie Hovenden in her origin. Danforth, not Warland, is her appropriate mate. She is one of that excellent and unexciting sisterhood in Hawthorne who might be called the watchers of the fireside, a species of faithful vestal matrons. This company is headed by Phoebe Pyncheon, the model of gentle domestic grace, the cultivated garden flower in whom all trace of wildness has been carefully bred out. Rose Garfield, the mate of Robert Hagburn in *Septimius Felton,* is also a close relation, as is the slightly drawn but most attractive Dorothy, the faithful wife in "The Gentle Boy." It is to be noticed of these women that, with all but the crowning virtues, they generally lack the final insight which would bring them fully to life. There is a kind of spiritual coarseness about them which makes them fail to do justice to a lofty nature. So Annie lets Warland down in the crisis; Rose Hagburn is unequal to Septimius Felton; and Phoebe Pyncheon is far from comprehending the depths of her lover Holgrave.

Hawthorne's intention clearly is to present Owen Warland as the spiritual norm of his tale and to proclaim through him the superior significance and intensity and the greater value of the artist's experience and interpretation of reality. As we have seen, however, Warland does not always show up well in his environment. This fact is a tribute to Hawthorne's imaginative honesty. The artist is in some degree Hawthorne himself, and therefore it is all the more necessary that he avoid manipulating the fictional truth in his favor. So, as is his custom, Hawthorne leans backward—at times a little too far backward. Although the parallel is not exact, his treatment of the artist may be compared to his treatment of the Puritans in *The Scarlet Letter* and "The Maypole of Merry Mount." Himself Puritan in temperament, and possessed of a deep comprehension of the Puritan mind, he manhandles them unmercifully and yet with a certain affectionate familiarity. While Puritan, he is artist as well, and the Puritan in him is well able to take the world's part. The deprecation of Warland, consequently, comes from both sides of Hawthorne's nature—as Hawthorne portrays himself he deprecates, while as Puritan he reprehends with a "How shall the world be served?"

More important, however, is the Platonic fashion in which Hawthorne envisions the artist's gift. The notion of a transcendent reality is itself a paradox, for our imaginations fail to grasp it. Warland's physical smallness and his delicate minuteness of craftsmanship are intended to imply no lack of essential magnitude. His tiny butterfly transcends its spatial limitations; "In its perfect beauty, the consideration of size was entirely lost. Had its wings overreached the firmament, the mind could not have been more filled or satisfied." Undoubtedly the repeated emphasis upon Warland's physical smallness and weakness are meant to underline the opposition of ideal-material. What is true in the lower world is false in the higher; and Warland and his butterfly mock the pretensions of mere material bulk. But the imagination is at times inclined to prefer the lower truth, seeing with the eyes of a Hovenden or a Danforth. Faced with this paradox, Hawthorne does not attempt to solve it; rather, he dramatizes it. Danforth is superior to Warland as strength is to weakness, and he has the advantage of a sturdy masculinity. In a sense he is a greater artist. In the forge scene he is depicted as lifting from the fire a white-hot bar of iron, then shaping it with powerful strokes of the hammer. This is an image of creation, the molding of recalcitrant materials into unity, which calls to mind the mighty artist of Blake's "Tiger":

> What the hammer? what the chain?
> In what furnace was thy brain?
> What the anvil? what dread grasp
> Dare its deadly terrors clasp?

Blake, however, conceives a synthesis of strength and beauty which Hawthorne explicitly disavows, although he admits the hope of it as an ideal. The artist is disappointed in his faith that Annie is "imbued . . . with a finer grace, that might enable her to be the interpreter between strength and beauty."

The fact that Warland is a watchmaker lessens his dignity. The worker with mechanisms is soiled by the touch, even though he transforms his materials to living beauty. We cannot wholly forget the artisan in the artist. Warland is nearly unique in Hawthorne's work in that he successfully executes his ideal conception, and one cannot avoid considering that his success is partly due to the slightness of the archetype. He is unique in another respect: because of the peculiar nature of his art he runs no risk of violating the human heart, of losing the respect for the sanctity of the human spirit, as do those who imitate the human form or delve into human psychology. The painter of "The Phophetic Pictures" is one of the latter, as is Miles Coverdale, the "spiritualized Paul Pry" of *The Blithedale Romance*. It is perhaps significant that Hawthorne, in this his most extensive and explicit study of the problem of the artist, has exempted Warland from a danger with which he himself was undoubtedly preoccupied. In painting the ideal artist he has from affection freed him from this temptation, left him unstained by "Earth's common lot of care and sorrow," and in so doing weakened him.

Warland is isolated from society, as in Hawthorne are all artists and indeed all men of extraordinary aspirations, capacity, or achievements. His isolation, however, is that of an unfallen nature in a fallen world, which will not brook his pure pursuit of beauty, his urge for freedom from the prison house of life. His isolation is not self-inflicted but is forced upon him. From Annie he seeks love, and through love to link himself with human society, but his overtures are rejected. Love, the touching of the heart, is itself a kind of Fall and is incompatible with the attainment of the pure ideal. This fulfillment in Warland would probably have precluded the fulfillment of art, and the resulting disillusion with actuality might have achieved the same end as his final perception of the meaning of the butterfly.

> Had he become convinced of his mistake through the medium of successful love,—had he won Annie to his bosom, and there beheld her fade from angel into ordinary woman,—the disappointment might have driven him back, with concentrated energy, upon his sole remaining object. On the other hand, had he found Annie what he fancied, his lot would have been so rich in beauty that out of its mere redundancy he might have wrought the beautiful into many a worthier type than he had toiled for. . . .

But neither of these alternatives occurs; one feels that the possible choice is confined to an "either-or." Love awakens to life, as Hawthorne proclaims in a famous letter; but it binds as well, as he suggests in the young lovers of "The Maypole of Merry Mount." Love would be inappropriate to Warland, symbol of the free and soaring, whose triumph results from accepting his isolation and from perceiving the difference between the actual and the longed-for ideal. His wonderful butterfly, so pitilessly destroyed, is the scapegoat, the price of his freedom. It is the Warland of pure sensibility, Warland the seeker for sympathy and love, without the protective armor of knowledge which he himself has acquired painfully from conflict.

The Logic of Compulsion in
"Roger Malvin's Burial"

by Frederick C. Crews

    ... I choose this one tale to analyze because it illustrates the indispensability, and I should even say the priority, of understanding the literal psychological dramas in Hawthorne's fiction. Like all of his best tales, this one is packed with symbolic suggestions that invite a moralistic reading, and the problem it explores appears to be a problem of ethics. Yet a scrupulous examination of the main character's motives reveals that Hawthorne has approached his subject on a deeper level than the ethical—that he has not asked what someone in a certain predicament *should* do, but rather how a man may become the victim of unconscious hypocrisies over which he has no ethical control at all. Indeed, the working-out of this plot is strictly dependent, not on a religious attitude of Hawthorne's, but on an amazingly rigid logic of unconscious compulsion in the protagonist.[1] Nor, in my opinion, is this an exceptional case. "Roger Malvin's Burial" is a particularly clear example of an amoral, problematic embodiment of a psychological theory, but in nearly all Hawthorne's tales, I would maintain, the moral "message" is a secondary

"The Logic of Compulsion in 'Roger Malvin's Burial,' " by Frederick C. Crews. *PMLA*, LXXIX (September 1964, Part 1), 457-65. Copyright © 1964 by the Modern Language Association of America. Reprinted by permission of the Modern Language Association. With the author's permission a few preliminary remarks have been omitted and the footnotes reduced.

    [1] The argument of this paper is not altogether original. It is partly anticipated by Waggoner, *Hawthorne* (1955 edition), pp. 78-86; Richard P. Adams, "Hawthorne's *Provincial Tales*," *NEQ*, xxx (March 1957), 39-57; Louis B. Salomon, "Hawthorne and His Father: A Conjecture," *Literature and Psychology*, xiii (Winter 1963), 13-16; and Agnes McNeill Donohue, " 'From Whose Bourn No Traveller Returns': A Reading of 'Roger Malvin's Burial'," *NCF*, xviii (June 1963), 1-19. The last of these articles, which appeared after the present one was submitted for publication, admirably characterizes the spirit of Hawthorne's plot. Miss Donohue rests her argument, however, on "the consistent symbolism of the tale" (p. 14) rather than on its psychology, and she thus leaves herself vulnerable to the objection that Hawthorne's symbolism can bear other readings than her own. In reality Miss Donohue is right about "Roger Malvin's Burial" because she has intuitively grasped Reuben Bourne's motivation. My purpose is to demonstrate that the evidence for a reading like Miss Donohue's is entirely contained within the literal plot of the tale.

element. As Melvin W. Askew has observed, Hawthorne's allusively Biblical situations are ultimately resolved on the plane of the characters' psychological maturity or immaturity, not on that of their salvation or damnation. Hawthorne's insight into human motives is frequently so penetrating as to leave us with a sense of psychological fatalism that robs the implicit or explicit "moral" of its relevance.

The story in "Roger Malvin's Burial" is as follows. Roger Malvin, an old Indian-fighter who has been seriously wounded and finds himself unable to survive the homeward journey through a forest, persuades his young companion, Reuben Bourne, to leave him to die. Reuben will thereby gain a chance to survive, whereas to remain would simply mean two deaths instead of one. After promising to return some day to bury his old friend, Reuben departs and is eventually rescued by a search party. Though he marries Roger's daughter Dorcas, he is unable to explain to her that he left her father alive, preferring tacitly to accept her belief that he has already been buried. Reuben's public character and fortunes soon begin to go awry, until finally he is forced to take his wife and adolescent son off into the wilderness to seek a new life. Yet his steps bring him, not to the intended destination, but to the clearing where he left Roger Malvin many years before. There, detecting what might be a deer behind some undergrowth, he fires his musket, only to discover that he has killed his son Cyrus on the very spot where Roger died. The story ends, nonetheless, on an affirmative and extremely pious note:

> Then Reuben's heart was stricken, and the tears gushed out like water from a rock. The vow that the wounded youth had made the blighted man had come to redeem. His sin was expiated,—the curse was gone from him; and in the hour when he had shed blood dearer to him than his own, a prayer, the first for years, went up to Heaven from the lips of Reuben Bourne.

Such language naturally leads us to interpret "Roger Malvin's Burial" as a parable of atonement, for Reuben's act of manslaughter has melted his heart and enabled him to beg God for forgiveness. But forgiveness for what? It is unclear whether Reuben has atoned merely for not burying Roger or for some other failing, and critics disagree as to what he has done wrong. In Harry Levin's view, Reuben is "innocent" of Roger Malvin's death and only "inadvertently guilty" of his son's. Mark Van Doren, on the other hand, holds Reuben accountable for both the desertion of Roger and the hypocrisy of silence toward Dorcas: "he has committed a sin and he has failed to confess it when he could." A third interpretation is that of Arlin Turner, who finds that Hawthorne "relieves Reuben Bourne of any guilt for abandoning Malvin" but shows the ill effects of his failure to be honest with Dorcas. The only point of general agreement is that the slaying of Reuben's son Cyrus is accidental.

For Van Doren it is "Fate" that engineers the final catastrophe, and that event strikes Levin as "one of those coincidences that seem to lay bare the design of the universe."

All of these opinions, including the unquestioned one about Cyrus' death, miss the essence of Hawthorne's story by not recognizing a difference between the feeling of guilt and the state of being guilty. Turner, to be sure, makes the point that Reuben's guilt is subjective, but in regard to the desertion scene he apparently confuses a moral absolving of Rueben by Hawthorne with an absence of guilty feeling on Reuben's part. We can see, however, in this scene and throughout the story, that Hawthorne is concerned *only* with subjective guilt as Reuben's conscience manufactures it, independently of the moral "sinfulness" or "innocence" of his outward deeds. That this is so at the end of the tale is obvious, for how could we take seriously the religious notion that a man can make his peace with the Christian God by shooting his innocent son? It is clear that Reuben has not performed a Christian expiation but simply rid himself of his burden of guilty feeling. It can be shown, furthermore, that this guilty feeling was never generated by a committed sin or crime in the first place. Once we have recognized this, the task of deciding whether Reuben has been morally absolved becomes pointless, and Reuben's own theory that his steps have been led by "a supernatural power" appears in its true light—as a delusion fostered by, and serving to cloak, a process of unconscious compulsion that is evidenced in great detail.

Everyone agrees that Reuben feels guilty after misleading Dorcas, and it seems quite evident that Reuben's behavior in that scene is governed by an inner discomfort over his having left Roger Malvin behind. But why should Reuben feel this discomfort? The scene of desertion is presented in such a way as to put every justification on Reuben's side; Roger's arguments have persuaded not only Reuben but most of the tale's critics to feel that there is only one reasonable decision to be made. Why, then, does Reuben find it so difficult to explain the true circumstances to Dorcas? The answer seems to be that in some deep way Reuben feels more responsible for Roger's death than he actually is. "By a certain association of ideas," as Hawthorne says of him later, "he at times almost imagined himself a murderer."

How could Reuben feel himself even remotely to be Roger's murderer? If there is no factual basis for the self-accusation, perhaps there is a psychological basis. The charge seems, indeed, to be true to fantasy if not true to life, for Reuben shows definite signs of looking forward to deserting Roger in spite of his comradely feeling for him. When Roger adduces the point that Dorcas must not be left desolate, Reuben feels reminded "that there were other and less questionable duties than that of sharing the fate of a man whom his death could not benefit. Nor," adds Hawthorne significantly, "can it be affirmed that no selfish feeling strove to enter Reuben's heart, though the consciousness made him more earnestly resist his companion's entreaties." This would seem to be the source of all Reuben's trouble. It is obviously advantageous as well as reasonable for him to go on without Roger, since he faces a prospect of married bliss if he survives. The contrast between Roger's altruism and his own self-seeking motives is painful to his conscience; his personal claims must strive for recognition, and Reuben feels a need to counter-attack them with a redoubled dedication to remain with Roger. "He felt as if it were both sin and folly to think of happiness at such a moment." Thus we see that his feelings of guilt have already set in before he has made a final decision to leave. He feels guilty, not for anything he has done, but for thoughts of happiness—a happiness that will be bought at the price of a man's life.

The more closely we look at the scene of desertion, the more ironical Hawthorne's view of Reuben's mental struggle appears. The mention of Dorcas marks a turning-point between a series of melodramatic, self-sacrificing protestations of faithfulness and a new tone of puzzlement, self-doubt, and finally insincerity. Reuben is no longer really combatting Roger's wishes after this point, but posing objections that he knows Roger will easily refute. "How terrible to wait the slow approach of death in this solitude!" But a brave man, answers Roger, knows how to die. "And your daughter,—how shall I dare to meet her eye?" The question is already how *shall* I, not how *would* I! When this too has been answered, Reuben needs only to be assured of the possibility of his returning with a rescue party.

> No merely selfish motive, nor even the desolate condition of Dorcas, could have induced him to desert his companion at such a moment—but his wishes seized on the thought that Malvin's life might be preserved, and his sanguine nature heightened almost to certainty the remote possibility of procuring human aid.

There follows a grim comedy in which Roger pretends to see a similarity between the present case and another one, twenty years previously, that turned out well, and Reuben fatuously allows himself to be convinced. Hawthorne leaves no doubt that Reuben is semi-deliberately deceiving himself in order to silence his conscience. "This example, powerful in affecting Reuben's decision, was aided, unconsciously to himself, by the hidden strength of many another motive." When he finally does leave, the act is presented as a triumph of these other motives over his human sympathy: "His generous nature would fain have delayed him, at what-ever risk, till the dying scene were past; but the desire of existence and the hope of happiness had strengthened in his heart, and he was unable to resist them."

These citations from the story's first scene make it evident that Hawthorne, by having Reuben's self-seeking wishes concur with a morally legitimate but painful decision, has set in bold relief the purely psychological problem of guilt. Unlike his critics, Hawthorne does not dwell on the moral defensibility of Reuben's leaving; rather, he demonstrates how this act appears to Reuben as a fulfillment of his egoistic wishes, so that he is already beginning to punish himself *as if* he had positively brought about Roger's death. Hawthorne has anticipated Freud's discovery that (in Freud's terminology) the superego takes revenge for unfulfilled death-wishes as well as for actual murder.[2]

Indeed, Hawthorne's whole rendering of Reuben's mind seems remarkably "Freudian." Some of Reuben's motives, as we have seen, operate "unconsciously to himself," which is to say that they have been repressed; and once this repression has circumvented conscious moral control, Reuben becomes a classic example of the man who, because he can neither overcome his thoughts nor admit them into consciousness, becomes their victim. The real reason for his inability to state the outward facts of the case to Dorcas is that these facts have become associated with the unbearable fantasy that he has murdered his friend. Guilty feeling leads to a superficially uncalled-for hypocrisy, which in turn provides further reinforcement of guilt; "and Reuben, while reason told him that he had done right, experienced in no small degree the mental horrors which punish the perpetrator of undiscovered crime."

One other inconspicuous, but absolutely crucial, element in the scene of desertion remains to be mentioned. As Hyatt Waggoner has perceptively emphasized, the relationship between Roger and Reuben is essentially that of a father to a son. Roger repeatedly calls him "my boy" and "my son," and at a certain point he turns this language to an argumentative use: "I have loved you like a father, Reuben; and at a time like this I should have something of a father's authority." Reuben's reply is interesting: "And because you have been a father to me, should I therefore leave you to perish and to lie unburied in the wilderness?" From a strictly Freudian point of view the answer to this rhetorical question could be *yes;* the "son" feels murderous impulses toward the "father" simply because he *is* the father, i.e., the sexual rival. It is unlikely that Hawthorne's thinking has gone quite this far. Yet it remains true that Reuben, in leaving Roger to die, will get to have Dorcas' affections all to himself, and we cannot say that such a consideration is

[2] I do not mean, however, that Reuben actively wills Roger's death at any point. The link between his prospective happiness and Roger's imminent, already inevitable death is originally a fortuitous irony of circumstance and nothing more. But Reuben's punctilious conscience turns this link into one of causality; he will no longer be able to contemplate his own welfare without imagining, quite falsely, that he has bought it with Roger Malvin's blood. As always in Hawthorne's works, guilt is suffered more through an excessive moral scrupulosity than through actual wrongdoing.

not among the "many another motive" for his departure.[3] The "father's authority" of which Roger ingenuously speaks is going to be left behind in the forest. In terms of the unconscious role he has assumed in relation to Roger, Reuben must think of himself not simply as a murderer but as a parricide.

This conclusion, which looks so speculative and over-sophisticated, receives ample confirmation from the remainder of the story. Reuben, who henceforth is occupied in "defending himself against an imaginary accusation," gradually turns his interest to his son Cyrus. "The boy was loved by his father with a deep and silent strength, as if whatever was good and happy in his own nature had been transferred to his child, carrying his affections with it. Even Dorcas, though loving and beloved, was far less dear to him; for Reuben's secret thoughts and insulated emotions had gradually made him a selfish man, and he could no longer love deeply except where he saw or imagined some reflection or likeness of his own mind. In Cyrus he recognized what he had himself been in other days. . . ." Reuben has, in a word, projected himself into his son. And what is to be the conclusive deed of "Roger Malvin's Burial"? Reuben, who harbors an accusation of having murdered a "father" and who cannot bring this accusation up to the rational criticism of consciousness, shoots and kills the boy who has come to stand for himself. In killing Cyrus he is destroying the "guilty" side of himself, and hence avenging Roger Malvin's death in an appallingly primitive way. The blood of a "father" rests on the "son," who disburdens himself of it by becoming a father and slaying his son. This is the terrible logic of Hawthorne's tale.

Thus I would maintain, in opposition to the generally held view, that the slaying of Cyrus is not at all the hunting accident it appears to be. It is a sacrificial murder dictated by Reuben's unconscious charge of parricide and by his inability to bring the charge directly against himself. He has become the accusing Roger at the same time that he has projected his own guilty self into Cyrus. These unconscious stratagems are his means of dealing with the contradictory repressed wishes (the desire to atone and the unwillingness to accept blame) that have transformed him into an irritable, moody, and misanthropic man over the course of years. The killing of Cyrus, by cancelling Reuben's imaginary blood-debt, frees his whole mind at last for the task of making peace with God; yet this religious achievement becomes possible, as Hawthorne stresses in the closing sentence, only "in the hour when he had shed blood dearer to him than his own."

[3] We could even purport to find an incest theme here, for if Roger is to be taken seriously as Reuben's "father," Dorcas becomes his sister. Again, real evidence is lacking, and my argument does not rest on such conjectures as this. It may be added in passing, however, that the nature of Dorcas' later feeling for her son—"my beautiful young hunter!"—does not dispel the pervasive atmosphere of over-intimacy in the tale.

There are two main obstacles to the theory that Reuben's shooting his son is intentional. One is that Reuben has no idea that his target is Cyrus instead of a deer; he simply fires at a noise and a motion in the distance. Secondly, there is the possibility that not Reuben but God is responsible for bringing the tale to its catastrophe. The final paragraph, after all, speaks of the lifting of a curse, and Roger Malvin has imposed a religious vow on Reuben to "return to this wild rock, and lay my bones in the grave, and say a prayer over them." Both Roger and Reuben are religious men, and Reuben "trusted that it was Heaven's intent to afford him an opportunity of expiating his sin." Perhaps we are meant to read the story in divine rather than psychological terms.

The answer to this latter point is provided by Hawthorne in a single sentence describing Reuben in the final scene: "Unable to penetrate to the secret place of his soul where his motives lay hidden, he believed that a supernatural voice had called him onward, and that a supernatural power had obstructed his retreat." No one who ponders these words can imagine that Hawthorne's famous ambiguity between natural and supernatural causality is really sustained in "Roger Malvin's Burial." As for the other objection, it is certainly true that Reuben shows no conscious awareness that he is firing at his son. But does this make the act wholly unintentional? Before investigating the actual shooting we must see just what Hawthorne means by intention. His theory is evidently somewhat deeper than that of our law courts, which would surely have acquitted Reuben in a trial for murder. "Roger Malvin's Burial" discriminates from the first between surface intentions and buried ones, between outward tokens of generous concern and inward selfishness, between total ignorance and a knowledge that is temporarily unavailable to consciousness. For this last distinction we may point to the statement that Reuben cannot choose to return and bury Roger because he does not know how to find his way back: "his remembrance of every portion of his travel thence was indistinct, and the latter part had left no impression upon his mind." Yet we have just seen that Reuben will be guided by "his motives," residing in a "secret place of his soul." Furthermore, he has always "had a strange impression that, were he to make the trial, he would be led straight to Malvin's bones." We can only conclude that his unconscious does remember the route he took in that traumatic flight from the deserted comrade. The knowledge is repressed, not lost, and when Reuben finally gives himself over to the guidance of his unconscious he is led infallibly back to the scene.

In order to see the killing of Cyrus in its true light we must observe Reuben's prior behavior rather closely. Although Cyrus reminds him again and again that he is taking the family in a different direction from the announced one, Reuben keeps resuming his original course after each correction. His thoughts are obviously dwelling on something other than the relocation of his home. "His quick and wandering glances were sent

forward, apparently in search of enemies lurking behind the tree trunks;
and, seeing nothing there, he would cast his eyes backwards as if in fear
of some pursuer." Reuben would appear to be projecting his self-accusa-
tions into multiple exterior threats to himself. The internalized Roger
Malvin—the Roger Malvin created by Reuben's unwarranted self-accusation of murder—is evidently redoubling his demand to be avenged as
the anniversary of his death draws near. When the fifth day's encampment
is made, Dorcas reminds Reuben of the date. " 'The twelfth of May! I
should remember it well,' muttered he, while many thoughts occasioned a
momentary confusion in his mind. 'Where am I? Whither am I wandering? Where did I leave him?' " Among those "many thoughts" that have
suddenly been jolted into consciousness are probably the answers to all
three of Reuben's questions. Dorcas has accidentally brought to the surface, though only for a moment, Reuben's feeling that he is on a deliberate mission. Is the mission simply to bury Roger's bones? Evidently something further is involved, for in reply to Dorcas' next words, praising
Reuben for having loyally stayed with Roger to the end, Reuben replies,
"Pray Heaven, Dorcas, . . . pray Heaven that neither of us three dies
solitary and lies unburied in this howling wilderness!" And on this fore-
boding note he hastens away at once. It seems to me obvious that Reuben's terribly sincere "prayer" is a response to his own unconscious urge
to commit the sacrificial killing—an urge that has been screwed to the
sticking place by Dorcas's unwitting irony. Like all men in the grip of a
destructive obsession, Reuben hopes desperately that his own deep wishes
will be thwarted; yet he rushes off in the next moment, and a few min-
utes later Cyrus will be dead.

We have, then, an abundance of evidence to show that one side of Reuben's nature, the compulsive side, has gained mastery over his conscious
intentions. The evidence continues to accumulate as the moment of the
shooting draws nearer. Reuben is assaulted by "many strange reflections"
that keep him from governing his steps in the supposed hunt for a deer;
"and, straying onward rather like a sleep walker than a hunter, it was
attributable to no care of his own that his devious course kept him in
the vicinity of the encampment." No *conscious* care, that is, for Reuben
has a very good compulsive reason for his movements. Cyrus has previously set out on another deer hunt, "promising not to quit *the vicinity of
the encampment*" (italics mine). Surely Hawthorne's repetition of these
five words within the space of two pages is meant to strike our attention.
Without quite realizing what he is doing, Reuben is stalking his son.
His conscious thoughts are straying vaguely over the puzzle of his having
reached this spot on this date, and he arrives at a conscious interpretation
—explicitly rejected by Hawthorne, as we have already seen—that "it was
Heaven's intent to afford him an opportunity of expiating his sin." The
consciously accepted "sin" is that of leaving Roger Malvin unburied, but
while Reuben busies himself with this lesser anxiety he is going about

the business of squaring his deeper unconscious debt. Here is the deed itself:

> From these thoughts he was aroused by a rustling in the forest at some distance from the spot to which he had wandered. Perceiving the motion of some object behind a thick veil of undergrowth, he fired, with the instinct of a hunter and the aim of a practised marksman. A low moan, which told his success, and by which even animals can express their dying agony, was unheeded by Reuben Bourne. What were the recollections now breaking upon him?

These are brilliantly suggestive lines. Reuben is supposedly deer-hunting, but Hawthorne leaves no implication that Reuben thinks he has spotted a deer; he fires at a "rustling" and a "motion." To say that he does this with a hunter's instinct is slyly ironical, for of course a good hunter does not shoot at ambiguous noises, particularly in "the vicinity of the encampment"! The moan that would tell Reuben of his ironic "success," if he were sufficiently in command of himself to heed it, is said to be one "by which *even* animals can express their dying agony"—perhaps a hint that animals have not been his primary target. And finally, the question at the end serves to put the blame for Cyrus' death where it properly belongs. The repressed "recollections" of the original scene are now free to become wholly conscious because the guilt compulsion that protected them has finally completed its work.

I have as yet made no mention of literary symbolism in "Roger Malvin's Burial." It seemed more important to establish the sequence of psychological events in the plot than to move directly to other levels of meaning. The tale is not wanting in symbolism, however. As W. R. Thompson has recently shown, the names of three of the four major characters are Biblical and suggest various parallels to Scripture. The Biblical Reuben leaves a loved one (Joseph) in the wilderness, intending to return and rescue him, but eventually lies about the whole affair. Dorcas is mentioned briefly in Acts ix.36-41 as a good, long-suffering woman, and Cyrus is the Lord's anointed soldier in Isaiah xliv-xlv. One can only agree with Thompson that these parallels must have some symbolic relevance to Hawthorne's story. But how do we arrive at an explication of the name-symbolism? Thompson, approaching the tale, as he says, "on the level of the source material," is inclined to see Reuben as an allegorical figure in the second half of the story; the Biblical Cyrus' role suggests that Reuben is no longer an individual but "a people seeking redemption and deliverance from their bondage," since Israel was to receive such redemption from the original Cyrus. Again, the Cyrus prototype "makes it mandatory that Reuben somehow achieve salvation through the medium of Cyrus Bourne." "Thus Cyrus in death leads Reuben to the only spot in creation where he can make good his pledge of so many years' standing." Now, it is evident from our tracing of the tale's literal action that these inferences are strained. Reasoning purely about the symbolism, Thompson has distorted the plot. Hawthorne leaves no implication that Reuben stands for a captive people, and it is not Cyrus, dead or alive, who leads Reuben to his fateful appointment. Nor is it at all clear that Reuben has achieved "salvation" at the end of the tale. Assuming, with other critics who have been anxious to interpret "Roger Malvin's Burial" before seeing exactly what happens in it, that the killing of Cyrus is done "accidentally," Thompson reduces Hawthorne's grim irony to a minimum and leaves the impression that the ultimate point of view behind the story is a pious one. The emphasis must be on salvation because this is what we find in Isaiah!

I suggest that a sounder procedure would be to relate the Biblical allusions to what Hawthorne has created, not vice-versa. Once we have grasped the point that the slaying of Cyrus obeys an unconscious intention, no strictly religious interpretation seems possible. Even the Abraham-Isaac parallel, which seems to me as pertinent as any other Biblical analogue, must be taken in an ironic spirit, for Reuben's "sacrifice" of his son is dictated not by God by by self-loathing. The portent of the story's ending is heretical, to say the least; Reuben's "redemption" has been earned through murder, while the guilt from which he has thereby freed himself was attached to a crime that had been committed only in his imagination. The real murder is unrepented yet—indeed, Reuben seems to show little concern for his dead son—while the fantasy-murder brings forth tears and prayer. The Biblical allusions suggesting redemption serve the purpose, in my opinion, of placing in relief the merely pathological nature of the case at hand. The idea of divine care for a chosen people is cruelly mocked by Hawthorne's plot, in which all exhortations to Heaven spring from self-delusion, and in this story the "redeemer" performs his redemptive function by unintentionally stopping a musket ball.

The other symbols in Hawthorne's story ought likewise to be considered in relationship to its essential savagery. The most conspicuous symbol is, of course, the oak sapling upon which Reuben placed a blood-stained handkerchief, partly as a signal of rescue for Roger and partly to symbolize his own vow to return. When he does return the tree has grown into "luxuriant life," with "an excess of vegetation" on the trunk, but its "very topmost bough was withered, sapless, and utterly dead." This branch, which is the one that formerly bore the emblem of the vow, falls in fragments upon the *tableau vivant* of the living and dead at the very end. The symbolic meaning is, if anything, too obvious. The sapling is Reuben, whose innocent young life has been "bent" (he bends the sapling downward to affix the handkerchief to it) to a sworn purpose and to a secret self-reproach; Reuben grows as the tree grows, becoming mature in outward respects but blasted at the top, in his soul or mind; and when the withered bough crumbles we are doubtless meant to conclude that the guilt has been cancelled and that a possibility now exists for more normal development. I would call particular attention, however, to the *excessive* vegetation and *luxuriant* lower branches. Luxuriance in Hawthorne almost always has something faintly sick about it, and the word "excess" speaks for itself. I would surmise that these aspects of the tree represent the compensatory elements in Reuben's character, the gradual accumulation of defenses against the tormenting thoughts that he has been fighting down for years. His peace of mind is partly restored at the end of the tale, but he will never again be the simple person we met in the beginning.

Finally, let us consider the symbolic value of the forest itself. Reuben's initiation into guilt, like Young Goodman Brown's and Arthur Dimmesdale's, occurs in the forest, and it is in the forest that he will bring forth what his guilty feelings have hatched. "He was," as Hawthorne says of Reuben's desire to seek a new home, "to throw sunlight into some deep recess of the forest." The forest is of course his own mind, in which is deeply buried a secret spot, a trauma, to which he will have to return. He thinks he does not know the way back, he resists the opportunity to go, but ultimately he is overruled by the strength of what he has repressed. Self-knowledge is knowledge of what lies almost inaccessibly remote in the forest of the mind, and Reuben will not be free until he has reached this point and released what lies imprisoned there. The expression and purgation of this secret will be a crime of violence, a murder which is symbolically a suicide, since the victim stands for Reuben himself.

Hawthorne's interest in the forest as a conveyer of these grave implications accounts for a good deal of the nature description in the second half of the story. In this demonic tale it is not enough for Hawthorne to bind his characters to a "dark necessity" of one man's compulsion; he must also tease us with the possibility that God's in His Heaven after all. Hawthorne waxes lyrical as the dénouement approaches: "Oh, who, in the enthusiasm of a daydream, has not wished that he were a wanderer in a world of summer wilderness . . . ?" In an expansive paragraph he fancies the possibility of a life of sheer innocence, purity, and harmony with nature. The purpose of all this is to set up an antithesis: "The tangled and gloomy forest through which the personages of my tale were wandering differed widely from the dreamer's land of fantasy. . . ." There are resemblances, to be sure, and there are moments of joy in which nature seems to echo the family's resurgent hopes. But this is near the start of the journey, when Reuben has not yet veered toward his real destination. When this happens the effect is quite different: "They were now keeping farther to the north, striking out more directly from the settlements, and into a region of which savage beasts and savage men were as yet the sole possessors." This is the "howling wilderness" that Reuben mentions in the last sentence spoken to Dorcas before the slaying; it is the wilderness of his own inner world, and his own murderous intent toward Cyrus is the savage beast that inhabits it. Though Dorcas, unaware that the killing has taken place, makes one final effort to humanize the forest by domesticating it in her imagination, the measure of her success is what she finds at the base of the rock where her father died.

The relative critical neglect of "Roger Malvin's Burial" has sprung, I believe, from the general failure to see Reuben's motivation. It is interesting that the few critics who have grasped the main outline of the tale have also been impressed by its high quality, for the apparent flaw in "Roger Malvin's Burial" is the improbability of its coincidences. If we eliminate the psychological justification for Reuben's finding his way back to the very spot where the story began, the plot of course becomes over-neat, and no talk about Fate, Providence, or "the design of the universe" can atone for the banality of it all. We have seen, however, that Roger Malvin's real "burial" takes place in what Hawthorne calls "the sepulchre of [Reuben's] heart"; in that organ the dead man lives again, directing the self-accused "killer" to perform an expiation that is not simply plausible, but absolutely necessary and inevitable.

The Ethical Dimension of "The Custom House"

by *Larzer Ziff*

Perhaps the chief interest "The Custom House" Introduction holds for the reader today is its statement of Hawthorne's theory of romance, a theory which, as many have noted, profoundly governs the form and content of *The Scarlet Letter*. What has not been as well noted is the relationship between that theory and Hawthorne's theory of the good life. The experiences surrounding Hawthorne's definition of the romance as the meeting ground of the actual and the imaginary are more moral than aesthetic, and the realization of the theory in *The Scarlet Letter* governs the moral conclusions Hawthorne would like his reader to draw as well as the subject-matter and its arrangement.

Talking of his experiences as Surveyor of the Customs at Salem, in "The Custom House," Hawthorne asserts that for the most part his colleagues are a "set of wearisome old souls, who had gathered nothing worth preservation from their varied experience of life." We can appreciate why these men are wearisome when we consider the two whom he singles out for particular discussion: one is the epitome of what he finds distasteful in his colleagues; the other is an exception who serves to underline his general observation.

The epitome of wearisomeness is the Inspector who has stored his memory with husks and thereby stunted his moral development. He has numbered in his experience three wives, now dead, and twenty children, most of them also dead. "Here," Hawthorne says, "one would suppose, might have been sorrow enough to imbue the sunniest disposition, through and through, with a sable tinge." But this is not so. All the Inspector seems to have gained from life is a concern with the physical present. His main interest and chief topic of conversation is food—the mutton-chop he ate, the hindquarter of veal he will eat—so that he has, in Hawthorne's words, "no higher moral responsibilities than the beasts of the field," and shares the beasts' "blessed immunity from the dreariness and duskiness of age."

"The Ethical Dimension of 'The Custom House,'" by Larzer Ziff. *Modern Language Notes*, LXXIII (May 1958), 338-44. Copyright © 1958 by *Modern Language Notes*. Reprinted by permission of Johns Hopkins Press and Larzer Ziff.

The exception to the moral desert which Hawthorne finds in the custom house is the old retired General who is Collector of Customs. Hawthorne sees him as noble and heroic, yet his actual contact with the General is less than with most of his other colleagues:

> He seemed away from us, although we saw him but a few yards off; remote, though we passed close beside his chair; unattainable, though we might have stretched forth our hands and touched his own. It might be that he lived a more real life within his thoughts than amid the unappropriate environment of the Collector's office. The evolutions of the parade; the tumult of the battle; the flourish of old, heroic music, heard thirty years before,—such scenes and sounds, perhaps, were all alive before his intellectual sense.

From these descriptions of character we can infer an important precept which links Hawthorne's aesthetics to his ethics. The implied proposition might be phrased as follows: "Man's inner life can be more real than his outer life." It can be applied in fiction by dealing with the thoughts and emotions of characters as well as with their actions. It is also an ethical proposition because Hawthorne obviously finds that the Collector's inner life makes him a better man than the Inspector, who is much more alive physically but does not seem ever to have reflected.

The old General, like Hester Prynne, indulges in his reveries beside a fire, and it is pertinent that the "dim glow of a coal-fire" in the Introduction is as necessary an element of the room which analogizes the romance as are the moon-light and the familiar objects. The ethical formula which precedes the aesthetic equation of the actual and the imaginary is one which characterizes the good life as a life which blends the reveries of the past with the actions of the present, which combines morality and materiality. Just as the good romance strikes a balance between the actual and the imaginary, so the man of good character strikes a balance between his inner state and the materiality of the world.

The formula is further developed in "The Custom House" when Hawthorne discusses his own moral condition. He represents himself as the descendant of a family associated with Salem ever since its founding, and he takes sentimental comfort in this genealogy. Indeed, there is the flavor of semiconscious snobbism in his later reference to the modern aristocracy of Salem as families who can be traced "from the petty and obscure beginnings of their traffic, at periods generally much posterior to the Revolution, upward to what their children look upon as long-established rank." Hawthorne claims a moral quality for his sentiment because it has provided him with a "home-feeling with the past," a feeling which, he goes on to say, he can "scarcely claim with reference to the present phase of the town." Too much of this sentiment can be unhealthy—he is glad his children (like Phoebe Pyncheon) were born and are being bred free of a Salem in which the legacy would be weightier by another generation—

but for him it is a good thing. It provides him with a background of experience, albeit vicarious, so that like the old General he can face the materiality of life with a hidden life of his own.

Instead of sitting next to the custom house fire surrounded by his memories, the Surveyor Hawthorne we are presented to pokes about the attic reading the dusty documents of New England's past—his past. The effect, of course, is similar. And just as his life has been given moral quality by its familial link with the past, so when he turns to fiction he develops an artistic link with the past. Surveyor Pue is his literary ancestor, and accounts for the century which lies between that in which the action of *The Scarlet Letter* takes place and that in which Hawthorne occupies the custom house.

The past and present, then, enter into Hawthorne's theory of experience as counterparts of the distinction between inner state and materiality; as necessary elements of the view of life which informs the actual-imaginary view of fiction. Romance is an enrichment of the actual by the imaginary. The good life is an enrichment of the material by the inner self, an appreciation of the present through a consciousness of the past. The elements of the good life find their dramatic counterparts in the two basic elements of the romance, and such a good life is, then, the material of the romance.

For this very reason, Hawthorne professed himself dissatisfied with the total achievement of *The Scarlet Letter*. His romance seemed to him too complete an escape into the past, too much concerned with the hidden and too little concerned with the open. A better book than he has written, he tells us in "The Custom House," would be written by the man who could see the "true and indestructible value that lay hidden in the petty and wearisome incidents, and ordinary characters" which surrounded him in Salem; the man who could fathom "the deeper import" of what seemed "dull and commonplace" to Hawthorne. When reading these remarks, one thinks of William Dean Howells' description of the crowd on the boat which is taking Tom Corey and Silas Lapham to the latter's summer cottage: "In face they were commonplace, with nothing but the American poetry of vivid purpose to light them up, where they did wholly lack fire." But whereas Howells' problem was to reveal the fire that lit up commonplace characters and events, Hawthorne's was to discover the commonplace settings which would display his sense of the past's importance. His quarrel with *The Scarlet Letter* is addressed to the overbalance in that book of the half of the dualism embodying the past, the inner state, and the imaginary, so that the virtues of the present, the material, and the actual are underdeveloped. What he wishes is to be able to write about the present, although it may fictionally appear as an earlier period, giving it the values which he associates with the past, but, nevertheless, keeping the actual always in focus so that whatever his characters' dramatic reconciliations with their environment may be they are also reconciliations with materiality. He notes, at the end of "The Custom House," that if he is remembered at all in Salem he will be remembered as the historian of the town pump, the author of the little temperance piece about Salem's early source of water. He wants the contemporaneity of "A Rill from the Town Pump" to be informed with the morality of *The Scarlet Letter,* but he also wants *The Scarlet Letter* to bear a more immediate relationship to the actual than he feels it does. *The House of the Seven Gables,* for instance, can be seen as Hawthorne's attempt to fuse what he found satisfying in the aforementioned two works so as to produce a work which better balanced the past with the present.

Of course, the generally accepted opinion is that Hawthorne did in *The Scarlet Letter* achieve just such a balance between the actual and the imaginary as he talked of in the introductory sketch, so that the discontent expressed in "The Custom House" should be read merely as an expression of the artist's customary discontent with his finished product in view of the perfection he envisioned. However, if we bear in mind the ethical as well as the aesthetic connotation of his theory of romance, we can see that as sound as this opinion may be for the critic of the novel, Hawthorne could not have shared it because he refused to separate the ethics of his content from the beauty of his form. The critic is correct, of course. Hawthorne did achieve a superb balance between the actual and the imaginary in *The Scarlet Letter.* But there was an imbalance for Hawthorne because his theory of the good life did not achieve as successful an embodiment as did his theory of romance: the balancing of the actual and the imaginary should also have been the balancing of the inner state and materiality and the latter blend was not, for Hawthorne, satisfactorily composed.

This can be appreciated by considering the Puritan past which serves as the scene of *The Scarlet Letter.* It provides the characters with precisely that environment in which the secret acts of the soul are matters of public concern, in which the sin of adultery is a crime against the state, in which the scarlet letter, making public the hidden, can be worn with probability. But as aesthetically appropriate as the setting may seem, Hawthorne, in the last analysis, found it ethically inappropriate. The Puritan commonwealth might artistically stand for the actual while the superstitions and torments of its citizens might stand for the imaginary, but Hawthorne wanted his actual also to correspond to what he regarded as materiality so that when the dramatic reconciliation of his characters with their environment took place, so would the ethical reconciliation between inner state and materiality occur. This, however, is not the case in *The Scarlet Letter* because the fictional Boston is far too remote from materiality. Any reconciliation of a character's private life with its public life could hardly be viewed as an instructive achievement with obvious parallels in the nineteenth century America which Hawthorne viewed from his window.

The idea can be illustrated with reference to Pearl who aesthetically stands so well for the meeting place of the actual and the imaginary. However, she also serves to remind us that Boston itself is a dark place. Governor Bellingham sees her at his home, a place reminiscent of old England—of the wider world—with its liveried servant, its old furniture, and its garden, which, significantly, has failed to develop after its English model but has degenerated into little more than a cabbage patch. In this setting, Pearl is a reminder for Bellingham of his "days of vanity in old King James's time." In the same scene, the Reverend John Wilson says of Pearl, "Methinks I have seen just such figures, when the sun has been shining through a richly painted window, and tracing out the golden and crimson images across the floor." He adds, "But that was in the old land."

As Pearl is the organic embodiment of the sin of her parents, that which Dimmesdales must acknowledge in the market place, so she is also for the Puritan community the embodiment of what they attempted to leave behind when they went into the forest but what they cannot reconcile with their present life, although, to be ethically sound, they must. Boston, which aesthetically may stand for the actual, ethically partakes of the hidden half of the dualism because of its suppressed materiality.

Such a community, then, did not ultimately satisfy its creator's moral demands, for it failed to have the hearty materiality, the indulgence in the senses, which he saw in the Salem about him. He comments that the Puritans were, after all, "Native Englishmen, whose fathers had lived in the sunny richness of the Elizabethan epoch; a time when the life of England, viewed as one great mass, would appear to have been as stately, magnificent, and joyous, as the world has ever witnessed." He makes it clear that they should not have denied this heritage, and that the extravagances they have permitted themselves are, unfortunately, exceptions. Aesthetically, daily Boston might balance the secret lives of its citizens, but morally it is too much of the same. Chillingworth, for all of the dire effect he has upon Dimmesdale, opens the windows of Dimmesdale's mind to European thoughts, to what is happening in the market place of the world. If Hester's attempt to get to that world with Dimmesdale is ill-fated, it is not because Boston is ethically the best place, but because Hester and Dimmesdale have not yet given Boston its due meed. Pearl does so, and is no longer required to languish there but is permitted to mingle the morality which Boston has imposed upon her with the materiality which Boston unhealthily denies.

For *The Scarlet Letter* to have lived up to the theory of romance's ethical demands, then, its Boston would have to have been much more like the Salem which Hawthorne saw from his windows. He did not regret, he tells us, his initial entrance into his duties as Surveyor of Customs. Because he had worked at Brook Farm, mingled with Channing and Thoreau, and been influenced by Emerson and Longfellow, it was a healthy thing for him to get into active life. The Inspector was a necessary antidote for Alcott. He tells us this immediately before expressing his sense of his inability to write a good book about the life around him, in order to absolve the daily activity of the custom house from responsibility for its apparent sterility, a responsibility which, he believed, actually resided in his perception of it. *The Scarlet Letter* disappoints him because the materiality of the life in it is, ultimately, too close to an objectification of the hidden lives of its characters so that his interpretation of the actual and the imaginary is not matched by its ethical counterpart.

This supposed shortcoming of *The Scarlet Letter* explains why Hawthorne's subsequent romances took the direction they did. After his first full length work, the historical past ceases to be the scene in which Hawthorne set his work, because he wished his scene to provide more of the materiality which entered into his view of the good life than it did in *The Scarlet Letter*. The past, of course, remained an important element of that good life, and, therefore, of the romance's subject matter, but it was subordinated to the demands of the immediate world of the work, and shaped but did not constitute it. The living are very much in control of *The House of the Seven Gables* as its reaches its resolution.

The Scarlet Letter

by Mark Van Doren

The Scarlet Letter is in a sense the last of Hawthorne's tales, and of course their climax. Afterwards, made ambitious by success, he planned novels and romances, and sought to enlarge his scope. His masterpiece, however, is this culmination, achieved at forty-five, of the narrower effort which for a quarter century he had been putting forth. "It has about it that charm," says James, "very hard to express, which we find in an artist's work the first time he has touched his highest mark—a sort of straightness and naturalness of execution, an unconsciousness of his public, and freshness of interest in his theme." It was the last as well as the first time Hawthorne touched this mark, and as for the freshness of interest—there is mystery in that, for the theme was old. Hawthorne was doing again what he had done so many times that he thought he was weary of it. He could not have been, as he now discovered; but exactly what had happened, to his mind and to his theme, neither he nor anyone else was wholly to know. It is not enough to speak, as he himself often did in other connections, of inspiration and grace, though neither explanation is bad. When he saw the Houses of Parliament in London he decided with some disappointment that the architect had "felt no power higher and wiser than himself, making him its instrument," and therefore had "missed the crowning glory—that being a happiness which God, out of his pure grace, mixes up with only the simple-hearted, best efforts of men." In "Drowne's Wooden Image" he had told how the sculptor in pine and oak had failed to find in himself "that deep quality, be it of soul or of intellect, which bestows life upon the lifeless and warmth upon the cold" until the day when, working "in a kind of dream" because "kindled by love," he wrought the miracle of a lady in wood who walked in mirth and fluttered her fan. All this is interesting and true, but to speak thus of *The Scarlet Letter* would be saying less than we know, for we know in detail the materials he is treating again, even for

"*The Scarlet Letter.*" From *Nathaniel Hawthorne* by Mark Van Doren (New York, William Sloane Associates, 1949). Copyright 1949 by William Sloane Associates, Inc. Reprinted by permission of William Sloane Associates and Mark Van Doren. The first two transitional pages of the chapter and the synopsis of the novel have been omitted with the author's permission.

the hundredth time. The only thing we do not know for certain is how or why he suddenly converted them to greatness.

The persons of the tale were long since types to him, as were their souls' predicaments. The broken law, the hidden guilt, the hunger for confession, the studious, cold heart that watches and does not feel— no one of these was new. There was a new symbol, to be sure, though even that had lain in Hawthorne's memory for years. In "Endicott and the Red Cross," as early as 1837, he had written:

> There was likewise a young woman, with no mean share of beauty, whose doom it was to wear the leter A on the breast of her grown, in the eyes of all the world and her own children. And even her own children knew what that initial signified. Sporting with her infamy, the lost and desperate creature had embroidered the fatal token in scarlet cloth with golden thread and the nicest art of needlework; so that the capital A might have been thought to mean Admirable, or anything rather than Adulteress.

In 1844 he had entered in his note-book, evidently as the idea for a story: "The life of a woman, who, by the old colony law, was condemned always to wear the letter A, sewed on her garment, in token of her having committed adultery." And three years later, with or without the husband of such a woman in mind, he had made the entry: "A story of the effects of revenge, diabolizing him who indulges in it." Here was Roger Chillingworth, the familiar devil of the tales, supplied at last with a human motive; as here in Hester Prynne, the wife he had sacrificed to his learning, was a woman into whom Hawthorne could pour every feeling and idea he had about her sex. About sin, too; though in his third person, Arthur Dimmesdale, Hester's lover and Roger's victim, he had a still more perfect vessel for that purpose. It is Dimmesdale whom secrecy tortures; it is he who must confess and die. But Dimmesdale is merely one more ideal scholar in a procession that marches back as far as Fanshawe, merely one more sensitive man rendered helpless before the world. And yet not merely, for his intensity absorbs all of his predecessors and makes them pale by comparison; as Chillingworth surpasses each previous villain; and as Hester becomes a heroine, almost a goddess, into whom the character of every other woman in Hawthorne flows. Hawthorne's witch-lady is here also, in Mistress Hibbins; Hester's elf-daughter, Pearl, is a descendant both of the sweet children who fashioned a play-maiden out of snow and of the fiend's infants who stoned the Gentle Boy; the dignitaries of the book, from Governor Bellingham down, are done in the august style of the provincial tales; and the familiar crowd of citizens, the feeling mob, has all of its old function, its double function of population and chorus.

The difference, at least so far as the three principals are concerned, is in the degree to which Hawthorne feels and honors them as individuals. Formerly his temptation had been to decorate ideas, to produce rhetoric about emotions, at the expense of the persons in whom he placed them.

This had caused a certain coldness in the persons, over and above the coldness with which it became conventional for him to charge them. But worse than that, it meant a vagueness, a want of force, consistent with his practice of refusing to define the good or the evil—usually the evil—that was in them. Hawthorne had cultivated in himself a weakness for the abstract. Abstraction is necessary to narrative, but at a deeper level than any which the poet lets us see. It is what makes the people finally important and utterly exciting. But exhibited before our eyes, in the refractory medium of accident and character, of speech and deed, it distracts us so that we can neither believe nor feel. In *The Scarlet Letter* Hawthorne has at last found individuals who can hold all of his thought, and so naturally that even he forgets what his thought is. His thought can be of them, not what they signify.

This in part is because their predicament can state itself. It is simple, it is immemorial. . . . Never before has Hawthorne dealt with stuff so solid; and never again will he be so able or content to let his people determine his plot. His plot in this case is his people.

Above all it is Hester Prynne, whose passion and beauty dominate every other person, and color each event. Hawthorne has conceived her as he has conceived his scene, in the full strength of his feeling for ancient New England. He is the Homer of that New England, as Hester is its most heroic creature. Tall, with dark and abundant hair and deep black eyes, a rich complexion that makes modern woman (says Hawthorne) pale and thin by comparison, and a dignity that throws into low relief the "delicate, evanescent, and indescribable grace" by which gentility in girls has since come to be known, from the very first—and we believe it—she is said to cast a spell over those who behold her; and this is not merely because of the scarlet letter, "so fantastically embroidered and illuminated," upon the bosom of her always magnificent dress. It is because of herself, into whom Hawthorne has known how to put a unique importance. Nor is this a remote, a merely stately importance. We are close to her all of the time, and completely convinced of her flesh and blood, of her heart and mind. She is a passionate woman whom Hawthorne does not need to call passionate, for he has the evidence: her state of excitement, bordering on frenzy, in the prison after her first exposure to the crowd—her "moral agony," reflected in the convulsions that have seized the child; her pride, her daring, in after days when she makes more show than she needs to make of the letter on her bosom, the symbol she insists upon adorning with such "wild and picturesque peculiarity"; her alternations of despair and defiance; her continuing love, so unconfessed that we can only assume it to be there, for the man whose weakness seems so little to deserve it; her power of speech, so economical and so tender, when at last she is with this man; her sudden revelation that through years of loneliness she has not consented to let her soul be killed.

"I pity thee," says Chillingworth near the close, "for the good that has

been wasted in thy nature." These are terrible words, for they express a
fear we have had, the fear that this magnificent woman has lived for
nothing; for a few days of love, and then for dreary years of less indeed
than nothing. Hawthorne has known how to fasten this fear upon us
—it could exist in us only if we loved her too—but he also has known
how to make Chillingworth's words untrue. The life of Hester increases,
not diminishes, in the bleak world whose best citizen she is. Nor is this
done by Hawthorne at the expense of that world. He deplores the "dismal severity" of its moral code, and for all we know he is presenting
Hester as the blackest sacrifice it ever offered on its altar. But he is not
doctrinaire against the code. His Puritan world is in its own way beautiful.
It fully exists, as Hester fully exists. If their existences conflict, then that is
the tragedy to be understood. Hester, whose solitary thought takes her
far beyond the confines of the code, is nevertheless respectful of the
strength in it that could kill her were she not even stronger. She is not
the subject of a sermon; she is the heroine of a tragedy, and she understands the tragedy. She understands it because Hawthorne does; because
at the same time that he recoils from the Puritan view of sin he honors
its capacity to be a view at all. Sin for him, for Hester, and for the people
who punish her is equally a solemn fact, a problem for which there is no
solution in life. There was no other solution for his story, given Hester's
strength, Dimmesdale's weakness, and Chillingworth's perversion, than
the one he found. Rather, as we read, it finds itself. And if the conclusion is not depressing, the reason is that nothing before it has been meaningless. This world has not been really bleak. It has been as beautiful as
it was terrible; Hester's life has not been hollow, nor has her great nature
been wasted.

The weakness of Dimmesdale is personal to him and a part of the story,
whose power it magnifies rather than lessens. He is "tremulous," and he
holds his hand over his heart—these are two facts about him of which
Hawthorne keeps us constantly informed. So constantly, indeed, that
we might grow tired of the information were it not so relevant to the
agony within. His penances, which extend even to scourging himself
until he laughs bitterly at the blood that flows, still do not give him
peace. The blood comes, but not his soul, for there is no penitence. He
tortures but cannot purify himself. And there is no man for whom purity
is more important, no man who more loves the truth and loathes the lie.
Yet he maintains the lie, and so diminshes his very existence. "It is the
unspeakable misery of a life so false as his," says Hawthorne at one
point, "that it steals the pith and substance out of whatever realities
there are around us, and which were meant by Heaven to be the spirit's
joy and nutriment. To the untrue man the whole universe is false—it
is impalpable—it shrinks to nothing within his grasp. And he himself, in
so far as he shows himself in a false light, becomes a shadow, or, indeed,
ceases to exist. The only truth that continued to give Mr. Dimmesdale a

real existence on this earth was the anguish in his inmost soul, and the undissembled expression of it in his aspect. Had he once found power to smile, and wear a face of gayety, there would have been no such man!"

He is redeemed for us only because his suffering makes him beautiful and because Hester continues to love him. He would be fantastic, he would be one of Hawthorne's figments, had she not loved him in the first place. We believe this because we believe everything about her, and understand how much distinction she gives the objects of her love. The explanation for her superior strength, which never shows itself more clearly than when "with sudden and desperate tenderness" she throws her arms around him in the forest, is not merely that she has had the comparative luck to live in public shame. We are convinced that she would have been strong in any case, with the wisdom not to pervert either herself or him. As always with Hawthorne's women, she has more courage than the man with whom her lot is joined. This was true of Dorcas Bourne, of Faith Brown, of Dorothy Pearson, of Martha Pierson, of Beatrice Rappaccini; it was even true, in *Fanshawe*, of Mrs. Melmoth and Ellen Langton; it will be true of Phoebe, Zenobia, and Miriam. Somewhere, if not in the New England of his time, Hawthorne unearthed the image of a goddess supreme in beauty and power; and this included, whether he planned it or not, erotic power. "Those words 'genteel' and 'lady-like,'" he said, "are terrible ones, and do us infinite mischief, but it is because (at least, I hope so) we are in a transition state, and shall emerge into a higher mode of simplicity than has ever been known to past ages." One of the reasons he set so many of his tales in the past must have been that there, and there only, he could find the women he wanted for his art. As early as 1829, in his sketch "The Canal Boat," he had written:

> Here was the pure, modest, sensitive, and shrinking woman of America— shrinking when no evil is intended, and sensitive like diseased flesh, that thrills if you but point at it; and strangely modest, without confidence in the modesty of other people; and admirably pure, with such a quick apprehension of all impurity.

And as late as 1863, in *Our Old Home*, he was to assess his "dear country-women" as having "a certain meagreness, . . . a deficiency of physical development, a scantiness, so to speak, in the pattern of their material make, a paleness of complexion, a thinness of voice." Sir Peter Lely's Nell Gwyn, he decided, was "one of the few beautiful women" he had seen on canvas. Nor was the woman of his imagination's choice deficient in the mysterious powers belonging to her sex. D. H. Lawrence found these powers terrible in Hester, and supposed them so destructive of Dimmesdale that he died hating her. Hawthorne, a profounder psychologist, did not so protest against the might he recognized. He recorded it as true, and let it work. It seldom worked for him with such intensity as here, but it is present in all of his interesting tales—more mild, more submerged, in "The Wives of the Dead" and "The Great Carbuncle," but certainly present. It is why he can suggest in so few words that love exists between two persons, and can interest us so deeply in this fact; it is why, for instance, *The Scarlet Letter* is one of the great love stories of the world although it gives us no details of love. Hawthorne went to the center of woman's secret, her sexual power, and stayed there. For him it was not intellectual power. The women he considered, from Mrs. Hutchinson on, he never could praise if their minds had got the better of them. Hester threatens to become a feminist in the injustice of her solitude, but he saves her from that fate. "We may be sure," says Henry James, "that in women his taste was conservative." It was more than that. It was classic.

Yet Dimmesdale, for all he lives exclusively in Hester's love, is a remarkable person in his own right. His haunted, emaciated, all but sanctified figure will never be forgotten by anyone who has seen it reeling through this ancient world which Hawthorne has known how to keep so dark and clear; so little, and yet so alive. Hawthorne liked nothing better than to discover a man with a hidden mind; especially, a mind that hid monsters. Dimmesdale, walking home from his one interview with Hester, becomes for that short while a comic figure, bursting with thoughts of impossible, irreverent revelations which remind us of those more somber ones that afflicted Goodman Brown. He can barely resist his ghastly desire to shout them out; he does resist, however, and becomes once more the tremulous man whom Chillingworth had tortured.

He is more a person than Chillingworth is because he is more simply and directly seen. Chillingworth is necessary to the tale, and convincing enough; but he cannot shake off certain articles of dress and look which for Hawthorne were literary conventions. He is that unreal thing, a villain; he is Archimago still, stooping as he walks. "A writhing horror twisted itself across his features, like a snake gliding swiftly over them, and making one little pause, with all its wreathed intervolutions in open sight. His face darkened with some powerful emotion, which, nevertheless, he so instantaneously controlled by an effort of his will, that, save at a single moment, its expression might have passed for calmness. After a brief space, the convulsion grew almost imperceptible, and finally subsided into the depths of his nature." This was when he stood by the scaffold and recognized Hester Prynne. He had come there out of melodrama, and in melodrama he remains. If Hawthorne makes him acceptable nevertheless, the reason is the vitality of the whole world here envisioned; like Homer's world, it is sure enough on its foundation not to be weakened by appearances of the supernatural—in Hawthorne's case, of the diabolical. Chillingworth is the devil again. Yet at one point he is better than that. He is one man playing with another, hideously, in a fashion that since has become a science. Hawthorne could not have fore-

seen the science—which, being a science, is doubtless no longer hideous.
But he described its process perfectly. The minister's physician

> deemed it essential, it would seem, to know the man, before attempting to
> do him good. Wherever there is a heart and an intellect, the diseases of the
> physical frame are tinged with the peculiarities of these. In Arthur Dimmes-
> dale, thought and imagination were so active, and sensibility so intense, that
> the bodily infirmity would be likely to have its groundwork there. So Roger
> Chillingworth—the man of skill, the kind and friendly physician—strove
> to go deep into his patient's bosom, delving among his principles, prying
> into his recollections, and probing everything with a cautious torch, like a
> treasure seeker in a dark cavern. Few secrets can escape an investigator who
> has the opportunity and license to undertake such a quest, and skill to fol-
> low it up. A man burdened with a secret should especially avoid the in-
> timacy of his physician. If the latter possess native sagacity, and a nameless
> something more—let us call it intuition; if he show no intrusive egotism,
> nor disagreeably prominent characteristics of his own; if he have the power,
> which must be born with him, to bring his mind into such affinity with his
> patient's, that this last shall unawares have spoken what he imagines him-
> self only to have thought; if such revelations be received without tumult,
> and acknowledged not so often by an uttered sympathy as by silence, an
> inarticulate breath, and here and there a word, to indicate that all is un-
> derstood; if to these qualifications of a confidant be joined the advantages
> afforded by his recognized character as a physician—then, at some inevitable
> moment, will the soul of the sufferer be dissolved, and flow forth in a dark
> but transparent stream, bringing all its mysteries into the daylight.

The precision of this passage is a sign that Hawthorne knew everything
about the burden imposed by secrecy upon the soul. Nobody misses this
knowledge in him, early or late; nor misses his further knowledge that
confession is the only cure. The same precision, however, warns us that
man cannot be man's confessor, whether or not his motives are benign.
Dimmesdale's confession is finally to Hester, but even that is not enough;
it still must be to heaven, as—doubtfully and darkly—at the end it is.
No such doubt darkens the figure of Dr. Johnson at Uttoxeter, or of
Hilda in St. Peter's.

Pearl has for every reader some unreality too, though again the force
of the whole tale is natural enough to contain her. She also has something
of the supernatural about her; she may even be the devil's child. Something sinister in her, something unpredictable, equals her charm. She
is sunshine in her mother's life, and yet her pouts and scowls, her frenzies
and her furies, are not the least of Hester's desperations. Her behavior in
the forest, when she insists that Hester don again the letter she has cast
off, has more meaning than it has at other times. When it is meaningless,
as it sometimes is, Hawthorne may be supposed not to have absorbed well

enough the notes he made about Una when she was a child of five in
Salem.

Hawthorne, watching her then, had been struck by her eccentricity—
"a wild grimace, an unnatural tone." She seemed "an unripe apple, that
may be prefected to a mellow deliciousness hereafter," but that now was
all "acerbity" and discord.

> It seems to me that, like many sensitive people, her sensibility is more read-
> ily awakened by fiction than realities. . . . She is never graceful or beau-
> tiful, except when perfectly quiet. Violence—exhibitions of passion—strong
> expressions of any kind—destroy her beauty. . . . She plays, sits down on
> the floor, and complains grievously of warmth. This is the physical mani-
> festation of the evil spirit that struggles for the mastery of her; he is not a
> spirit at all, but an earthly monster, who lays his grasp on her spinal mar-
> row, her brain, and other parts of her body that lie in closest contiguity to
> her soul; so that the soul has the discredit of these evil deeds. . . . There is
> something that almost frightens me about the child—I know not whether
> elfish or angelic, but, at all events, supernatural. She steps so boldly into
> the midst of everything, shrinks from nothing, has such a comprehension of
> everything, seems at times to have but little delicacy, and anon shows that
> she possesses the finest essence of it; now so hard, now so tender; now so
> perfectly unreasonable, soon again so wise. In short, I now and then catch
> an aspect of her in which I cannot believe her to be my own human child,
> but a spirit strangely mingled with good and evil, haunting the house where
> I dwell.

These notes are somehow more convincing than their result in *The
Scarlet Letter*. Hawthorne in them is puzzled, not only by what he sees
but by the nature of his response—he is not sure he believes any of this,
but he says it anyway, and doubtless hopes to forget it. For Pearl, since
she exists in public, he has to be more responsible, yet his art does not
show him how. Not wholly, that is. Pearl too has her fascinations, and
some of them may stem from his very failure to forget the actuality of
Una. At any rate, just as Chillingworth is more interesting than Hawthorne's other villains because we know why he behaves as he does—he
is no mere monster of art like Aylmer, Rappaccini, and Ethan Brand—
Pearl is Hawthorne's most interesting accident of nature because she is
indeed so accidental; and because the fact of her being at all is so painful, so mixed a joy to the more important person, Hester Prynne, by
whom she lives.

Something of the same sort can be said of the crowd in this book—
the crowd, that "species of solitude" to which Hawthorne was so addicted.
The crowd here is the whole of society, which when it appears, as Con-
stance Rourke has said, "appears mainly as a mob under strong emotion."
Hawthorne has created other crowds, and in *The Marble Faun* he will
set all Rome in carnival movement. He was bound to do so, lest his nar-

ratives ignore the hum of human life. Here, however, it becomes a roar. No crowd in Hawthorne is like this one, either at the beginning, around Hester's scaffold, or at the conclusion, on Election Day. Again the reason lies in the fierceness of its relevance to his individuals. Hester and Arthur Dimmesdale have all of life for their audience. They want no audience, yet they need one too. They have it, ironically, in this mob whose repulsive is equal to its attractive power.

But *The Scarlet Letter* contains still other persons, and they are chief among the number even though they have no names. The protagonists of the tale are abstractions, and this time they are neither cold nor empty. Sin, Guilt, Isolation, Pride were not the husks of Hawthorne's thought, they were its deep, warm center, and here for once they operate as personalities, no less divine in their power because they are hidden from sight. The eight satires he had written at the Old Manse, the comprehensive allegories in which he surveyed the contemporary world and found it wanting, had not succeeded even with him. The contemporary world was worth that much of his attention, but he had scattered his fire; had even withheld it, out of a doubt that he knew where he stood. For he was of that world, and much of it he liked. He merely knew that it was wrong when it said with Emerson that self-reliance is a sufficient virtue comprehending all other virtues. "The world has done its best to secure repose without relinquishing evil." The man who could write this could see how little repose was in store for the complacent. He was certain that evil cannot be relinquished—that is, forgotten or wished away. It is the common human heritage, it is the one thing that makes all men, as men, alike. "In Adam's fall we sinnèd all." And if evil in its extreme forms makes men inhuman by isolating them from their brothers, so does arrogance of spirit. The Transcendental brethren worshipped solitude, which Hawthorne could see only as isolation. His hell, like Dante's, was cold and solitary, a wilderness where nothing blossomed but the will. A warmer world would be one in which men recognized together the ineradicable weakness and corruption of their nature. To him the Puritan world was warmer than his own.

Yet there was much about it that he disliked. It was dismal, it was confined; he would not have had it back. *The Scarlet Letter* in no sense recommends it as a system of thought or a way of life. Hawthorne did not need to believe in Puritanism in order to write a great novel about it. He had only to understand it, which for a man of his time was harder. If it was not impossible for him, the reason is less his experience than his genius, and the fact that something of supreme importance had survived in his lonely thought. He was so alone, so aloof, because he found so few around him whose seriousness equaled his; and by seriousness he meant the real thing, a thing consistent with irony and love, a thing indeed for which comedy might be as suitable an expression as tragedy. If one were serious, one never forgot the eternal importance of every soul, and

never doubted that the consequences of deeds, even of impulses, last forever. The Puritans had known this all too well, and their resulting behavior was at times abominable. *The Scarlet Letter* is saying so at the
same time that it is revealing a world where tragedy and comedy are possible.

The conflict in Hawthorne of two worlds between which he hung, exposing the fanaticism of one, despising the blandness of the other, is not
the least source of *The Scarlet Letter*'s power. The book was and is a
reminder to modern man, who still talks about his conscience, of where
that conscience came from. For Hawthorne it came from a dark world
where human injustice was done, but only because men fumbled in
their understanding of justice. Justice itself was a form of fate; or, for
Hawthorne, so it must seem to any mortal and therefore limited intelligence. To any man "the rickety machine and crazy action of the universe"
must appear all but incomprehensible, as at times it did to Hester Prynne.
She might have felt as Hawthorne did when at Florence he looked into
the faces of Michelangelo's Fates; and came another day to look again.
He remembered having seen an etching of them when he was a child,
"and being struck, even then, with the terrible, stern, passionless severity,
neither loving us nor hating us, that characterizes these ugly old women."
It was like looking at the Sphinx, but he could look; and come to look
again. For such an imagination the drama of guilt did not lose its drama
by being terrible. As an artist he was committed to drama; which was
why he could see so clearly the differences between men. He saw these
differences in terms of the evil they did or did not recognize—did recognize, and so were warm in peace; did not, and so were merciless to those
for whom concealment was impossible, or else were corrupted by the sup-
pression involved in evil's "turning its poison back among the inner vitali-
ties" of their souls. For such an imagination also there was no social gospel, of Brook Farm or of any other place, that could serve as a substitute
for the simple act of recognizing that every soul, beginning with one's
own, is sadly imperfect. Hester does good deeds, but in themselves they
are not enough; they do not give her mind the rest it desires. In "The
Custom House" Hawthorne even wonders whether the compulsion to do
them had not made her at times "an intruder and a nuisance."

Out of such ideas as these, possessed for once by Hawthorne in the
available form of a perfect balance, the force of *The Scarlet Letter* surely
derives. He was an artist, and so he knew how to use the ideas; but it
would be wrong to deny that he had them, as Henry James substantially
does when he discovers in Hawthorne "no general views in the least
uncomfortable." Hawthorne's "general views" were so serious, so profound, that they left him free to write a tragedy. Duplicity is not de-
nounced in Dimmesdale; it is comprehended, and so made terrible. If
the views of Hawthorne did not extend to the understanding that the
isolation of modern man—so much more awful than the solitude of the

Puritan who at least was alone with God—is an isolation for which no
cure exists, we have perhaps the reason for his failure to equal *The
Scarlet Letter* in any subsequent effort. It was written, we may admit,
with more feeling than thought—though with the deepest and most
delicate feeling. We need not suppose, however, that it was done with
tricks.

The structure of the tale is justly celebrated, and its economy, and its
lighting—"densely dark," says James, "with a single spot of vivid color
in it." That spot is not the letter A alone; it is the meaning this letter
keeps, and the power it has to illuminate the soul of Hester Prynne. We
see her with it at the start, stationary on the scaffold, and we see her
beneath it at the close, stationary in her grave. The story moves rapidly,
as fate moves, but through a series of tableaux in which everything seems
to stand still. The scaffold is the scene to which Hawthorne always returns; it is the place where Dimmesdale, his breast torn open to expose
the letter he also wears, a scarlet stigma branded in his very flesh, dies
in Hester's arms. But midway of the tale, in the chapter called The
Minister's Vigil, the scaffold has performed its supreme function. In the
obscure night which swallows up the shrieks of Dimmesdale so that even
if they were intended as confession they have failed, in the impenetrable
darkness which fits his state so well, the minister has to stand, one after
another, with the principals of the drama: with Hester and Pearl, and
finally with Roger Chillingworth. For all its lack of light it is more brilliant than any other chapter, though each of them rivals it in a different
way. The ironies latent in certain early scenes where Hester and Dimmesdale, face to face in public, can only look into each other's eyes and communicate in words which no third person understands—these ironies, so
pure and so immense, are dissolved in the forest scene where at last they
are alone together, alone with only Pearl.

The four chapters devoted to this interview are more than brilliant;
they are overwhelming, and they are the heart of the book. They are
overwhelming because the speeches that adorn them can be so brief. "Art
thou in life?" "Dost thou yet live?" "Hester, hast thou found peace?"
"Hast thou?" "That old man!—the physician!—he whom they call Roger
Chillingworth!—he was my husband!" "I might have known it. I did
know it! . . . Why did I not understand? O Hester Prynne, thou little,
little knowest all the horror of this thing! . . . I cannot forgive thee!"
"Thou shalt forgive me! Let God punish! Thou shalt forgive!" . . . "I
do forgive you, Hester. I freely forgive you now. May God forgive us
both! We are not, Hester, the worst sinners in the world. There is one
worse than even the polluted priest! That old man's revenge has been
blacker than my sin. He has violated, in cold blood, the sanctity of a
human heart. Thou and I, Hester, never did so!" "Never, never! What we
did had a consecration of its own. We felt it so! We said so to each other!
Hast thou forgotten it?" "Hush, Hester! No; I have not forgotten!" This

is still the high mark in American fiction—this, and many another moment before or after. For *The Scarlet Letter*, like any masterpiece, is powerful everywhere and all the time. If its scene is bleak, itself is blended of the richest, most moving, most splendid things, put densely and inseparably together.

Yet Hawthorne doubted that it could stand alone, and so recalled the author of the sketches to write for him the introductory section which he called "The Custom House." It is the best of his works in the comic kind. It is witty, it is serene, it is detached—absolutely detached, thought Mrs. Fields, who noted almost with a shudder how he "described the ancient adherents of the custom-house service and the signs of decay in Salem with the terrible keenness and truth of one who had dropped there from another planet." It is detached even from himself, whom he discusses with the mock intimacy he can make so charming. He even suggests that *The Scarlet Letter* had been no trouble to write; "a small roll of dingy paper," discovered upstairs in the Custom House, had provided "a reasonably complete explanation of the whole affair." He was never to admit how much his masterpiece had cost him, or to subject himself to such cost again. For one thing, he was through forever with the Salem that had caused it if any outward circumstance can be supposed to have done so. "Henceforth," says Hawthorne of his town, "it ceases to be a reality of my life. I am a citizen of somewhere else."

The House of the Seven Gables

by F. O. Matthiessen

. . . It is small wonder that turning away from what he considered the unrelieved gloom of *The Scarlet Letter,* Hawthorne thought *The Seven Gables* "more characteristic of my mind, and more proper and natural for me to write." The measure in which he intended the latter book as a criticism of his own age is somewhat obscured by his treatment of time. Even while he was examining his changing New England, he felt the past weighing heavily on the present's back. Unlike virtually all the other spokesmen for his day, he could never feel that America was a new world. Looking back over the whole history of his province, he was more struck by decay than by potentiality, by the broken ends to which the Puritan effort had finally come, by the rigidity that had been integral to its thought at its best, by modes of life in which nothing beautiful had developed. Furthermore, his contemporaries seemed still to be branded with lasting marks from the weight and strain of such effort. He was often reflecting on the loss in vitality, on such facts as that the "broad shoulders and well-developed busts" of the women of Hester Prynne's day had long since tended, along with their "boldness and rotundity of speech," to wither away like trees transplanted in too thin a soil. Even at Brook Farm, he had not been able to share in the declaration that the new age was the dawn of untried possibilities. Even there he had thought about how much old material enters into the freshest novelty, about the ages of experience that had passed over the world, about the fact that the very ground under their feet was "fathom-deep with the dust of deluded generations, on every one of which, as on ourselves, the world had imposed itself as a hitherto unwedded bride."

Consequently, as he meditated on time in this story of the old house with its "mysterious and terrible past," the present often seemed "this visionary and impalpable Now, which, if you once look closely at it, is nothing." He was not, however, in any doubt as to the focus of his plot;

"The House of the Seven Gables." From *American Renaissance: Art and Expression in the Age of Emerson and Whitman* by F. O. Matthiessen. Copyright 1941 by Oxford University Press, Inc. Reprinted by permission of Oxford University Press. The pages reprinted here are a part of the chapter entitled "Hawthorne's Politics, with the Economic Structure of *The Seven Gables.*" Footnotes have been omitted.

in fact, he held that the only basis for calling this book a romance rather than a novel was its attempt "to connect a bygone time with the very present that is flitting away from us. It is a legend prolonging itself . . . down into our own broad daylight." His treatment of this legend constituted his nearest approach to everyday contemporary life, since he did not cast it in the special circumstances of a Utopian community or of an art colony, but chose materials more naturally at hand. His attitude towards them was in no sense different from that in his other books. He was always concerned with the enduring elements in human nature, but the structure he devised here enabled him to disclose better than elsewhere how "the Colonel Pyncheon of two centuries ago steps forward as the Judge of the passing moment." As a result Lowell wrote at once to tell him that this book was "the most valuable contribution to New England history that has been made," since it typified the intimate connections between heredity and descent, which more mechanical historians had failed to establish. On the other hand, James, sending a letter half a century later to the celebration at Salem of its novelist's centenary, was impressed most by the "presentness," by Hawthorne's instinctive gift in finding his romance, "the quaintness or the weirdness, the interest *behind* the interest of things, as continuous with the very life we are leading . . . round about him and under his eyes." He saw it in *The Seven Gables* "as something deeply within us, not as something infinitely disconnected from us," and could consequently make this book a "singularly fruitful" example "of the real as distinguished from the artificial romantic note." Therefore, it will serve better than any of his others to answer the first of our two main questions about his equipment for writing tragedy: to what degree could he conceive of individuals who were representative of a whole interrelated condition of society?

The seventeenth century house, grown black in the prevailing east wind, itself took on the status of a major theme. Hawthorne wrote to Fields that "many passages of this book ought to be finished with the minuteness of a Dutch picture, in order to give them their proper effect"; and that aim can be read in his careful drawing of the thick central chimney, the gigantic elm at the door, the long-since exhausted garden, the monotony of occurrences in the by-street in which the mansion now fronts, the faint stir of the outside world as heard in the church bells or the far whistle of a train. As he dwelt on this example of "the best and stateliest architecture" in a town whose houses, unaccountably to our eyes, generally struck him as having little pretense to varied beauty, he could feel that it had been "the scene of events more full of human interest, perhaps, than those of a gray feudal castle." This is worth noting since he seems to have forgotten it by the time he was writing the preface to *The Marble Faun*, where, developing the thought that romance needs ruin to make it grow, he took the conventional attitude about the thinness of material for the artist in America. Since this, in turn, gave the lead to James' famous enumeration of all "the items of high civilization," all the complexity of customs and manners that were left out of Hawthorne's scene, it is important that the Hawthorne of *The Seven Gables* believed that no matter how familiar and humble its incidents, "they had the earth-smell in them." He believed far more than that, for within the oak frame of the house, "so much of mankind's varied experience had passed . . . so much had been suffered, and something, too, enjoyed, that . . . it was itself like a great human heart, with a life of its own, and full of rich and sombre reminiscences."

These furnished him with several other themes that were central to American history. The old spinster Hepzibah Pyncheon, at the opening of the book the sole possessor of the dark recesses of the mansion, is the embodiment of decayed gentility, sustained only by her delusion of family importance, lacking any revivifying touch with outward existence. Hawthorne knew how fully her predicament corresponded to the movement of the age, since "in this republican country, amid the fluctuating waves of our social life, somebody is always at the drowning-point." He made the young reformer Holgrave confront her with the unreality of her existence by declaring that the names of gentleman and lady, though they had once had a meaning and had conferred a value on their owners, "in the present—and still more in the future condition of society—they imply, not privilege, but restriction!" Indeed, by imprisoning herself so long in one place and in the unvarying round of a single chain of ideas, Hepzibah had grown to be a kind of lunatic, pathetic in her efforts to merge with human sympathies, since no longer capable of doing so. Hawthorne posed her genteel helplessness against the demurely charming self-reliance of her niece Phoebe. By pointing out that it was owing to her father's having married beneath his rank that Phoebe possessed such plebeian capabilities as being able to manage a kitchen or conduct a school, Hawthorne deliberately etched a contrast between the Pyncheon family and the rising democracy. This contrast is sustained even down to the inbred hens in the garden, who have a "rusty, withered aspect, and a gouty kind of movement," in consequence of too strict a watchfulness to maintain their purity of race. This accords again with Holgrave's statement to Phoebe that "once in every half-century, at longest, a family should be merged into the great, obscure mass of humanity, and forget all about its ancestors. Human blood, in order to keep its freshness, should run in hidden streams."

But there is more substance to Hawthorne's contrast than the tenuous if accurate notation of the gradual waning of the aristocracy, as against the solidly based energy of common life. He had observed in one of his early sketches of Salem that the influence of wealth and the sway of class "had held firmer dominion here than in any other New England town"; and he now traced those abuses to their source. The original power of the Pyncheons had been founded on a great wrong: the very land on which the house was built had first been occupied by the thatched hut of Matthew Maule, who had settled there because of the spring of fresh water, "a rare treasure on the sea-girt peninsula." But as the town expanded during its first generation, this treasure took on the aspect of a desired asset in real estate to the eyes of Colonel Pyncheon. A man of iron energy of purpose in obtaining whatever he had set his mind upon, he asserted a plausible claim to Maule's lot and a large adjacent tract of land, on the strength of a prior grant.

Hawthorne's treatment of this material is characteristic of his effort to suggest social complexity. He stated that since no written record of the dispute remained in existence, he could merely enter the doubt as to whether the Colonel's claim had not been unduly stretched. What strengthened that suspicion was the fact that notwithstanding the inequality of the two antagonists, in a period when well-to-do personal influence had great hereditary weight, the dispute remained unsettled for years and came to a close only with the death of Maule, who had clung stubbornly to what he considered his right. Moreover, the manner of his death affected the mind differently than it had at the time, since he was executed as one of the obscure "martyrs to that terrible delusion, which should teach us, among its other morals, that the influential classes, and those who take upon themselves to be leaders of the people, are fully liable to all the passionate error that has ever characterized the maddest mob." In the general frenzy it was hardly noted that Colonel Pyncheon had applied his whole bitter force to the persecution of Maule, though by stressing this origin of the condemned man's curse upon his enemy— "God will give him blood to drink"—Hawthorne recognized how economic motives could enter even into the charge of witchcraft.

By the time the justification for that curse began to be whispered around, the mansion was built, and "there is something so massive, stable, and almost irresistibly imposing in the exterior presentment of established rank and great possessions, that their very existence seems to give them a right to exist; at least, so excellent a counterfeit of right, that few poor and humble men have moral force enough to question it." The Maules, at any rate, kept their resentment to themselves; and as the generations went on, they were usually poverty-stricken, always plebeian. They worked with "unsuccessful diligence" at handicrafts, labored on the wharves, or went to sea before the mast. They lived here and there about the town in tenements, and went to the almshouse "as the natural home of their old age." Finally they had taken "the downright plunge" that awaits all families; and for the past thirty years no one of their name had appeared in the local directory.

The main theme that Hawthorne evolved from this history of the Pyncheons and the Maules was not the original curse on the house, but the curse that the Pyncheons have continued to bring upon themselves. Clifford may phrase it wildly in his sense of release at the Judge's death:

> What we call real estate—the solid ground to build a house on—is the broad foundation on which nearly all the guilt of this world rests. A man will commit almost any wrong,—he will heap up an immense pile of wickedness, as hard as granite, and which will weigh as heavily upon his soul, to eternal ages,—only to build a great gloomy, dark-chambered mansion, for himself to die in, and for his posterity to be miserable in.

But this also corresponds to Hawthorne's view in his preface, a view from which the dominating forces of his country had just begun to diverge most widely with the opening of California: "the folly of tumbling down an avalanche of ill-gotten gold, or real estate, on the heads of an unfortunate posterity, thereby to maim and crush them, until the accumulated mass shall be scattered abroad in its original atoms." Hawthorne's objections to the incumbrance of property often ran close to Thoreau's.

What Hawthorne set himself to analyze is this "energy of disease," this lust for wealth that has held the dominating Pyncheons in its inflexible grasp. After their original victory, their drive for power had long since shifted its ground, but had retained its form of oppressing the poor, for the present Judge steps forward to seize the property of his feeble cousins Hepzibah and Clifford, with the same cold unscrupulousness that had actuated the original Colonel in his dealings with the Maules. The only variation is that, "as is customary with the rich, when they aim at the honors of a republic," he had learned the expediency, which had not been forced upon his freer ancestor, of masking his relentless will beneath a veneer of "paternal benevolence." Thus what Hawthorne saw handed down from one generation to another were not—and this paradoxical phrase was marked by Melville—"the big, heavy, solid unrealities" such as gold and hereditary position, but inescapable traits of character.

He did not, however, make the mistake of simplifying, by casting all his Pyncheons into one monotonous image. If the Judge typified the dominant strain in the family, Clifford, the most complex character in the book, could stand for the recessive. His gently sensuous, almost feminine face had received years ago its perfect recording in a Malbone miniature, since as a young man he had loved just such delicate charm. Hawthorne suggested the helplessness of his aesthetic temperament before the ruthless energy of the Judge, by saying that any conflict between them would be "like flinging a porcelain vase, with already a crack in it, against a granite column." By using that symbolic, almost Jamesian image, he gave further embodiment to the kind of contrast he had drawn between Owen Warland and his hostile environment. His implications also extended beyond the Pyncheon family, for the hard competitive drives that had crushed many potentialities of richer, less aggressive living, had been a distorting factor throughout the length of American experience.

But Hawthorne made no effort to idealize Clifford. Holgrave calls him an "abortive lover of the beautiful," and it is true that the fragile mainspring of his life has been shattered by his long imprisonment for the supposed murder of his uncle. This punishment had been especially cruel since the old man had actually died of an apoplectic seizure, the traditional Pyncheon disease, but under such suspicious circumstances that his other nephew Jaffrey, who coveted the whole inheritance, could cause it to appear an act of violence. As a result he had gained the fortune on which he was to build the career that led to the eminent respectability of a judgeship; and Hepzibah was left with only the life occupancy of the house. And to the house she clung tenaciously, though its proper maintenance was far beyond her impoverished means, in the hope that is finally realized, of welcoming home her brother after his belated release. But the man who returns no longer possesses any intellectual or moral fibre to control his sensibility. His tastes express themselves only in a selfish demand for luxuries and in an animal delight in food, an exaggeration of the defects that Hawthorne always felt to lie as a danger for the artistic temperament, whose too exclusive fondness for beauty might end by wearing away all human affections. Clifford has retrogressed until he is hardly more than an idiot, a spoiled child who takes a childish pleasure in any passing attraction that can divert him from the confused memories of his terrible years of gloom. But, occasionally, deeper forces stir within him, as one day when he is watching, from the arched window at the head of the stairs, a political procession of marching men with fifes and drums. With a sudden, irrepressible gesture, from which he is restrained just in time by Hepzibah and Phoebe, he starts forward as though to jump down into the street, in a kind of desperate effort at renewed contact with life outside himself, "but whether impelled by the species of terror that sometimes urges its victim over the very precipice which he shrinks from, or by a natural magnetism, tending towards the great centre of humanity," Hawthorne found it not easy to decide.

Melville considered this one of the two most impressive scenes in the book; and the currents that are stirring here rise to their climax in the chapter in which Hawthorne's imagination moves most freely, "The Flight of Two Owls," the poignant account of how Hepzibah is swept away by her brother's strange exhilaration at finding the Judge, who had come to threaten him, dead of a seizure. Clifford is now determined to leave the whole past behind, and impels Hepzibah to start off at once with him crazily in the rain. With no definite goal, his attention is suddenly attracted by a feature of the Salem scene unknown at the time of his imprisonment, a train at the depot. Before Hepzibah can protest, they are aboard and are started on a local towards Portsmouth. The fact that Hawthorne had made a record in his notebook, just the year before, of this very trip, seems to have helped him to catch the rhythm of kaleido-scopic impressions into which the two old people are caught up. With a giddy sense that he has finally merged with life, Clifford's excitement mounts in ever more reckless talk with a man across the aisle, in which Hawthorne ironically makes him develop the transcendental doctrine that evil is bound to disappear in the ascending spiral of human improve-ment. But just as the hard-eyed stranger's suspicions of his insanity are crystallizing into certitude, Clifford is seized by the impulse that he has now gone far enough. Taking advantage of the fact that the train has stopped for a moment, he again draws the bewildered Hepzibah after him and both get off. Another moment and they are alone on the open plat-form of a deserted way-station, under a sullen rain-swept sky. Clifford's unreal courage deserts him all at once, and he is once more helplessly dependent on his sister to get him home. The impression that Haw-thorne has thus created of their solitude, of their decrepit inexperience in an uncomprehending and hostile world, may well have been part of the stimulus for the most effectively intense chapter in *Pierre,* where the adolescent couple arrive in New York at night, for the luridly brutal first impact of corruption upon innocence.

Still another theme is introduced through the role that is played by Holgrave. At the start of the book Hepzibah has taken him as her sole lodger, though she has become increasingly startled by his strange com-panions, "men with long beards, and dressed in linen blouses, and other such new-fangled and ill-fitting garments; reformers, temperance lec-turers, and all manner of cross-looking philanthropists; community-men, and come-outers, as Hepzibah believed, who acknowledged no law, and ate no solid food." Moreover, she has read a paragraph in a paper accus-ing him of delivering a speech "full of wild and disorganizing matter." But though this has made her have misgivings whether she ought not send him away, she has to admit from her own contact with him that even by her formal standards he is a quiet and orderly young man. His first effect on Phoebe, after she has come to visit her aunt and really to take over the burden of running the house, is more disquieting, for his conversation seemed "to unsettle everything around her, by his lack of reverence for what was fixed."

In unrolling Holgrave's past history, which is made up in part from the histories of various characters whom Hawthorne had picked up in his country rambles, the novelist made clear that he believed he was tapping one of the richest sources of native material. He said at more explicit length than was customary to him:

A romance on the plan of Gil Blas, adapted to American society and man-ners, would cease to be a romance. The experience of many individuals among us, who think it hardly worth the telling, would equal the vicissitudes

of the Spaniard's earlier life; while their ultimate success, or the point
whither they tend, may be incomparably higher than any that a novelist
would imagine for his hero.

Holgrave himself told Phoebe somewhat proudly that he

. . . could not boast of his origin, unless as being exceedingly humble, nor
of his education, except that it had been the scantiest possible, and obtained
by a few winter-months' attendance at a district school. Left early to his own
guidance, he had begun to be self-dependent while yet a boy; and it was a
condition aptly suited to his natural force of will. Though now but twenty-
two years old (lacking some months, which are years in such a life), he had
already been, first, a country schoolmaster; next, a salesman in a country
store; and either at the same time or afterwards, the political editor of a
country newspaper. He had subsequently travelled New England and the
Middle States, as a pedlar, in the employment of a Connecticut manufactory
of cologne-water and other essences. In an episodical way he had studied
and practiced dentistry, and with very flattering success, especially in many
of the factory-towns along our inland streams. As a supernumerary official,
of some kind or other, aboard a packet-ship, he had visited Europe, and
found means, before his return, to see Italy, and part of France and Germany. At a later period he had spent some months in a community of
Fourierists. Still more recently he had been a public lecturer on Mesmerism.

His present phase, as a daguerreotypist, was no more likely to be permanent than any of the preceding ones. He had taken it up "with the careless alacrity of an adventurer, who had his bread to earn."

Yet homeless as he had been, and continually changing his whereabouts, "and, therefore, responsible neither to public opinion nor to
individuals," he had never violated his inner integrity of conscience, as
Phoebe soon came to recognize. His hatred of the dead burden of the past
was as thoroughgoing as possible; but he had read very little, and
though he considered himself a thinker, with his own path to discover,
he "had perhaps hardly yet reached the point where an educated man begins to think." "Altogether in his culture and want of culture"—as Hawthorne summed him up, somewhat laboriously, but with telling accuracy—"in his crude, wild, and misty philosophy, and the practical
experience that counteracted some of its tendencies; in his magnanimous
zeal for man's welfare, and his recklessness of whatever the ages had
established in man's behalf; in his faith, and in his infidelity; in what
he had and in what he lacked,—the artist might fitly enough stand forth
as the representative of many compeers in his native land." His saving
grace was the absence of arrogance in his ideas, which could otherwise
have become those of a crank. He had learned enough of the world to be
perplexed by it, and to begin to suspect "that a man's bewilderment is
the measure of his wisdom." Melville checked that, as he did also the re-

flection that it would be hard to prefigure Holgrave's future, since in this country we are always meeting such jacks-of-all-trades, "for whom we anticipate wonderful things, but of whom, even after much and careful inquiry, we never happen to hear another word." In short, Hawthorne has presented a detailed portrait of one of Emerson's promising Young Americans.

The course that is actually foreshadowed for him is devastating in its limitations. In consequence of the awakening of his love for Phoebe and her acceptance of him, society no longer looks hostile. When Phoebe is afraid that he will lead her out of her own quiet path, he already knows that the influence is likely to be all the other way. As he says, "the world owes all its onward impulses to men ill at ease," and he has a presentiment that it will hereafter be his lot to set out trees and to make fences, and to build a house for another generation. Thus he admits, with a half-melancholy laugh, that he feels the traditional values already asserting their power over him, even while he and Phoebe are still standing under the gaze of the portrait of Colonel Pyncheon, whom Holgrave recognizes as "a model conservative, who, in that very character, rendered himself so long the evil destiny of his race."

The conclusion of this book has satisfied very few. Although Phoebe's marriage with Holgrave, who discloses himself at length as a descendant of the Maules, is meant finally to transcend the old brutal separation of classes that has hardened the poor family against its oppressors, the reconciliation is somewhat too lightly made. It is quite out of keeping with Hawthorne's seemingly deliberate answer in his preface to the new thought's doctrine of Compensation, of the way good arises out of evil. For Hawthorne said there that his book might illustrate the truth "that the wrong-doing of one generation lives into the successive ones, and, divesting itself of every temporary advantage, becomes a pure and uncontrollable mischief." That unrelenting strain was still at the fore in his final reflections about Clifford. Although his feeble spirits revived once the Judge's death had removed him from the sphere of that malevolent influence, "after such wrong as he had suffered, there is no reparation . . . No great mistake, whether acted or endured, in our mortal sphere, is ever really set right. Time, the continual vicissitude of circumstances, and the invariable inopportunity of death, render it impossible. If, after long lapse of years, the right seems to be in our power, we find no niche to set it in."

In contrast to that tragic thought, Hawthorne's comparatively flimsy interpretation of the young lovers derives from the fact that he has not visualized their future with any precision. Trollope objected to this on the basic level of plot:

The hurrying up of the marriage, and all the dollars which they inherit from the wicked Judge, and the "handsome dark-green barouche" prepared for their departure, which is altogether unfitted to the ideas which the reader has formed respecting them, are quite unlike Hawthorne, and would seem almost to have been added by some every-day, beef-and-ale, realistic novelist, into whose hands the unfinished story had unfortunately fallen.

As they leave for the new country house that has tumbled into their hands, they seem to have made the successful gesture of renouncing the worst of the past. The tone of the last page could hardly be more different from that of the end of *The Cherry Orchard*, where Chekhov dwells not on what lies ahead, but on the mingled happiness and despair that have been interwoven with the old house. But the Russian was aware of the frustration and impending breakdown of a whole social class, whereas Hawthorne assumed with confidence the continuance of democratic opportunity. Yet in the poetic justice of bestowing opulence on all those who had previously been deprived of it by the Judge, Hawthorne overlooked the fact that he was sowing all over again the same seeds of evil.

The world that both Phoebe and Holgrave had previously belonged to, as conservative and radical manifestations, was the New England into which both Sophia and Hawthorne had been born. Julian Hawthorne suggested its engaging innocence in the same passage where he commented on the democratic closeness between work and culture:

> Plain living and high thinking can seldom have been more fully united and exemplified than in certain circles of Boston and Salem during the first thirty or forty years of this century . . . Religious feeling was deep and earnest, owing in part to the recent schism between the severe and liberal interpretations of Christian destiny and obligations; and the development of commerce and other material interests had not more than foreshadowed its present proportions, nor distracted people's attention from less practical matters. Such a state of things can hardly be reproduced, and, in our brief annals, possesses some historic value.

But the implications that lay ahead in the young couple's inheritance of several hundred thousand were equally beyond both Hawthorne's experience and imagination. He took for granted that in a democratic society the domineering influence of private wealth would not be able to hold the evil sway that it did in the narrowly autocratic era of Colonel Pyncheon. But the fact that he hardly cast a glance to examine what would prevail at the Holgraves' countryseat, prevented him from suggesting their participation in any definite state of existence, as, for instance, Tolstoy could suggest the Russia of which Pierre and Natasha had become part at the close of *War and Peace*.

Out of his savage revulsion from the America that had followed—the America of Sinclair Lewis's early satires, whose roots Veblen had probed with deeper thoroughness—Lawrence could make his free interpretation of Hawthorne's conclusion: "The new generation is having no ghosts or cobwebs. It is setting up in the photography line, and is just going to make a sound financial thing out of it." With all the old hates swept out of sight, "the vendetta-born young couple effect a perfect understanding under the black cloth of a camera and prosperity. *Vivat industria!* . . . How you'd have *hated* it if you'd had nothing but the prosperous, 'dear' young couple to write about! If you'd lived to the day when America was nothing but a Main Street."

Hawthorne's inability, despite all his latent irony, to conceive any such world, made Eliot reflect, when he was about to start *The Waste Land,* that the thinness of the novelist's milieu was owing to no lack of intellectual life, but to the fact that "it was not corrupt enough." This circumstance involved also "the difficult fact that the soil which produced him with his essential flavor is the soil which produced, just as inevitably, the environment which stunted him." What that means in the evidence furnished by *The Seven Gables* is that Hawthorne could conceive evil in the world, but not an evil world. As a result his final pages drift away into unreal complacence. No such blindness is to be found in his direct reckoning with the forces surrounding him and with the problem of embracing them in an imaginative construction. He never ceased to be acutely conscious of the difficulty in doing what he wanted most, of opening an intercourse with society. He was aware that he was presenting in *The Seven Gables* hardly more of society's larger movements than could be glimpsed in "one of the retired streets of a not very populous city." He knew how hard it was to make his slender store of homely details extend over the surfaces of a whole book, for, no matter how authentic, their poverty would be revealed by the diffuseness with which they were spun out. But his basic problem was even harder, and was always the same, no matter what his chosen material: how was he to bridge the gap between foreground and background, how to suggest the whole scene of which his characters were part?

He never really succeeded. Although he could see his characters in a definite environment, he could not give the sense of their being in continuous contact with that larger outside world. It seems in his pages more like a backdrop than an enfolding atmosphere. He spoke apologetically in *Blithedale* of his method of "insulating" his few characters from other relations in order to keep them so long upon his "mental stage, as actors in a drama." The resulting isolation enforces itself in a double degree: not only do they seem to be cut off from any full participation in society beyond their immediate circle, but, in addition, with the absence of the usual novelist's filling of other people and events, you become conscious of how Hawthorne's customary four or five principals are separated one from another by wide, unoccupied spaces. They often seem to move in a void as lonely as that which, notwithstanding the smallness of their seventeenth century village, kept Hester and Dimmesdale from meeting by themselves for seven years. Furthermore, when Hawthorne centers directly on the presentation of his individuals, he can ordinarily manage no more than to give a careful notation of their traits—as we have just seen with Holgrave—instead of revealing them gradually through significant incidents. Even in their conflicts with one another, description nearly always usurps the place of immediate action. Hawthorne tells us that Hepzibah has struggled through a scene "of passion and terror" in confronting the Judge; we recognize it, but we hardly feel it directly. Drama, at least the highly realized form that Granville-Barker speaks of, was beyond him: he could not project individuals against a fully developed society. For no such thing had yet been evolved in the individualistic career of our democracy.

What is too often neglected in the current demand that a work of art should be a criticism of its age is that it becomes so, not by a mere frontal attack, not by virtue of any abstract statements of right and wrong, nor by bare demonstrations of social and economic abuses, but by the degree to which it can create a sustained vision of man's existence. Such a vision possessess validity and urgency just in proportion as it corresponds to *felt* experience. Hawthorne recognized this fact, in remarking in his preface to *The Seven Gables* that "when romances do really teach anything, or produce any effective operation, it is usually through a far more subtle process than the ostensible one." By subscribing to Hawthorne's success in doing that very thing in this book, Melville arrived at his conception of the way in which the artist creates "the usable truth," "the absolute condition of present things as they strike the eye of the man who fears them not." Although neither Hawthorne nor Melville would have thought in such terms, they were not unaware of what Engels later formulated concerning the role of the artist in contrast to that of the social theorist: "The father of tragedy, Aeschylus, and the father of comedy, Aristophanes, were both very clearly poets with a thesis, as were Dante and Cervantes . . . But I believe that the thesis must inhere in the situation and the action, without being explicitly formulated; and it is not the poet's duty to supply the reader in advance with the future historical solution of the conflict he describes."

Measured by the standard of this reasoning, Hawthorne fulfilled his chief function, since his work was a mirror of its age by virtue both of its searching honesty and of its inevitable unconscious limitations.

The Blithedale Romance

by A. N. Kaul

In *The Scarlet Letter* Hawthorne had noted the utopian aspect of the Puritan migration to New England. In *The Blithedale Romance* he presents the utopian experiment of Brook Farm as an extension of the Puritan tradition. The backward glance of comparison runs like a rich thread through the pattern of the latter novel, making explicit the significance which the American romancer saw in this otherwise quixotic enterprise.

The day on which the visionaries assemble at Blithedale—to begin "the life of Paradise anew"—is bleaker and less encouraging than the day of the Pilgrims' landing as described by William Bradford. How conscious Hawthorne's narrator is of the suggested parallel we notice when, seated by the blazing hearth of the farmhouse at the end of the tempestuous journey, he reflects that "the old Pilgrims might have swung their kettle over precisely such a fire as this" and that, though Blithedale was hardly a day's walk from the old city, "we had transported ourselves a world-wide distance from the system of society that shackled us at breakfast-time." The Blithedalers are careful to distinguish the moral idealism of their motivation from the guiding principles of other contemporary communitarians. When Miles Coverdale reads the works of Fourier during his convalescence, he concludes that the world was mistaken in equating Blithedale with Fourierism "inasmuch as the two theories differed, as widely as the zenith from the nadir, in their main principles." Hollingsworth, to whom Coverdale puts the case, dismisses the Frenchman in an impassioned speech which is a curious amalgam of Hawthorne and the elder James. Fourier, Hollingsworth declares, "has committed the unpardonable sin; for what more monstrous iniquity could the Devil himself contrive than to choose the selfish principle— the principle of all human wrong, the very blackness of man's heart, the portion of ourselves which we shudder at, and which it is the whole aim of spiritual discipline to eradicate—to choose it as the master work-man of his system? To seize upon and foster whatever vile, petty, sordid, filthy, bestial, and abominable corruptions have cankered into our na-ture, to be the efficient instruments of his infernal regeneration!" Since "the selfish principle" at the base of organized society is also the chief reason for the Blithedalers' withdrawal from it, in denouncing Fourier, Hollingsworth is stating by implication their own different purpose. The irony here, however, lies in the fact—which will be noted more fully later—that this criticism of Fourier remains the ultimate comment on Hollingsworth himself. The true importance of the Blithedale experi-ment, as Hawthorne presents it, is that it embodies the visionary hope for mankind which was coeval with the American settlement itself. Miles Coverdale puts the claim for it explicitly when he opens a later chapter, "Eliot's Pulpit," by saying: "Our Sundays at Blithedale were not or-dinarily kept with such rigid observance as might have befitted the de-scendants of the Pilgrims, whose high enterprise, as we sometimes flattered ourselves, we had taken up, and were carrying it onward and aloft, to a point which they never dreamed of attaining."

In many ways Hawthorne was, as Mrs. Q. D. Leavis says, the unwilling heir of the Puritans. But this is far from being true with regard to the tradition of idealism which was a part of his inheritance. On the con-trary, he affirmed it in the only serious way in which an artist can affirm tradition: by becoming its critic. It must be said in passing that as far as the actual experiment of Brook Farm is concerned, Hawthorne's motives in joining it were as mixed as those of his ancestors in coming to America. On the one hand, there was the practical expectation of a comfortable livelihood for himself and Sophia. On the other, there was a good deal of simple faith in the theory behind the venture—enough faith, at any rate, to induce him to stake a thousand dollars from his meager resources on its success. Brook Farm, as he says in the preface to the novel, was "essentially a day-dream, and yet a fact," and indeed, in the curious episode of his association with it, one finds it difficult to separate the hard-headed Yankee from the wild-eyed dreamer. Perhaps, like Coverdale, he hoped that in the long run "between theory and practice, a true and available mode of life might be struck out."

However, be his personal motivation what it may, the important thing to realize is that Brook Farm presented Hawthorne with an appropriate subject for his theme. In "Earth's Holocaust," the fantasy which describes an attempted regeneration, he had observed that it mattered little whether the attempt was made in the time past or time to come. The contours of the action were indeed hidden in the whole history of Amer-ica. *The Scarlet Letter* had dealt with it at its very source in the seven-teenth century. In *Blithedale* Hawthorne brought the action up to date. Here again was an embodiment of the archetypal American experience:

withdrawal from a corrupt society to form a regenerate community. The basis for regeneration had of course shifted from theological to economic theory; social morality was no longer embedded in metaphysics. In this sense Hawthorne was marking realistically enough the shift in tradition that had occurred over the centuries, for, although in America, unlike Europe, the communitarian tradition developed in unbroken continuity from its chiliastic source in the seventeenth century, the experimenters of the nineteenth century were communitarians first and sectarians only in the second place—or not at all. Moreover, it was no longer confined to alien groups. Ripley's community was both native in composition and secular in purpose.

It is to emphasize the action of withdrawal and to underline the exercise of that radical choice which America was supposed to have made permanently available to mankind that the novel opens in society, with Coverdale about to take the plunge which he later compares to the Pilgrim's world-wide leap across the Atlantic. In the temporary movement of the story back to society, which occurs in the middle of the novel, we get some richly evoked scenes of Boston life. This is the most detailed body of social description in Hawthorne, and it comes very close to the best manner of European fiction. Hawthorne is not, however, a "social" novelist, and this presentation is the background rather than the milieu of the action, which explores not a social problem but the possibility of repudiating organized society in its entirety. The subject is not Boston life but rather the drama of Boston and Blithedale, or the American dialectic between actual society and ideal community. The theme is not reform but social regeneration.

While the Blithedalean visionaries acknowledge their kinship with the American Puritans of the seventeenth century, their own enterprise arises primarily from a repugnance to the principle of economic individualism, from the fact that society has come to be organized exclusively on the basis of the force which had caused the failure of Bradford's communitarian experiment but which Bradford had accepted as an inevitable factor of God's dispensation for the New World. Of course the Blithedale community has other avowed objectives, like the belief in agriculture as the true foundation of the good life. This, however, constitutes the ridiculous part of their venture, and is treated uniformly as such by Hawthorne. It is indeed the chief target of the mild but persistent comedy in which Silas Foster, together with the pigs and the manure dump, serves to point out the reality behind the masquerade, while Miles Coverdale, like Shakespeare's Touchstone, performs the function of more articulate comic exposure. Hawthorne, as much as Melville, faced but overcame the nineteenth century temptation toward the Arcadian relapse. It is true that outdoor life helps both Priscilla and Coverdale to add sunburn to their cheeks. But, as Coverdale observes:

The peril of our new way of life was not lest we should fail in becoming practical agriculturists, but that we should probably cease to be anything else. . . . The clods of earth, which we so constantly belabored and turned over and over, were never etherealized into thought. Our thoughts, on the contrary, were fast becoming cloddish. Our labor symbolized nothing, and left us mentally sluggish in the dusk of the evening. Intellectual activity is incompatible with any large amount of bodily exercise. The yeoman and the scholar—the yeoman and the man of finest moral culture, though not the man of sturdiest sense and integrity—are two distinct individuals, and can never be melted or welded into one substance.

Hawthorne is exposing here again the fallacy of the virgin scene: the assumption that a new and regenerated life demands the total repudiation of man's accumulated moral and material achievement, and that, as soon as the heritage of the past is abandoned, regeneration begins of its own accord. In a later chapter, while describing the exciting bustle of city life, Coverdale goes on to say how all this "was just as valuable, in its way, as the sighing of the breeze among the birch-trees that overshadowed Eliot's pulpit." When in the same chapter he observes a scene of simple domestic affection, being fresh from the discords he has witnessed at Blithedale, he reflects that he had not "seen a prettier bit of nature" during his summer in the country than the actors in that scene had shown him here "in a rather stylish boarding-house."

One should be careful, however, not to divert the ridicule that Hawthorne reserves for the Arcadia to other aspects of the community idea. As a matter of fact, though he presents Blithedale in its single corporate image, he clearly distinguishes between the different values involved in its broad spectrum. For instance, he does not debunk the issue of the equality of the sexes as he does the cult of agriculture. His attitude toward it is ambiguous in the sense that he accords to it the dignity of a serious though not one-sided argument. It is true that even the ardent feminist Zenobia gives in to Hollingsworth's view that should women ever dream of straying from their natural subservience to man, the male sex must "use its physical force, that unmistakable evidence of sovereignty, to scourge them back within their proper bounds!" But as Coverdale reflects a moment later, is such submission to male egotism a token of woman's true nature or is it "the result of ages of compelled degradation?" Together with this goes the further reflection that "women, however intellectually superior, so seldom disquiet themselves about the rights or wrongs of their sex, unless their own individual affections chance to lie in idleness, or to be ill at ease." Thus, while Zenobia's side of the case is presented as unquestionably superior to Hollingsworth's Nietzschean bombast, the whole issue of feminist reform is seen as a secondary question—an unfortunate consequence of the general distortion of human relations in society. With regard to the primary cause of such dislocations—which is indeed the cause of the Blithedalean withdrawal—Hawthorne leaves us in no doubt. Early in the novel, while commenting on the first day's assembly at Blithedale, Coverdale observes:

> If ever men might lawfully dream awake, and give utterance to their wildest visions without dread of laughter or scorn on the part of the audience,—yes, and speak of earthly happiness, for themselves and mankind, as an object to be hopefully striven for, and probably attained,—we who made that little semicircle round the blazing fire were those very men. We had left the rusty iron framework of society behind us; we had broken through many hindrances that are powerful enough to keep most people on the weary tread-mill of the established system, even while they feel its irksomeness almost as intolerable as we did. We had stepped down from the pulpit; we had flung aside the pen; we had shut up the ledger . . . It was our purpose . . . [to show] mankind the example of a life governed by other than the false and cruel principles on which human society has all along been based.
>
> And, first of all, we had divorced ourselves from pride, and were striving to supply its place with familiar love. . . . We sought our profit by mutual aid, instead of wresting it by the strong hand from an enemy, or filching it craftily from those less shrewd than ourselves (if, indeed, there were any such in New England), or winning it by selfish competition with a neighbor; in one or another of which fashions every son of woman both perpetrates and suffers his share of the common evil, whether he chooses it or no.

Whatever one may say of Blithedale and its members as things eventually turn out, there is no question about the force with which the vision of an ideal community is presented here. Nor is there any ambiguity about the distribution of sympathies as between the values avowed by Coverdale and those which govern the "iron framework of society." The visionaries stand—in theory at least—upon the principle of human brotherhood as against the predatory competitiveness of the established system. Blithedale itself, as we shall see, is finally judged in terms of its own professed values and not by the standards and norms of society. It is only when, and insofar as, the visionaries themselves turn out to be men of iron masquerading in Arcadian costume, that Blithedale is dismissed as a humbug—as false as society but more hypocritical. But this process of criticism—of exposing the same basic drives twice over and of showing the corrupted rebel as more reprehensible than the original villain—does not lead to a reversal of values involved in the challenge. It makes for a more clear-sighted affirmation. Nor does the novelist, as distinct from the characters who are all more or less ironically presented, abandon his position with regard to "the common evil" of exploitative individualism which every person in society either suffers from or perpetrates. Hawthorne's attitude, it must be said, does not involve the repudiation of individual freedom and choice. On the contrary, like the elder James, he insists on the primacy of the moral person in all social arrangements. But the individualism he champions is not incompatible with, but rather tends toward and finds its richest fulfillment in, the human community.

Since the story is mainly concerned with the fortunes of the Blithedale community, the image of the surrounding society occupies of necessity a marginal position. Yet this is strictly true only in a physical sense. In reality, the main characters of the story, who are all communitarians, carry with themselves, more or less visibly, the outwardly repudiated social values and attitudes—like old earth clinging to tufts of transplanted grass. It is this fact which makes *Blithedale* an exploration of the dialectical rather than simply the oppositional relation between actual society and the aspiration toward a better community life. But, apart from this, one of the most remarkable feats of the novel is the manner in which the two peripheral characters—old Moodie and Westervelt—are made to suggest concretely certain sinister forces working in the depths of the social world. Although one would at first sight suppose them to belong wholly to the machinery of romance, even their connection with the central theme of *Blithedale* is close enough for one to conclude that Hawthorne's apologia in the preface with regard to the introduction of the communitarian experiment into the romance should be treated in the same light as Mark Twain's celebrated warning against finding a moral in *Huckleberry Finn*. Where Hawthorne maintains cautiously that the whole treatment of Brook Farm is "altogether incidental to the main purpose of the romance," one feels the whole romance is in reality a characteristically modulated projection of the main society-community theme.

In *The Seven Gables* Hawthorne had observed that in nineteenth century America, "amid the fluctuating waves of our social life, somebody is always at the drowning-point." This process and the consequent sense of insecurity are exemplified in *Blithedale*—more starkly and less sentimentally than in the case of Hepzibah Pyncheon—by old Moodie: the grandee of yesterday become the pauper of today; Fauntleroy turned into "a gray kennel-rat." This is a motif which recurs in a good deal of later American fiction, the career of George Hurstwood in *Sister Carrie* being a case which readily comes to mind. Hawthorne's method, however, is one of poetic, or "romantic," evocation rather than the "realistic" accumulation of minute detail, and his purpose is not so much to show the impassable gulf between classes as to point out the morally untenable nature of those distinctions which separate man from man in society. It is only in this sense that the fact of the relation between Zenobia and Priscilla becomes more meaningful than a mere contrivance of romantic plotting, for the sisterhood that is avowed at Blithedale but denied in society is not a playful masquerade as Zenobia seems to think; it is a reflection of the true nature of things.

In Westervelt, who is also connected with Zenobia and Priscilla, the projected force is one of secret power. The relation between him and the poor seamstress Priscilla is not unlike that between Ethan Brand and Esther, and mesmerism is to that extent presented as a peculiarly sinister variation of exploitative science. It makes "a delusive show of spirituality" but is "really imbued throughout with a cold and dead materialism." Westervelt represents in this sense the final degradation of the Puritan tradition. However, just as Hawthorne has explored the social implications of Puritan theology, he uses here the new psychic phenomenon to embody a sociological insight. These subtle transferences and suggested correlations are characteristic of Hawthorne's complex fictional method. Westervelt is in many ways the polished gentleman, a representative of the social type in which Coverdale sees a partial reflection of his own pre-Blithedale existence. But he is also a wizard the gold band around whose false teeth reveals him somehow as a "moral and physical humbug." Yet his power, though exerted invisibly, is real enough. In its remote control it suggests the exploitative power which technology was putting into the hands of men: the power to bring individuals into total bondage while leaving them outwardly free and untouched. Westervelt's human shape is thus "a necromantic, or perhaps a mechanical contrivance, in which a demon walked about." He, too, affirms faith in a golden future and speaks publicly of the dawning era "that would link soul to soul" in "mutually conscious brotherhood," but he speaks of it "as if it were a matter of chemical discovery." As against the brotherhood of voluntary love, which is based upon the magnetic chain of human sympathy, Westervelt's mesmeric union is enforced bondage, destructive of true individuality as well as true community.

The brotherhood of love and mutual sympathy, which is lacking or perverted in an individualist social system, is precisely what the Blithedale community has taken for the foundation of its life. It is likewise the basis of Hawthorne's criticism of Blithedale itself. What the novel finally calls in doubt is not the values avowed by the visionaries but their means, materials, and ultimately the depth and sincerity of their professions. Zenobia is a dilettante who, until she meets Hollingsworth, expects from Blithedale nothing worse than a naughty frolic and hardly anything better than a pleasant interlude in rusticity. She takes the experiment as a stage set for an unaccustomed personal role, and a curious theatricality accompanies her doings at Blithedale right up to the manner of her suicide. Coverdale is at heart a well meaning sybarite who has joined the community out of boredom with an aimless life, although the sense of direction and purpose he develops while there is a different matter. He and Zenobia share between themselves the accusation that the Veiled Lady levels at Theodore in Zenobia's own legend: "Dost thou come hither, not in holy faith, nor with a pure and generous purpose, but in scornful skepticism and idle curiosity?" For his detachment and lack of faith Coverdale indeed suffers the same fate as Theodore does for not saving from her bondage the girl he eventually loves: he relapses into a purposeless life haunted by his lost dream. Zenobia pays for her scorn and impure motives by a gruesome death.

The one person at Blithedale who lacks neither faith nor energy is Hollingsworth. But his faith is not the faith in a regenerate community, and his energy, like that of the Puritan magistrates with whom he is explicitly compared, drives him into a moral blindness of unique opacity. Unlike the dilettantish triflers, he is in deadly earnest, and he is a true builder rather than a dreamer of schemes. What he seeks to build, however, is not a regenerate community but an enduring edifice for the treatment of criminals. His monomaniacal preoccupation with crime is the nineteenth century equivalent of the Puritan absorption with sin. If Coverdale testifies to the ineffectuality of nineteenth century American idealism, Hollingsworth remains a permanently frightening symbol of what happens to a visionary scheme when it is geared to an individual's ruthless egotism and overwhelming energy. As Hawthorne insists in several places, Hollingsworth's plan of criminal reform was motivated by an initially noble impulse. But he has fallen into the reformer's occupational disease of monomania—a danger which Emerson noted in "New England Reformers": "Do not be so vain of your one objection. Do you think there is only one? Alas! my good friend, there is no part of society or of life better than any other part." Hawthorne, a true visionary of the hopeful American years, had the same objection to reformist zeal; and Hollingsworth's scheme becomes truly criminal when, in pursuit of its success, he subverts the nobler purpose of total regeneration embodied in the Blithedale community, destroying in the process also the faith and happiness of its other members. The key chapter for understanding the developments which lead eventually to the failure of the community, is the one appropriately entitled "A Crisis." It is here that Hollingsworth repudiates the communitarian idea, and we realize how he has used the experiment as a covert base for his own operations. He has made arrangements with Zenobia, on morally dubious grounds, for the financial support of his reformist enterprise. Nor is he prepared to accept Coverdale's suggestion that he reveal his design to the other members of the community. On the contrary, he invites Coverdale, too, to become his collaborator and join in the subversion of the Blithedale experiment.

> And have you no regrets, [Coverdale inquires] in overthrowing this fair system of our new life, which has been planned so deeply, and is now beginning to flourish so hopefully around us? How beautiful it is, and, so far as we can yet see, how practicable! The ages have waited for us, and here we are, the very first that have essayed to carry on our mortal existence in love and mutual help! Hollingsworth, I would be loath to take the ruin of this enterprise upon my conscience.

To which the indomitable man replies: "Then let it rest wholly upon mine!" When Coverdale refuses to join him finally, rather than tolerate a friend who does not share his own fanatical purpose Hollingsworth repudiates the bond of personal friendship too.

This man of iron thus possesses all those attributes that Hawthorne had enumerated in *The Seven Gables* as constituting the essential moral continuity between the Puritan of the seventeenth century and his descendant of the nineteenth. Like the members of that persistent clan, he is brutal in personal relations and dishonest in public ones, "laying his purposes deep, and following them out with an inveteracy of pursuit that knew neither rest nor conscience; trampling on the weak, and, when essential to his ends, doing his utmost to beat down the strong." His altruistic professions notwithstanding, Hollingsworth reveals in himself finally the same egotism, selfish principle, or ruthless individualism which the Blithedalean visionaries identified as the "common evil" of the established system. In *The Seven Gables* Hawthorne had said that the truth about a public man is often best discovered in a woman's view of him, and in *Blithedale* it is indeed a disillusioned Zenobia who gives utterance to the moral obliquity of Hollingsworth's character. "It is all self!" she declares in one of the climactic scenes of the novel. "Nothing else; nothing but self, self, self! The fiend, I doubt not, has made his choicest mirth of you these seven years past, and especially in the mad summer which we have spent together. I see it now! I am awake, disenchanted, disinthralled! Self, self, self!"

Thus at Blithedale, too, instead of brotherhood there is selfhood, instead of faith there is skepticism, and instead of love there is fresh antagonism. It is not that, as Coverdale puts it, the Blithedaleans stand in a position of "new hostility, rather than new brotherhood" with regard to the society at large; because, as Coverdale himself adds, this could not fail to be the case so long as they were in "so pitiful a minority." Their estrangement from society is inevitable in "proportion with the strictness of our mutual bond among ourselves." The criticism of the Blithedale community therefore lies not in its hostile relation to the surrounding social system but rather in the absence of the promised bond within itself and in the divergence between its theory of mutual sympathy on the one hand and its reality of fresh antagonisms and mutual suspicions on the other. When Coverdale returns to Blithedale toward the end of the novel it has become a grim battlefield, with Hollingsworth resembling a Puritan magistrate holding an inquest of life and death in a case of witchcraft. The succeeding scenes enact Zenobia's tragedy, which, as Mark Van Doren says, is trash.[1] But it seems to me that Van Doren misses the whole force of this calculated vulgarity, for the point is precisely that the com-

[1] Mark Van Doren, *Nathaniel Hawthorne*, American Men of Letters Series (New York, William Sloane Associates, 1949), pp. 189-90.

munity, built on a premise of high idealism, should resolve itself finally
into the same old story of love, jealousy, and sensational suicide. Zenobia's
fate only illustrates the true tragedy of Blithedale.

The great test of the experiment's human worth is of course Priscilla.
It is not for nothing that Coverdale is made to put the question of
Blithedale's success or failure to her avatar as the Veiled Lady in the
opening chapter. Unless the visionaries can save this daughter of poverty
from her bondage, their enterprise will be a mockery of their principles.
It is, indeed, Hollingsworth who declares: "As we do by this friendless
girl, so shall we prosper." After vanishing from her enslavement to
Westervelt, she has arisen, as Zenobia says in her legend, among this knot
of visionary people to await her new destiny. What volumes of meaning
this conveys with regard to the hope that was associated with the whole
experiment of America! But the visionaries deliver Priscilla back to
Westervelt, Zenobia being the chief instrument of her renewed bondage.
A long line of critics has taken Hawthorne to task for not revealing the
precise nature of Zenobia's relation with Westervelt. To me it seems that
the ambiguity with which he surrounds their connection detracts nothing
from, but rather adds to, the intended effect of obscure but intimate collusion. It is a collusion in which Hollingsworth is somewhat vaguely but
quite unquestionably implicated, for, when Coverdale asks Priscilla in
town if Hollingsworth knows where she is, the girl replies that she has
come at his bidding. Coverdale himself, though honest, plays the limited
role that befits his self-appointed position as chorus to the action.

Blithedale is thus not the regenerate community it professes to be. It
is a company bound together, as the younger Henry James said in words
that might have come from his father, rather by "its mutual suspicions
and frictions, than by any successful surrender of self." [2] It has repeated
rather than eliminated the cardinal sin of the outwardly repudiated society. "Alas," the narrator says at the end of the novel, "what faith is
requisite to bear up against such results of generous effort!" Hawthorne
had taken for his theme the exploration of such generous effort over the
whole field of American history. Faced with the corruption which inevitably overtook the visionary schemes, it is not surprising that, like Cooper,
he seems to conclude that nothing like social perfection is possible upon
this earth. But, like Cooper again, he knew that it was foolish to expect
perfection before its time. Because his faith was matched by his historical
understanding, he did not become cynical. He realized that the nineteenth
century belonged to gold-toothed wizards and narrow-minded reformers,
and, what is more, the visionaries were themselves imbued with the spirit
of their age. Blithedale was accordingly doomed from the outset, not only
to failure, but to unreality. As Coverdale says of the experiment from the
perspective of his retreat to Boston: "But, considered in a profounder
relation, it was part of another age, a different state of society, a segment

---

[2] Henry James, *Library of the World's Best Literature*, XII, 7058.

of an existence peculiar in its aims and methods, a leaf of some mysterious volume interpolated into the current history which time was writing off."

Set out of its time and place, the community remains thus only a noble and anticipatory gesture of hope. There is, however, no unreality about the values it affirms even in failure. The true measure of these values is neither Hollingsworth nor Zenobia. They constitute the destructive element. One must look elsewhere—to Priscilla and Coverdale—for their tragic affirmation. Whatever her ultimate destiny, it is only at Blithedale that Priscilla comes into her proper heritage of freedom, happiness, dignity, and even love—such as it is. With regard to Coverdale, though his end is not very different from his beginning, we must not overlook the development that lies in between. After he sheds the more frivolous part of his skepticism together with his illness, he is reborn into a new existence. He is not, it is true, converted to the Arcadia of pigs and masquerades. Nor does he by any means abandon the serious part of his critical attitude toward the enterprise. The important change lies in the new sense of community which he acquires and which gives meaning to his otherwise empty life. He returns to Boston only because of the break with Hollingsworth and the consequent feeling of excommunication. How much he still belongs inwardly to Blithedale, however, we see from the tumultuous excitement with which he returns to it and the deep response with which he greets its distant glimpse:

> In the sweat of my brow I had there earned bread and eaten it, and so established my claim to be on earth, and my fellowship with all the sons of labor. I could have knelt down, and have laid my breast against that soil. The red clay of which my frame was moulded seemed nearer akin to those crumbling furrows than to any other portion of the world's dust. There was my home, and there might be my grave.

Years later the middle-aged Coverdale voices the same sentiment:

> Often, however, in these years that are darkening around me, I remember our beautiful scheme of a noble and unselfish life; and how fair, in that first summer, appeared the prospect that it might endure for generations, and be perfected, as the ages rolled away, into the system of a people and a world! Were my former associates now there,—were there only three or four of those true-hearted men still laboring in the sun,—I sometimes fancy that I should direct my world-weary footsteps thitherward, and entreat them to receive me, for old friendship's sake.

To seek an affirmation of visionary hope, Cooper had read American history backward. Hawthorne, who started with the past, had moved up to his own time, and from there referred the faith in a sane community life to some possible future age. "More and more I feel that we had struck upon what ought to be a truth," as Coverdale says. "Posterity may dig it up, and profit by it."

The Marble Faun

by Hyatt H. Waggoner

I

Hawthorne's whole career had prepared him to write *The Marble Faun,* his "story of the fall of man." Loss of innocence, initiation into the complexities of experience in a world of ambiguously mingled good and evil, experiences of guilt so obscurely related to specific acts as to seem more "original" and necessary than avoidable, these had been his subjects in story after story. Eden had never been far in the background, whether he was writing of life in a decayed mansion in Salem or of the attempts of reformers to undo the fall in a utopian community. The analogy with the Garden of Biblical myth had supplied the basic metaphor in "Rappaccini's Daughter." When, just after his marriage, he had experienced a happiness greater than he had ever known before, he inevitably thought of Sophia and himself in the Old Manse as a new Adam and Eve in an unfallen world.

Several of his stories that we generally think of as stories of initiation are equally stories of the fall. Robin's encounter with sin becomes a fortunate fall in "My Kinsman, Major Molineux." The innocence of this self-reliant and naive country boy proves inadequate to guide him to his destination through the mazes of the city's streets, but thanks to a kindly Providence, he finds he may rise, after his fall, without the help he sought. Young Goodman Brown's experience in the forest was a less fortunate fall. Whether the evil he found universal there was only a dream, or a mirage contrived by the Devil to destroy him, or a false conclusion based on his inability to see the significance of his being there himself, at any rate he was destroyed by it when he lost faith in the reality of the good. From being an Innocent, he became a Cynic and so was lost because he could not accept the world as it really is. He prepares us for Giovanni in "Rappaccini's Daughter," who cannot accept the ambiguous mixture of good

"The Marble Faun." From *Hawthorne: A Critical Study* by Hyatt H. Waggoner, rev. ed. (Cambridge, The Belknap Press of Harvard University Press, 1963). Copyright © 1955, 1963 by the President and Fellows of Harvard College. Reprinted by permission of the publishers and Hyatt H. Waggoner.

and evil he finds in the garden. Brown's Faith wore pink ribbons until he lost it entirely; it never became mature. So Giovanni first thought Beatrice an angel, then decided she was a fiend, but never could accept her as a human being. The Adamic falls reenacted by Brown and Giovanni led to no subsequent rise. "My Kinsman" is perhaps the only story Hawthorne ever wrote in which there is a fall that is clearly fortunate. "Roger Malvin's Burial" ends in a reunion with God and man after isolation, to be sure, but whatever "rise" there is here is a very sad one. The vision of life it implies remains tragic.

The last story reminds us of another way in which Hawthorne's career had prepared him to write *The Marble Faun*. Hawthorne had so obscured Reuben's guilt as to make it seem like a general human condition rather than the result of a specific act which he might well have avoided. All men, Hawthorne had implied, rationalize their self interest as Reuben does, and none of us tells all the truth all the time—though in the end our evasions catch up with us, as Reuben's did with him, until at last we are guilty in fact, by a kind of negative choice, as well as by virtue of our sharing the human condition. Our sin, in short, is both "original" and ever-renewed. We are like the later Pyncheons, in part victims of the house, in part perpetrators of fresh sins—until love releases us from our inheritance. Hawthorne was more interested in guilt as a necessary human condition than he was in any specific sinful act. So he treated the central action in *The Marble Faun* in such a way that it is just as impossible to decide that Donatello is really responsible for the murder he committed as it is to decide that Reuben clearly did wrong when he left Roger Malvin to die. Miriam, herself a victim of a dreadful evil, is at least as responsible as Donatello, and the murdered man both invited and deserved his fate. All Rome, all history, made the crime inevitable, and its spreading effects leave no one untouched, not even the spotless Hilda. This murder is no ordinary crime but a reenactment of the archetypal fall.

II

If Hawthorne had told this story many times before, he had never told it quite so directly or with so conscious an effort to determine its ultimate significance. It had generally been in the background, perhaps not consciously intended at all, as in "Young Goodman Brown," or suggested in the form of enriching allusions, as in *The House of the Seven Gables*. Now it was made the explicit subject—the too explicit subject, the modern reader is likely to decide. When innocent, faun-like Donatello, who has grown up in a rural Arcadia where he has been "close to nature," encounters evil in the corrupt city and ends by committing a murder, but is apparently deepened and matured by the experience, Miriam sees the analogy with Eden and asks the question it prompts:

"The story of the fall of man! Is it not repeated in our romance of Monte Beni? And may we follow the analogy yet further? Was that very sin,—into which Adam precipitated himself and all his race,—was it the destined means by which, over a long pathway of toil and sorrow, we are to attain a higher, brighter, and more profound happiness, than our lost birthright gave?"

Should we think of Adam's sin as a Fortunate Fall, and therefore perhaps of each man's reenactment of the Fall as equally fortunate? Was Donatello's murder, in fact, a blessing in disguise? "Was it a means of education, bringing a simple and imperfect nature to a point of feeling and intelligence which it could have reached under no other discipline?" If sin is not educational, how else account for the fact that God permits it?

Kenyon, to whom Miriam addresses these questions, replies that he finds this line of speculation "too dangerous." He will not follow her into such "unfathomable abysses." Yet a little later, contemplating the significance of the fact that Donatello since his crime has perceptibly changed for the better, he *does* follow her:

"Here comes my perplexity," continued Kenyon. "Sin has educated Donatello, and elevated him. Is sin, then,—which we deem such a dreadful blackness in the universe,—is it, like sorrow, merely an element of human education, through which we struggle to a higher and purer state than we could otherwise have attained? Did Adam fall, that we might ultimately rise to a far loftier paradise than his?"

When Hilda demonstrates "the white shining purity" of her nature and the orthodoxy of her religious faith by responding to the sculptor's questions with horror, declaring herself shocked beyond words, he quickly retracts, asks her forgiveness, and declares he never did really believe it. He is in love with Hilda and has no answer ready to give to the question she asks him. "Do not you perceive what a mockery your creed makes, not only of all religious sentiments, but of moral law? and how it annuls and obliterates whatever precepts of Heaven are written deepest within us?"

For once, in this reply to Kenyon, Hilda may seem to the modern reader to demonstrate that moral sensitivity and insight that Hawthorne so emphatically, and to us for the most part so unaccountably, attributes to her. For she seems to have realized that one of the implications of the version of the old idea of the Fortunate Fall that both Miriam and Kenyon have put forth is that, since sin is educational, we *ought* to violate our consciences in order to attain the improvement in us that will result. In effect, whether she knows it or not, she sees that her friends are confusing history and myth. The myth describes the constant human condition: sin is "original" in man's nature, shared by all alike, present even in those not clearly guilty of any specific sin. It has nothing to say about what man ought to do about this fact. Only when it is taken as history does the question arise, Ought we then to imitate Adam and sin deliberately, so that Christ, the Second Adam, may come to redeem us? The idea of the Fortunate Fall arose when devout men contemplated the story of the old and new covenants as interpreted by Christians and felt a need to express their gratitude to God for the way He had brought good out of evil. Man had fallen but God had raised him again. Calamity had turned out, then, because "God so loved the world," to have unforeseeable, fortunate consequences: God sent His only son to die on the cross for our sins. Fortunately, the Atonement does for us what we cannot do for ourselves. The idea of the Fortunate Fall has immense theological implications, but no moral ones at all, or else the wrong ones, just as Hilda says.

The question as posed by Miriam and Kenyon is never resolved in the novel. It could not be without violating both Hawthorne's sense of the truth of life as he understood it and his sense of the limitations of words and rational thought in such areas, his sense of the mystery in which man finds himself. True, Miriam, who implies that she believes the fall *is* fortunate, is a sympathetic character and often speaks for the darker side of Hawthorne's mind, but she cannot be taken as always Hawthorne's spokesman. Hawthorne presents her as warped by her tragic experience even while he gives her his full sympathy. If her view of life is closer to Hawthorne's own than is Hilda's, Hawthorne admired Hilda more and wished he might more fully share her unquestioning faith. Miriam raised a question which Hawthorne too had pondered, and decided, apparently, he could not answer, at least not with a *yes* or a *no*.

Kenyon is much more a spokesman for Hawthorne than is Miriam, and Kenyon too rejects the implication of his own and Miriam's question. A good deal of the time in the novel there is very little distance between Kenyon and Hawthorne. Essentially, Kenyon and Hilda are Nathaniel and Sophia. When Hilda rebukes him for his speculation and he explains that he never really believed it, Kenyon goes on to explain his vagary:

> "But the mind wanders wild and wide; and, so lonely as I live and work, I have neither polestar above nor light of cottage windows here below, to bring me home. Were you my guide, my counsellor, my inmost friend, with that white wisdom which clothes you as a celestial garment, all would go well. O Hilda, guide me home!"

The parallel between this and many of Hawthorne's love letters to Sophia is very close. One of the things Hawthorne must have meant when he declared himself "saved" by his marriage was that he had found Sophia's buoyant faith a needed counterbalance to his own dark questionings. So Kenyon might be wiser in the ways of the world but Hilda, as we are often reminded, was wiser in religious truth. Kenyon might well ask her to guide him home, in Hawthorne's view of the matter. His refusal to carry on his line of speculation had Hawthorne's approval.

Depending on which aspect of it we look at, the plot either supports or does not support the rejection by Hilda and Kenyon of the idea of the Fortunate Fall. Though Donatello has been matured and human-ized by his suffering, he must go to prison. Though Miriam has been ennobled by love, she ends in sad penitence, without hope of happiness with Donatello. Kenyon and Hilda decide to leave Rome, thus in effect putting the problem behind them. The plot gives no clear answer to the largest question explicitly posed by the novel.

III

But perhaps the question itself is illegitimate, impossible to answer. Hawthorne has Kenyon say, after he has looked from Donatello's tower at the landscape mottled with patches of sunlight and shadow and seen it as a symbol of life, "It is a great mistake to try to put our best thoughts into human language. When we ascend into the higher regions of emo-tion and spiritual enjoyment, they are only expressible by such grand hieroglyphics as these around us." By symbols, in short, and myths. Speak-ing in his own person as narrator, Hawthorne has already noted the loss now that man has grown beyond the archaic expressiveness of gestures, and "words have been feebly substituted in the place of signs and sym-bols." What words cannot do, the visual arts sometimes can. Speaking again in his own person, in one of the passages lifted from the Note-books, Hawthorne says of Sodoma's Christ bound to a pillar that it shows what "pictorial art, devoutly exercised, might effect in behalf of religious truth; involving, as it does, deeper mysteries of revelation, and bringing them closer to man's heart, and making him tenderer to be impressed by them, than the most eloquent words of preacher or prophet." In his first chapter, describing the Faun, who was "neither man nor animal, and yet no monster," Hawthorne has despaired of putting his basic idea into abstract language: "The idea grows coarse as we handle it, and hard-ens in our grasp." The idea of the Faun, he decides, "may have been no dream, but rather a poet's reminiscence of a period when man's affinity with nature was more strict, and his fellowship with every living thing more intimate and dear." To discover what the novel finally, at its deepest level, means, then, we should turn from a consideration of the questions framed by Miriam and Kenyon to the myths which Hawthorne uses to shape his story.

Almost exactly in the center of his book Hawthorne has placed a chap-ter he calls simply "Myths." In it he gives us what Miriam, on another occasion, demands of Donatello, "the latest news from Arcady," which is, in effect, that nature has no cure for what ails us. However beautiful the old Arcadian myths are, however sad it is that we have lost our innocence, they are not true any longer in a fallen world. (In Hawthorne's terminology, the old pagan legends are "myths," the Bibilcal story in Genesis a symbolic truth, perhaps not literally true historeally but true as a type of the human condition. He never refers to the Genesis story as a "myth.") Donatello, now that he has known sin, cannot reenter Arcadia.

The chief substance of the chapter is the legend of Donatello's spring, which one of his ancestors found to be animated by a beautiful maiden, the spirit of the water, with whom he fell in love. On summer days she would cool his brow with her touch or make rainbows around him. Kenyon interrupts the story at this point with a skeptical comment:

> "It is a delightful story for the hot noon of your Tuscan summer . . . But the deportment of the watery lady must have had a most chilling influence in midwinter."

If this criticism seems the product only of the skeptical mind, another is implicit in the story itself. Eventually the dryad refused to appear to her lover, and Donatello explains that her refusal was caused by the effort of his ancestor to wash off a bloodstain in the water. While summer and innocence last, in short, being "close to nature" is perhaps enough; at least, Hawthorne says elsewhere, it is a very beautiful idea. But winter and guilt come, death and sin are in the world, and Arcadianism does not know how to deal with them. Attempting to communicate with the wild creatures as he once had, Donatello calls to them in the "voice and utterance of the natural man," but he is frustrated when a brown lizard "of the tarantula species" makes its appearance. "To all present appearance, this venomous reptile was the only creature that had responded to the young Count's efforts to renew his intercourse with the lower orders of nature." Donatello falls to the ground and Kenyon, alarmed, asks what has happened to him. " 'Death, death!' sobbed Donatello."

Kenyon himself supplies sufficient comment on the legend of the spring: "He understood it as an apologue, typifying the soothing and genial effects of an habitual intercourse with nature, in all ordinary cares and griefs; while, on the other hand, her mild influences fall short in their effect upon the ruder passions, and are altogether powerless in the dread fever-fit or deadly chill of guilt." After a little more talk, the two friends part, Donatello to climb up in his tower once more, Kenyon to go inside to read "an antique edition of Dante." We have met the venomous reptile and heard Donatello's answer to Kenyon before, in Rappaccini's garden, where Hawthorne also alluded to Dante to help us to get our metaphorical bearings. Sin and death have entered the world, to spoil the Arcadian dream. Whether the fall is "fortunate" or not may be impossible to answer, but at least the world we know is no unfallen earthly paradise. Evil is in it, and nature itself offers no satisfactory cure.

The cure, insofar as there is any, lies partly in repentance and love in this world, and partly in the hope of another life. These meanings emerge from the plot considered as symbolic action or myth and from the implications of the leading images with which Hawthorne supports his myth. The plot gives us three of the characters at least, and perhaps by intention four, growing in moral and spiritual stature as they experience sin and suffering. Miriam ceases to suffer in isolation and think only of herself, falls in love with Donatello, and dedicates her life to penitence and to the service of the one she has wronged. Donatello gains in wisdom and understanding, becomes in fact human. Hilda comes down from the tower of her perfect rectitude, repents having turned away Miriam in her need, and becomes human enough to marry Kenyon. All, in fact, come down from the isolation of their towers; all fall in love. That there is no cure for suffering is clear from the careers of Miriam and Donatello, but that suffering and acknowledgment of mutual complicity in guilt are necessary preludes to any redemption possible to man is clear from the careers of all of them.

The "higher hopes" of another life that will rectify the wrongs of this one are implied in Kenyon's deference to Hilda, in his plea that she lead him home, and in Hawthorne's own too often expressed admiration of her. Hilda is "the religious girl" as well as the girl of a shining purity of character, Kenyon the "thinker," potentially the skeptic. Not just Kenyon but the whole novel stands in awe of Hilda, whose precise function is to keep the lamp of religious faith, with its higher hopes, burning. (She can let the flame of the old Catholic lamp go out at the end because she herself in her own person emanates a better and purer light.)

Hilda is supported in her task of guarding religious faith and hope by much of the imagery, sometimes with images that Hawthorne makes very emphatic, sometimes with what seem mere reflexes of his habitual style. I shall give just two examples. At the end of the chapter called "The Owl Tower," in which Kenyon and Donatello have climbed to the top of Donatello's tower and Kenyon has had his vision of the symbolic landscape, Kenyon finds, growing out of the masonry of the tower, seemingly out of the very stone itself, "a little shrub, with green and glossy leaves." Donatello thinks, "If the wide valley has a great meaning, the plant ought to have at least a little one." Kenyon asks Donatello if he sees any meaning here and Donatello says he sees none, but, looking at the plant, he adds, "But here was a worm that would have killed it; an ugly creature, which I will fling over the battlements."

Kenyon does not voice the meaning he sees, and Hawthorne makes no comment. But the context makes reasonably clear what Donatello missed. We are reminded of Melville's "Bartleby the Scrivener," in which, in the Tombs, green grass could be seen by Bartleby if he would only turn his face from the wall. Kenyon's view of the valley has increased his "reliance on His providence" (whereas Donatello has seen only "sunshine on one spot, and cloud in another, and no reason for it in either case"), and he has just explained to Donatello that he "cannot preach": words will not express his "best" thoughts, that is, his religious thoughts. He has seen, as he looked at the earth spread below them, something of the way of "His dealings with mankind." Now, in the rarefied "upper atmosphere" of the tower, he finds a green shrub, the meaning of which he does not even attempt to state for his companion. Green is the traditional color of hope, and the plant is growing in a very unlikely place: "Heaven knows how its seeds had ever been planted . . ." But not only Heaven knew: Hawthorne knew how the seeds of such hope as he cherished had been planted. The chapter ends with Donatello's destruction of the "worm" that would destroy the plant.

My second example comes at the end of chapter three, "Subterranean Reminiscences," in which the four friends have been exploring one of the catacombs, where they "wandered by torchlight through a sort of dream." Hilda and Donatello, both Innocents, find the darkness especially repellent: their experience of life has in no way prepared them for it. Miriam thinks that "the most awful idea connected with the catacombs is their interminable extent, and the possibility of going astray in this labyrinth of darkness. . . ." When Kenyon wonders whether in fact any-one has ever been lost in the place, he is told of "a pagan of old Rome, who hid himself in order to spy out the blessed saints, who then dwelt and worshipped in these dismal places." The pagan has been "groping in the darkness" ever since, unable to find his way out.

At this point the party reaches a chapel carved out of the walls and stops to look at it; "and while their collected torches illuminated this one small, consecreated spot, the great darkness spread all round it, like that immenser mystery which envelops our little life, and into which friends vanish from us, one by one." Miriam, it turns out, has "vanished into the great darkness, even while they were shuddering at the remote possibility of such a misfortune." Miriam shares Hilda's strict orthodoxy even less than Kenyon, who at least longs for and admires what is not as much his as he would like it to be. She has something in common with the pagan of old Rome; she is not held by the brightly illuminated consecrated spot. (As it turns out, though, she is more a victim of persecution than an un-believer.)

We are reminded of the brightly lighted chamber in "Night Sketches," with the cold darkness all around, or of the darkness that seemed to press in on the little company at Blithedale. In the latter case, though, the hope suggested by the warmth and light was a secular one. Here everything about the context unites to suggest a purely "religious" hope —in the sense of a hope for immortality. The darkness into which our friends vanish is the darkness of death. Later, Kenyon will protest the presence of a skull in Donatello's bedroom: "It is absurdly monstrous, my dear friend, thus to fling the dead-weight of our mortality upon our immortal hopes. While we live on earth, 'tis true, we must needs carry our skeletons about with us; but, for Heaven's sake, do not let us burden our spirits with them, in our feeble efforts to soar upward." (Kenyon's higher hopes may have seemed to him feeble, but Hawthorne characterizes him elsewhere as he would have characterized himself, "a devout man in his way.") Those who know the extent of "the blackness that lies beneath us everywhere," who know that we are "dreaming on the edge of a precipice," who know that sinking into nature is equivalent to sinking into the grave and have explored the "dark caverns" of experience, will not need to keep a skull in the bedroom to remind them of man's mortality.

They will be likely to agree with the point of Hawthorne's moral and theological criticism of Sodoma's Siena fresco of Christ bound to a pillar. Hawthorne felt sure the picture sprang from sincere religious feeling: a shallow or worldly man could not have painted it. The picture is "inexpressibly touching" in its portrayal of the weariness and loneliness of the Savior:

> You behold Christ deserted both in heaven and earth; that despair is in him which wrung forth the saddest utterance man ever made, "Why hast Thou forsaken me?" Even in this extremity, however, he is still divine . . . He is as much, and as visibly, our Redeemer, there bound, there fainting, and bleeding from the scourge, with the cross in view, as if he sat on his throne of glory in the heavens! Sodoma, in this matchless picture, has done more towards reconciling the incongruity of Divine Omnipotence and outraged, suffering Humanity, combined in one person, than the theologians ever did.

IV

The Marble Faun ought to have been Hawthorne's finest novel. His career had pointed toward it from the beginning. In it the heart imagery that is implicit in "The Hollow of the Three Hills" has become the underground world of Rome, the catacombs, the tomb or dungeon of the heart and of dreams. In it Robin's initiation has become consciously archetypal, to be seen in the dimensions of its largest significance. In it the implications of "Earth's Holocaust" and "The Celestial Railroad" have been combined within the framework of man's basic myth. The most persistent preoccupations and the recurrent images of a lifetime of writing have been brought together in what ought to have been a definitive recapitulation.

Instead, the novel is clearly inferior to *The Scarlet Letter* and even, it seems to me, to *The House of the Seven Gables*. Richer in many respects than *Blithedale,* it is less consistently interesting: there are frequent stretches of it one wants to skip. There is a very large gap in it between intended and achieved meaning. Hawthorne failed with Rome, and he failed with Hilda, and both were essential to the achievement of his intention.

Hilda is at once a nineteenth century stereotype and Hawthorne's tribute to Sophia. The only way of interpreting her that will "save" Hawthorne and his novel is to take the portrait ironically, but this will not do if we consider all the evidence. True, Miriam points out that Hilda's innocence is like "a sharp steel sword"; so white a purity makes for judgments that are "terribly severe." And Miriam often speaks for Hawthorne. Here we should probably assume that he thought so too. But this is only a minor qualification of what, for Hawthorne, is Hilda's awe-inspiring virtue and compelling attractiveness. Once again, as in the case of Miriam's implied assent to the idea of the Fortunate Fall, we may not assume that Hawthorne is completely committed to Miriam as his spokesman. In his own person, as narrator, he pays Hilda lavish, and tiresomely repetitious, tribute, and as Kenyon he marries her and asks her to guide him home.

Yet to the modern reader Hilda is either ridiculous or, if we can take her seriously, self-righteous and uncharitable. She is not only a far less impressive character, as a literary character, than Miriam, she is far less attractive, and even less "good," as a person. Throughout most of the course of the novel her chief concern is to protect the spotlessness of the innocence assumed by her and asserted by Hawthorne. She finds everyone else's faith and everyone else's conduct corrupt. When called upon for help, she turns her friend away lest she be stained by the contact. Though the idea would have shocked Hawthorne immeasurably, it is impossible not to see her as a feminine version of the man of adamant—at least until the very end, when the rigor of her moralism is softened somewhat.

There is no consistent or effective irony in the portrait. Though this "daughter of the Puritans," as Hawthorne repeatedly calls her, comes down from her tower to marry Kenyon, the change is not so much one from spiritual pride to humility as from priestess to goddess: "Another hand must henceforth trim the lamp before the Virgin's shrine; for Hilda was coming down from her old tower, to be herself enshrined and worshipped as a household saint, in the light of her husband's fireside." It is true that Hilda thought right and wrong completely distinct, never in any degree mingled or ambiguous—the error of judgment that Hawthorne's innocent young men have to grow out of, the idea they have to unlearn by painful experience. But Hawthorne thought such an error— if indeed error it was, as he would have said—charming and admirable in innocent young girls. Hilda is like young Robin before his "evening of ambiguity and weariness"; the difference between them is that Hawthorne does not require that young girls should grow in knowledge of the world.

His century placed women on a pedestal just *because,* in their role of guardian of values that were being threatened, they knew nothing of the world. If their innocence rendered them helpless to deal with reality, it was nevertheless to be both protected and admired, for reality was very nasty. If they did not truly partake of the human condition, it was a good thing they didn't. A comment Hawthorne makes in the novel on a work of art, without suggesting any connection with his portrait of Hilda, suggests the chief reason for his failure with his heroine: "It was one of the few works of antique sculpture in which we recognize womanhood, and that, moreover, without prejudice to its divinity." Womanhood's "divinity"? Since Hilda was more than normally pretty and good, no wonder her destiny was to be "enshrined and worshipped" at the fireside.

As he depended greatly on Hilda to give his novel an affirmative meaning, so Hawthorne depended chiefly on Rome and its art treasures to give it thematic density. Here too he failed, though for quite different reasons. Again, recent efforts to "save" the novel do not really work. To be sure, Hawthorne anticipates James in developing the Europe versus America theme: Rome is the past, experience, culture, and corruption, in contrast with America's present, ideals, morality, and innocence: Miriam versus Hilda. This is fine, theoretically. But Hawthorne too often simply lifts long passages of description from the Notebooks, and the passages remain inert in the novel. There is too *much* of Rome, and too much about art. They are a burden the story is simply incapable of carrying.

Examples could easily be given of passages in which Hawthorne succeeds in making his comments on art and descriptions of Rome work for his story. Perhaps the best one is Miriam's comment on Guido's "dapper" Archangel, whose feathers are unruffled in his struggle with Satan: "Is it thus that virtue looks the moment after its death-struggle with evil? . . . A full third of the Archangel's feathers should have been torn from his wings . . ." But for page after page there is nothing like this, nothing in fact that is not very tedious. And Hawthorne seems to know it. At least he keeps apologizing for his descriptions while the story halts, sometimes for a chapter at a time, to accommodate them. This is simply awkward novel writing and no amount of demonstration that, where there are symbolic implications in the Notebook material they are consistent with the general theme, will really save the romance as a work of art. Thematic considerations alone cannot save any novel.

The effect on the reader of all this inert material is to suggest that Hawthorne was not sufficiently interested in his *story*—an effect reinforced by his embarrassed and coy protestations at the end, in the added conclusion, when he refused to make more than a slight gesture toward clearing up the mysteries of his plot. What he is really saying in his "Conclusion" is that he doesn't *care* whether Donatello had furry ears or not or who detained Hilda, and we the readers shouldn't either. But he had

cared about Hester, and Hepzibah, and Zenobia, cared about them as
people and not merely as allegoric or mythic symbols. Despite the elaborate density of its background, it might well be argued that *The Marble
Faun* is more allegorical than any of the three preceding romances.

V

Still, if it is true that the work has been generally underestimated, as
I think it has, the reason is not hard to find. Its weaknesses are very obvious, impossible I should think to overlook, while its strength is subtle
and delicate. It is easy to read this work in which "Adam falls anew,
and Paradise . . . is lost again" without responding to a good deal of
its multiple suggestiveness. There is nothing in its period quite like the
way it plays theological, philosophical, and psychological perspectives
against each other in the image of the catacombs. Here the characters
wandered in "a sort of dream," a dark labyrinth of guilt, an "ugly
dream" indeed: "For, in dreams, the conscience sleeps, and we often stain
ourselves with guilt of which we should be incapable in our waking
moments." The "dark caverns" of experience in Hawthorne's novel are
so richly meaningful that we should have to read the work for this if
there were nothing else to draw us.

There is of course much else. The scene at the precipice (we are all,
in some sense, "dreaming on the edge of a precipice"), the whole series of
chapters laid in Donatello's country, where the serpent is discovered in
nature's garden, the descriptions of the several studios (Miriam's is said
to be "the outward type of a poet's haunted imagination," and the description justifies the comment)—all these parts of the work, and more,
make it more worth reading than most American novels of the nineteenth
century, even if we are not already committed to Hawthorne before we
start it.

If we are, we shall find it an even more rewarding failure. For on the
thematic level it is, for the most part, such *good* Hawthorne. It is not
just Donatello but all of us who "travel in a circle, as all things heavenly
and earthly do." The loss of innocence is very sad, but it is at least naïve
and may be disastrous to suppose that we haven't lost it. Guilt is original,
a necessary aspect of the human condition, not something that sets conspicuous sinners apart from the rest of us. And it is mutual, so that in
our inevitable complicity we may not relieve ourselves of its burden by
pointing the finger, casting the stone. Still, we need not despair if only
we will acknowledge our complicity and enter the human circle.

"Outraged, suffering humanity" must learn to live with "the blackness
that lies beneath us, everywhere," but Kenyon, taking the long view from
the height of Donatello's tower, saw, above the stormy valley, "within the
domain of chaos, as it were,—hill-tops . . . brightening in the sunshine;

they looked like fragments of the world, broken adrift and based on nothingness, or like portions of a sphere destined to exist, but not yet finally compacted." Kenyon's images give us Hawthorne's answer to the question whether the fall was fortunate or not, an answer that springs from his "best thought" and that was otherwise inexpressible.

Chronology of Important Dates

1804	Nathaniel Hawthorne born on July 4, in Salem, Massachusetts. Descended on both sides from prominent New England ancestors.
1808	Death of his father, a sea captain, at Surinam, leaving the family poor and partially dependent on relatives.
1821-25	Attended Bowdoin College, Brunswick, Maine, where Longfellow and Franklin Pierce (later President of the United States) were his classmates. Upon graduation returned to Salem and spent the next twelve years in relative seclusion, reading and writing.
1828	*Fanshawe: A Tale,* published anonymously at his own expense. Later withdrawn.
1837	*Twice-Told Tales.*
1839	Became engaged to Sophia Peabody whom he married in 1842.
1839-40	Measurer in the Boston customhouse.
1841	Joined the Brook Farm Community at West Roxbury, Mass., in April. Invested over a thousand dollars in the venture but withdrew by the end of the year.
1842-45	Lived at the Old Manse, Concord, where his neighbors included Emerson, Thoreau, and Margaret Fuller.
1846	*Mosses from an Old Manse.*
1846-49	Surveyor in the Salem customhouse.
1850	*The Scarlet Letter.*
1851	*The House of the Seven Gables* and *The Snow Image.*
1852	*The Blithedale Romance.* Also the campaign biography of Franklin Pierce.
1853-57	Served as United States Consul at Liverpool.
1857-59	Lived in Rome and Florence.
1860	*The Marble Faun.* Returned to the United States. During the remaining four years of his life strove unsuccessfully to finish another romance and at his death left four fragments: *The Ancestral Footstep, Dr. Grimshawe's Secret, Septimius Felton,* and *The Dolliver Romance.*
1863	*Our Old Home.*
1864	Died on May 19, at Plymouth, New Hampshire.

Notes on the Editor and Authors

A. N. KAUL, the editor of this volume, has taught at the University of Delhi and now teaches at Yale University. He is the author of *The American Vision.*

YVOR WINTERS, professor at Stanford, poet, and pioneering critic of American literature, is the author of several volumes of criticism, among them *Maule's Curse.*

Q. D. LEAVIS (Mrs. F. R. Leavis) teaches at Cambridge. She has written *Fiction and the Reading Public* and several important critical essays.

CHARLES FEIDELSON, JR., author of *Symbolism and American Literature,* has recently co-edited (with Richard Ellman) an anthology entitled *The Modern Tradition: Backgrounds of Modern Literature.* He teaches at Yale.

R. W. B. LEWIS, who also teaches at Yale, is the author of *The American Adam, The Picaresque Saint,* and a number of articles on American literature and contemporary European fiction. He is the editor of *Malraux* in the Twentieth Century Views series.

H. J. LANG, of the University of Tübingen, has published several papers on American literature. His book *Hawthorne: Eine Einführung in symbolistische Erzählkunst* is to be published by Quelle and Meyer in the fall of 1965.

RICHARD HARTER FOGLE is the author of *Hawthorne's Fiction* and *The Imagery of Keats and Shelley.* He teaches at Tulane.

FREDERICK C. CREWS, of the University of California at Berkeley, has published critical studies of Henry James and E. M. Forster. He is also the author of a forthcoming book on Hawthorne to be published by Oxford University Press, entitled *The Sins of the Fathers: Hawthorne's Psychological Themes.*

LARZER ZIFF, also of the University of California at Berkeley, has written *The Career of John Cotton: Puritanism and American Experience.*

MARK VAN DOREN, man of letters and Professor of English at Columbia until his retirement a few years ago, has published a number of critical studies, among them *The Poetry of John Dryden* and *Nathaniel Hawthorne.*

F. O. MATTHIESSEN, one of the foremost critics of American literature, was Professor of English at Harvard at the time of his death in 1950. His works include *The Achievement of T. S. Eliot, American Renaissance,* and *Henry James: The Major Phase.*

HYATT H. WAGGONER, who teaches at Brown, has written *Hawthorne, The Heel of Elohim* and *William Faulkner.*

Selected Bibliography

Hawthorne's Text

The standard edition of the collected works has been for many years the Riverside Edition: *The Complete Works of Nathaniel Hawthorne*, 12 vols., Boston, Houghton Mifflin, 1883. Far from satisfactory, it will soon be superseded by *The Centenary Edition of the Works of Nathaniel Hawthorne*, which is being published by the Ohio State University Press. A convenient collection in one volume of all the completed novels, including *Fanshawe*, and of several important tales is *The Complete Novels and Selected Tales of Nathaniel Hawthorne* (Modern Library), with a valuable introduction by Norman Holmes Pearson. In addition one must cite Hawthorne's *American Notebooks*, New Haven, Yale University Press, 1932, edited, again with a valuable introduction, by Randall Stewart; and his *English Notebooks*, New York, Modern Language Association of America, 1941, also edited by Randall Stewart.

Biography and Criticism

Newton Arvin, *Hawthorne*. Boston: Little, Brown, & Co., 1929.

Walter Blair, "Color, Light, and Shadow in Hawthorne's Fiction," *New England Quarterly*, XV (1942), 74-94.

Paul Brodtkorb, Jr., "Art Allegory in *The Marble Faun*," *PMLA*, LXXVII (1962), 254-67.

Malcolm Cowley, "Hawthorne in the Looking-Glass," *Sewanee Review*, LVI (1948), 545-63.

Frederick C. Crews, "A New Reading of *The Blithedale Romance*," *American Literature*, XXIX (1957), 147-70.

Edward H. Davidson, *Hawthorne's Last Phase*. New Haven: Yale University Press, 1949.

Richard Harter Fogle, *Hawthorne's Fiction: The Light and the Dark*. Norman: University of Oklahoma Press, 1952.

John C. Gerber, "Form and Content in *The Scarlet Letter*," *New England Quarterly*, XVII (1944), 25-55.

Lawrence S. Hall, *Hawthorne: Critic of Society*. New Haven: Yale University Press, 1944.

R. B. Heilman, "'The Birthmark': Science as Religion," *South Atlantic Quarterly*, XLVIII (1949), 573-83.

Henry James, *Hawthorne* (English Men of Letters Series). London: Macmillan & Co., Ltd., 1879.

Q. D. Leavis, "Hawthorne as Poet," *Sewanee Review*, LIX (1951), 179-205, 426-58.

Roy Harvey Pearce, ed., *Hawthorne Centenary Essays*. Columbus: Ohio State University Press, 1964.

Donald A. Ringe, "Hawthorne's Psychology of the Head and Heart," *PMLA*, LXV (1950), 120-32.

John W. Schroeder, "'That Inward Sphere': Notes on Hawthorne's Heart Imagery and Symbolism," *PMLA*, LXV (1950), 106-19.

Randall Stewart, *Nathaniel Hawthorne: A Biography*. New Haven: Yale University Press, 1948.

Arlin Turner, *Nathaniel Hawthorne: An Introduction and Interpretation*. New York: Barnes & Noble, Inc., 1961.

Mark Van Doren, *Nathaniel Hawthorne*. New York: William Sloane Associates, Inc., 1949.

Hyatt H. Waggoner, *Hawthorne: A Critical Study*. Cambridge: Harvard University Press, 1955; rev. ed., 1963.

Dorothy Waples, "Suggestions for Interpreting *The Marble Faun*," *American Literature*, XIII (1941), 224-39.

In addition the following general studies contain essays or chapters on Hawthorne:

Marius Bewley, *The Complex Fate*. London: Chatto & Windus, Ltd., 1952.

————, *The Eccentric Design*. New York: Columbia University Press, 1959.

Richard Chase, *The American Novel and Its Tradition*. New York: Doubleday & Company, Inc., 1957.

Charles Feidelson, Jr., *Symbolism and American Literature*. Chicago: University of Chicago Press, 1953:

Irving Howe, *Politics and the Novel*. New York: Meridian, 1957.

A. N. Kaul, *The American Vision*. New Haven: Yale University Press, 1963.

Harry Levin, *The Power of Blackness*. New York: Alfred A. Knopf, Inc., 1958.

R. W. B. Lewis, *The American Adam*. Chicago: University of Chicago Press, 1955.

F. O. Matthiessen, *American Renaissance*. New York: Oxford University Press, 1941.

Yvor Winters, *Maule's Curse*. New York: New Directions, 1938.